LIFE APPLICATION® BIBLE COMMENTARY

REVELATION

Bruce B. Barton, D.Min.

Linda Taylor

Neil Wilson, M.R.E.

Dave Veerman, M.Div.

General Editor:

Grant Osborne, Ph.D.

Series Editor:

Philip W. Comfort, Ph.D., D.Litt. et Phil.

Tyndale House Publishers, Inc.
WHEATON, ILLINOIS

Library of Congress Cataloging-in-Publication data

Revelation / Bruce B. Barton—[et al.]; general editor, Grant Osborne.
    p.cm.—(Life application Bible commentary)
    Includes bibliographical references and index.
    ISBN 0-8423-2874-2 (sc : alk. paper)
    1. Bible. N.T. Revelation—Commentaries. I. Barton, Bruce B. II. Osborne,
Grant R. III. Series
BS2825.3.R45 2000
228′.077—dc21   99-048751

Printed in the United States of America

04   03
7   6   5   4

CONTENTS

Gospels

MATTHEW:
MARK: between
LUKE:

ACTS:

Paul's Epistles

ROMANS: about 57
1 CORINTHIANS: about 55
2 CORINTHIANS: about 56–57
GALATIANS: about 49

EPHESIANS:
PHILIPPIANS:
COLOSSIANS:
1 THESSALONIANS: about 51
2 THESSALONIANS: about 51–52
1 TIMOTHY:
2 TIMOTHY:
TITUS:
PHILEMON:

General Epistles   JAMES: about 49

1 PETER:
2 PETER:

JUDE:

NEW   TESTAMENT

AD 30	40	50	60

The church
begins
(Acts 1)
35
Paul's
conversion
(Acts 9)

46
Paul's first
missionary
journey
(Acts 13)

Jerusalem Council
and Paul's second
journey (Acts 15)
54
Paul's
third
journey
(Acts 18)
Nero
becomes
emperor

58
Paul
arrested
(Acts 21)

64
Rome
burns

61–63
Paul's
Roman
imprison-
ment
(Acts 28)

between 60–65
55–65
about 60

about 63–65

JOHN: probably 80–85

about 61
about 62
about 61

about 64
about 66–67
about 64
about 61

HEBREWS: probably before 70

about 62–64
about 67

1 JOHN: between 85–90
2 JOHN: about 90
3 JOHN: about 90

about 65

REVELATION: about 95

TIMELINE

| | 70 | 80 | 90 | 100 |

67–68
Paul and
Peter
executed

Jerusalem
destroyed

79 *Mt. Vesuvius
erupts in Italy*

About 98
John's
death
at Ephesus

68
*Essenes hide
their library
of Bible
manuscripts
in a cave
in Qumran
by the
Dead Sea*

About 75
*John begins
ministry in
Ephesus*

75
*Rome begins
construction
of Colosseum*

FOREWORD

The *Life Application Bible* Commentary series provides verse-by-verse explanation, background, and application for every verse in the New Testament. In addition, it gives personal help, teaching notes, and sermon ideas that will address needs, answer questions, and provide insight for applying the Word of God to life today. The content is highlighted so that particular verses and phrases are easy to find.

Each volume contains three sections: introduction, commentary, and reference. The introduction includes an overview of the book, the book's historical context, a time line, cultural background information, major themes, an overview map, and an explanation about the author and audience.

The commentary section includes running commentary on the Bible text with reference to several modern versions, especially the New International Version, the New Revised Standard Version, and the New Living Translation, accompanied by life applications interspersed throughout. Additional elements include charts, diagrams, maps, and illustrations. There are also insightful quotes from church leaders and theologians such as John Calvin, Martin Luther, John Wesley, and A. W. Tozer. These features are designed to help you quickly grasp the biblical information and be prepared to communicate it to others. The reference section includes an index and a bibliography.

INTRODUCTION

Hollywood studios produce spectacular displays for movie-theater entertainment. With computer-generated images and other high-tech tricks, movies present special effects that seem almost beyond comprehension. Aliens and dinosaurs come to life; explorers travel faster than light; animals and trees dance, sing, and talk. Viewers marvel at the show, then return to reality as the credits roll.

That's great entertainment. But we know it's not real. Now flip to the back of your Bible, to the last book—Revelation. As you read, you soon will become immersed in a fantastic display of sights, sounds, colors, and images. If you feel overwhelmed and amazed, think of what the original witness to these events, John, must have felt as vision after vision assaulted his senses. No adjectives can adequately describe *this* multimedia show. Trumpets, thrones, lightning, thunder, lampstands, awful creatures, millions of majestic angels, a mighty chorus, fiery horses, plagues, terrible bowls . . . one scene follows another, moving steadily and decisively toward the ultimate finale.

This is a story of martyrs and battles, of demons and angels, of things to come. Revelation reveals God and his plan for the future. And it's true.

AUTHOR

John the apostle, son of Zebedee and Salome and younger brother of James.

In a book filled with obscure images and vague allusions, one thing comes through loud and clear: the name of the author. At the very beginning, Revelation identifies its source: "This is a revelation from Jesus Christ . . . sent to God's servant John" (1:1 NLT). The statement asserts that Jesus Christ himself gave this revelation to a man named John.

The early church fathers—including Justin Martyr, Irenaeus, and Hippolytus—uniformly identified this John as the apostle of the same name, the one who abandoned his father's fishing nets to follow Jesus (Matthew 4:21-22). It is clear from the

Gospels that the apostle John was very close to Jesus. Jesus singled out Peter, James, and John to accompany him to Jairus's home to witness the resurrection of Jairus's daughter (Mark 5:37-43). Then, on two separate occasions, Jesus asked the three men to go away with him to a secluded place to spend time in prayer. At the first of these occasions, John witnessed the dazzling transfiguration of Jesus as he was joined by two heavenly guests, Moses and Elijah (Luke 9:28-31). The second occasion came during that agonizing night Jesus spent in the Garden of Gethsemane before his arrest (Matthew 26:36-38). John also helped make preparations for the Last Supper (Luke 22:8). What a great privilege to have been such a close confidant of the Lord Jesus himself!

Apparently, John's proximity to the Master made him quite bold. He didn't shrink from asking Jesus if he could sit in a place of honor in the coming kingdom (Mark 10:35-37). John even offered to call down fire from heaven to wipe out a Samaritan village that had rejected Jesus (Luke 9:54-55). In each case, Jesus reined in the misplaced enthusiasm of this "Son of Thunder" (see Mark 3:17). Yet John's clear loyalty to his Lord and Savior should be admired. His love for Jesus motivated him to stay close in the darkest hour. On the day of Jesus' crucifixion, John stood at the foot of the cross, where Jesus entrusted him with the care of Jesus' earthly mother (John 19:26-27). No wonder John humbly described himself as the disciple Jesus loved (John 13:23; 19:26; 20:2; 21:20-24).

It is certainly understandable, therefore, that Jesus would appear to this beloved apostle at a later date, to entrust him with a very special message for the church (Revelation 1:9-19). So, near the end of his life, John received a vision from Christ, which he recorded for the benefit of the seven churches in Asia and for Christians everywhere, throughout history.

Although much evidence affirms the apostle John as Revelation's author, a few scholars aren't convinced. Dionysius, a fourth-century bishop of Alexandria, was the first known doubter of this apostle's authorship of Revelation. Dionysius pointed out the following:

- Revelation has a completely different structure than John's other writings—including the Gospel of John, 1 John, 2 John, and 3 John.
- None of John's writings allude to Revelation.
- The rough and inaccurate Greek of Revelation sharply contrasts with the polished and faultless Greek of John's Gospel and letters.

Dionysius cautiously suggested that a prophet named John, who lived in Ephesus in the first century, had written this book.

The differences in Greek style between Revelation and John's writings are real but can be easily explained. The primary difference comes from the fact that John was writing apocalyptic literature—that is, he was recording the images he saw while he was seeing them. This style of writing, if left uncorrected, would account for its poor grammar and awkward syntax. The subject matter of Revelation also accounts for the difference in style. John's other writings are instructional or historical, while Revelation is the record of an extraordinary vision—a vision that couldn't be expressed with the precise syntax of the Greek language.

Although Bible scholars cannot assert with certainty that the "John" of Revelation is the apostle John, no other viable alternative has been offered. The evidence for Dionysius's "John of Ephesus" is slim. Thus, we have no substantial reasons to doubt that the apostle John was the one who witnessed the remarkable visions recorded in this book, appropriately titled "Revelation."

For more on John the apostle, see the "Introduction" in the *Life Application Bible Commentary* on the Gospel of John.

DATE AND SETTING

Written around A.D. 90–95 from the island of Patmos.

Readers don't have to guess or research where Revelation was written. The text clearly names the location as the island of Patmos: "I am John, your brother. In Jesus we are partners in suffering and in the Kingdom and in patient endurance. I was exiled to the island of Patmos for preaching the word of God and speaking about Jesus" (1:9 NLT). Patmos, with its rugged volcanic hills, lies about fifty-five kilometers off the southwest coast of Asia Minor and is only twelve kilometers long and seven kilometers wide.

John had been sent to that barren and rocky island off the coast of present-day Turkey because he had fearlessly proclaimed the gospel. John had been banished to Patmos as the Roman authorities continued moving against the church. Threatened by John's powerful ministry, they viewed John as a dangerous leader of the Christian sect. During this exile, while John was separated from his Christian brothers and sisters, the risen Jesus appeared to him in a spectacular vision.

Although the place of John's vision is identified in the text, the exact time is not. Most of the evidence seems to point to Emperor

Domitian's reign, around A.D. 90–95. The early church father Irenaeus made this case. Modern scholars agree with Irenaeus, believing that after writing Revelation, John was released from Patmos, whereupon he returned to Ephesus, where he had been ministering before his exile. Then, several years later, around A.D. 100, John died. This progression of events fits well with the evidence in Revelation itself.

The writer described himself as a brother and companion of the believers in Ephesus and nearby cities (1:9-11)—an appropriate statement for a leader of the Ephesian church.

The letters to the seven churches in Asia Minor in 2–3 speak of a spiritual decline—something that certainly could have occurred during the forty or so years after their foundings. The church of Laodicea is described as rich in 3:17. Since the city was completely destroyed by an earthquake in A.D. 60–61, it would have been difficult to say this of Laodicea much before A.D. 90.

Some believe that Revelation was written during Nero's reign, between the years A.D. 54 and 68, the time of Nero's greatest persecution of the Christians. The best argument for this date is that the apostle John may have written the description of the New Jerusalem (21:1-27) before the destruction of the old city in A.D. 70. Another explanation for an early date is that the number 666 works as a possible cryptic reference to Nero. When the words "Nero Caesar" are transcribed into Hebrew, the numeric value of the Hebrew letters can be calculated as 666. Another argument is that the persecution that Nero instigated against Christians could be coincidental with the persecution in the book of Revelation.

In the last analysis, however, the evidence seems to support the early church tradition that the apostle John wrote Revelation on the island of Patmos around A.D. 90–95.

AUDIENCE

The churches in Ephesus, Smyrna, Pergamum, Thyatira, Sardis, Philadelphia, and Laodicea and believers everywhere.

Although Revelation touches on all of human history, it is specifically addressed to seven churches located in what today is southwestern Turkey. Reliable historical sources from the second century A.D. describe the apostle John as ministering in Ephesus around A.D. 70–100, so he would have been intimately familiar with the strengths and weaknesses of the churches he was addressing.

Before John worked in Ephesus, Paul had labored there. Paul had founded the Ephesian church on his second missionary journey. At that time Paul had been on his way to Jerusalem, so he had left mature Christians—Aquila and Priscilla—to carry on the work (Acts 18:19-21, 24-26). On his third missionary journey, Paul stayed in Ephesus for three full years, making it a center for evangelistic activity for the present-day region of Turkey. The city was ideally suited for this strategic purpose because it was located at the intersection of two major overland routes: the coastal road running north to Troas and the western road that headed toward Laodicea. In addition, Ephesus sat on the Cayster River and, therefore, had easy access to the shipping traffic in the Aegean Sea. Because of this central and strategic location, Ephesus had become a commercial and cultural hub of the region. Another attraction in Ephesus was a great temple to Artemis, the fertility goddess. Visitors flocked to this temple every year (Acts 19:23-27). Paul envisioned Ephesus as the center of Christianity, rather than paganism, in the region.

In the lecture hall of Tyrannus, Paul organized an evangelism school to train teachers and preachers in the gospel message (Acts 19:9-10). For three years Paul stayed in Ephesus. (The "two years" of Acts 19:10 only account for part of Paul's stay there.) Most likely, during this time all the churches addressed in Revelation were founded. These churches—Ephesus, Smyrna, Pergamum, Thyatira, Sardis, Philadelphia, and Laodicea—were located on a circular postal route in southwestern Asia Minor (present-day Turkey).

PURPOSE

To reveal the full identity of Christ and to give warning and hope to believers.

Because of the description in Revelation of Christian martyrs and a beast who demands worship (13:1-8), many readers of Revelation have assumed that the cities to which the apostle John wrote were being severely persecuted. Indeed, these communities were experiencing *some* persecution. John himself had been exiled to Patmos for preaching the gospel (1:9), and Antipas in Pergamum had been put to death for his adherence to Christ (2:13). Nero was the first Roman emperor to persecute Christians. Yet his persecution of Christians was local and not Empire-wide. Nero blamed the Christians in Rome for the devastating fire that had destroyed much of the city.

It wasn't until the reign of Domitian (A.D. 81–96) that refusing to worship the Roman emperor became a punishable offense throughout the Empire. Before that time, emperor worship had been spread-

ing throughout the Roman Empire but hadn't been enforced. But
even with the decree that all should worship him as "God and
Lord," there isn't much evidence from Domitian's reign of widespread persecution of Christians. Most of the persecution of Christians in the first century consisted of local challenges to specific
groups of believers. Out of the seven churches addressed in Revelation, John encouraged only three (Smyrna, Pergamum, and Philadelphia) to endure suffering and persecution.

This book seems to be more concerned about false teaching,
sexual immorality, divisions within congregations, lack of love
for God and others, and complacency toward the things of God.
The greatest threat to these churches was internal, not external—
the spread of false teaching and spiritual compromise (2:14-16,
20-22; 3:4, 15-17). So Revelation wasn't necessarily addressed
to a persecuted minority. Instead, it was a wake-up call to a complacent, compromising church.

Revelation highlights the unseen realities that these congregations were ignoring. Vivid and terrifying visions illustrate a furi-
ous battle between good and evil—a battle of which the eventual
outcome has been already determined. Ultimately, God will win!
The only question was whether the members of these churches
would be on God's side or on Satan's side. The answer to this
question was a matter of life and death.

UNDERSTANDING APOCALYPTIC LITERATURE

To understand Revelation, we must recognize that John, the
author, wrote in a specific genre—apocalyptic literature. From
200 B.C. to A.D. 100, certain groups of Jews and Christians used
this writing style to describe the end of the world and God's judgment. Apocalyptic literature uses fantastic imagery to remind
readers of the invisible, supernatural battle occurring behind the
events of human history. Within the Bible, in addition to Revelation, the clearest examples of apocalyptic literature are Daniel
10–12 and Mark 13. Outside of Scripture, there are *The Assump-
tion of Moses, The Apocalypses of Ezra, The Shepherd of Her-
mas,* and *Baruch.* Non-canonical apocalypses usually name no
author but are written as though prominent Old Testament figures, such as Moses or Ezra, were seeing the future. There are
three key characteristics of apocalyptic literature.

1. All apocalyptic literature claims to be a revelation from God.
   The Greek word for "apocalypse" *(apokalupsis)* actually
   means "revelation." Thus, in the book of Revelation, God
   gives a glimpse into the future. Revelation consists of four

visions, each introduced by an invitation to see what the future holds (1:11; 4:1; 17:1; 21:9). In these visions world history is portrayed as a great war between God and Satan. In the end God defeats Satan and emerges as the winner of this great struggle. As you read Revelation, keep in mind the big picture—the cosmic warfare between good and evil.

2. Apocalypses are symbolic. Mysterious imagery, numerology, cosmic journeys, supernatural beings, and strange beasts fill the pages of apocalyptic works. This type of literature attempts to describe invisible, supernatural events in human terms. By their very nature, these images go beyond what is known, as apocalyptic writers point to supernatural realities through striking symbols. At this point it is important to note that in order to understand the symbols in Revelation, we must consider their meaning to the *first-century* readers and not impose contemporary events and people on the text. Apocalyptic writers never intended for the symbols to be interpreted as literal photographs of the future. Instead, they wanted their graphic and disturbing images to symbolize events, beings, or traits in the supernatural realm. For example, 1:16 describes Christ as having a sharp, double-edged sword in his mouth. By comparing this image to Hebrews 4:12-13 (which describes the Word of God as a double-edged sword that penetrates the soul and judges every thought), it becomes clear that this sword is a symbol for Christ's words. Christ's words are so full of truth that they can cleanly separate good from evil, truth from falsehood. Christ with his words of truth will be the ultimate Judge of all people.

3. Apocalyptic literature highlights God's supernatural intervention in history—the times when God decisively acts in ways that transcend natural laws. Revelation doesn't try to encourage people to discover God's workings within the natural laws that people take for granted. Instead, the visions in this book picture God acting purposefully to end the way things have always been. Revelation describes God defeating evil in this world once and for all and establishing peace and justice forever. In the end God will interrupt the natural world so dramatically that the earth and sky will flee from his presence (20:11). God will replace the old world with a radically new one (21:1). On the new earth, for example, neither sun nor moon will be needed (21:23).

Though most of this book is apocalyptic, not all of it is. Revelation also contains straightforward prophecy (1:3; 22:7, 10, 18-19) and seven letters of admonition from Jesus Christ (1:4–3:22). As prophecy, it focuses on believers' responsibilities in this world and their relationships to an eternal future spent with God. As an epistle to seven churches, it gives advice and encouragement to believers in seven separate churches. This is the only book in the Bible that promises a blessing to those who listen to its words and do what it says (1:3).

Revelation is a hybrid of apocalypse and prophecy written within the framework of an ancient Greek letter. The purpose of this letter was to inspire believers to overcome all obstacles by steadfastly holding on to their faith (2:7, 17, 25-26; 3:5, 11-12, 21). Despite the many strange images and mysterious symbols, the central message of Revelation is clear: God controls all of history, and Christ will return to earth to judge it and to reward those who have joined his side in the fight against evil and who have remained faithful to him (22:7, 12-13, 20).

Interpreting Revelation. Revelation is a book of symbols. Every symbol in this book was understandable by people in the first century. This was a first-century book, written to the believers of the first-century church; yet it also has significance for Christians two thousand years later. The questions to ask when reading the book are, What was God saying to John's original readers? What would they have understood from John's words? Why did God use a particular symbol to get across his message?

Revelation is a book about the future and about the present. It offers future hope to all believers, especially those who have suffered for their faith, by proclaiming Christ's total triumph over evil and the reality of eternal life with him. It also gives present guidance as it teaches us about Jesus Christ and how we should live for him now. Through graphic pictures, we learn that Jesus Christ is coming again, that evil will be judged, and that the dead will be raised to judgment, resulting in eternal life or eternal destruction.

Revelation is one of the most mysterious books of the Bible. For centuries people have debated various aspects of the book—for example, the timing of the rapture of the church, the nature of the millennial reign of Christ, and the timing of Christ's return (before, in the middle of, or after the Great Tribulation). And debates have raged over the identity of the Beast, the number 666, and the Great Prostitute. Unfortunately, these debates have fueled such great controversy that Christians have been divided, and churches have even split over these issues.

Every Christian who approaches this book must realize that if these questions have been debated over centuries, then God probably made them not clear on purpose. Churches and seminaries have made their interpretations of these debated issues part of their doctrinal statements. But they must understand that other Christians who disagree with their positions are doing only that—disagreeing. The positions regarding postmillennialism versus premillennialism do not make a difference as to whether one is a believer or not. The cardinal doctrine is whether a person believes that Christ, the Savior and King, will indeed one day return for his people and whether one has trusted in him as personal Savior. From there, the timing of Christ's return or when the church will be raptured are merely issues for discussion—not fundamental doctrines that affect a person's salvation.

Believers should study Revelation carefully, always realizing that whatever position they eventually take will meet with disagreement from other sincere Christians. Believers must have respect for those who, on the basis of the biblical evidence and their own studies, accept a different position. We must recognize and condemn heresy, teaching that directly contradicts Scripture, such as someone giving a date for Christ's return when Christ has clearly said no one can know the date. But when Scripture is not clear on certain issues, and especially when those issues have been debated throughout church history without agreement, then believers should lovingly accept people who disagree.

Historically, Christians have taken four main approaches to interpret Revelation.

1. One approach is to understand the book as describing the events immediately preceding and following Christ's second coming. Christians who interpret Revelation this way are called "futurists." These believers insist that the judgments of the seals, trumpets, and bowls (see 5:1–16:21) are future events that will occur at the end of history.

    Typically, futurists insist that the key to interpreting Revelation can be found in the description of the sealed scroll, which only the Lamb, Jesus, is worthy to open (5:1-14). Each time the Lamb opens one of the scroll's seven seals, the earth experiences a cataclysmic event. Thus, futurists believe that the descriptions of famine, war, and devastation in the central chapters of Revelation depict the final days of human history. According to this view, the Beast of Revelation 13 is the Antichrist, who will appear in the end times to deceive people.

2. Many of the Reformers—Luther, Calvin, and others—interpreted Revelation much differently. They understood this mysterious book as a prophetic survey of church history. Joachim of Fiore (1135–1202) was the first person to interpret Revelation this way; he considered that the book prophesies the events of Western history from the early church until his own time. In

this approach, called the "historicist" view, each one of the seven churches in Revelation 2–3 represents a certain stage of church history, from the early church to the church of the Middle Ages to, perhaps, even the modern-day church. According to this view, therefore, the Beast of Revelation would represent a specific person or institution in history. The historicist view doesn't enjoy much favor today because there hasn't been any agreement on the specific historical events that Revelation describes.

3. Other scholars believe that Revelation simply describes events confined to the apostle John's day. This is called the "preterist" view ("preterist" means "past action"). According to this perspective, for example, the Beast in Revelation 13 represents the Roman Empire because Revelation's original readers would have readily identified the Roman Empire as the primary opponent of the church.

4. Another group of interpreters understands Revelation as being primarily "symbolic." They believe that through symbols Revelation presents timeless truths that were relevant to the original readers and are relevant to readers today. According to the symbolic view, Revelation essentially describes a battle between good and evil that occurs throughout world history. Proponents of the symbolic perspective assert that Revelation's fundamental message can be understood by everyone—a person born in the Roman Empire in the first century, someone living in New Zealand in the nineteenth century, or someone living in America today. An extreme symbolic approach would spiritualize the entire book, asserting that Revelation predicts no specific historical events. The Beast, according to the symbolic view, would represent the power of all those who oppose Christ and who have opposed him throughout all of world history.

Whenever you hear someone talking about his or her view of Revelation, remember these four basic interpretative approaches. Some preachers and Bible teachers use more than one.

This commentary often presents several interpretations of a specific passage. Yet the basic approach of this commentary is to treat Revelation as a prophetic book, as the book itself claims to be (1:3; 22:7-21). Thus, this commentary will attempt to show how Revelation unveils the future and the end of human history. This commentary, however, will also describe what Revelation would have meant to its original readers in ancient Asia Minor.

In the final analysis, the central idea, on which all four basic interpretations agree, is that Christ will return some time in the future. This return will be a welcome sight to his people, for at that time Christ will defeat evil, judge evildoers, and reward the righteous. As you read Revelation, look beyond the symbols and interpretations to your sovereign God and to your Savior, Jesus Christ. And take hope—his victory is sure!

A QUICK JOURNEY THROUGH REVELATION

Revelation is a complex book that has baffled interpreters for centuries. We can avoid a great deal of confusion by understanding the literary structure of this book. This approach will allow us to understand the individual scenes within the overall structure of Revelation and keep us from getting unnecessarily bogged down in the details of each vision. John gives hints throughout the book to indicate a change of scene, a change of subject, or a flashback to an earlier scene.

John begins by relating the circumstances that led to the writing of this book (1:1-20), then relates special messages given him by Jesus for the seven churches of Asia Minor (2:1–3:22).

Suddenly caught up into heaven, John sees a vision of God Almighty on his throne. All of Christ's followers and the heavenly angels are worshiping God (4:1-11). John watches as God gives a scroll with seven seals to the worthy Lamb, Jesus Christ (5:1-14). The Lamb begins to open the seals one by one. As each seal is opened, a new vision appears.

As the first four seals are opened, riders appear on horses of various colors; war, famine, disease, and death are in their paths (6:1-8). As the fifth seal is opened, John sees those in heaven who have been martyred for their faith in Christ (6:9-11).

A set of contrasting images appears at the opening of the sixth seal. On one side, there is a huge earthquake, stars fall from the sky, and the sky rolls up like a scroll (6:12-17). On the other side, multitudes are before the great throne, worshiping and praising God and the Lamb (7:1-17).

Next, the seventh seal is opened (8:1-5), unveiling a series of God's judgments announced by seven angels with seven trumpets. The first four angels bring hail, fire, a burning mountain, and a falling star, and the sun and the moon are darkened (8:6-13). The fifth trumpet announces the coming of locusts with the power to sting (9:1-12). The sixth trumpet heralds the coming of an army of warriors on horses (9:13-21). In 10:1-11, John is given a little scroll to eat. Following this, John is commanded to measure the temple of God (11:1-2). He sees two witnesses, who proclaim God's judgment on the earth for three and a half years (11:3-14).

Finally, the seventh trumpet sounds, calling the rival forces of good and evil to a decisive battle. On one side is Satan and his forces; on the other side stands Jesus Christ with his forces (11:15–14:5). During this battle God reveals the absolute futility of Satan, who knows his time is short (12:12) and who, though he desires power and wants to rule, can only parody God and Christ. For example, the fatal wound that heals (13:3, 12) is an imitation of the Resurrection, and the mark of the Beast (13:16-18) imitates God's seal (7:3-4). In the midst of this call to battle, John sees three angels announcing the final judgment (14:6-13). Two angels begin to reap this harvest of judgment on the earth (14:14-20). Following on the heels of these two angels are seven more angels, who pour out God's judgment on the earth from seven bowls (15:1–16:21). One of these seven angels reveals to John a vision of a great prostitute called Babylon riding a scarlet beast (17:1-18). After the defeat of Babylon (18:1-24), a great multitude in heaven shouts praise to God for his mighty victory (19:1-10).

The last three and a half chapters of Revelation catalogue the events that complete Christ's victory over the enemy: the judgment of the rebellious nations, the Beast, and the false prophet (19:11-21); Satan's one-thousand-year imprisonment (20:1-10); the final judgment (20:11-15); and the creation of a new earth and a new Jerusalem (21:1–22:6). An angel then gives concluding instructions concerning the visions John has seen and what to do once he has written them all down (22:7-11).

Revelation concludes with the promise of Christ's return, an offer to drink of the water of life that flows through the great street of the new Jerusalem, and a warning to those who read the book (22:12-21). John finishes by praying, "Amen. Come, Lord Jesus" (22:20).

This book, and thus the whole Bible, ends with a message of warning and hope for men and women of every generation. Christ is victorious, and all evil has been conquered. As you read Revelation, marvel at God's grace in the salvation of the saints and his power over the evil forces of Satan, and take hope in the reality of his ultimate victory.

MESSAGE

God's sovereignty, Christ's return, God's faithful people, Judgment, Hope.

God's sovereignty (5:1-14; 11:15-18; 20:1–22:21). The sovereignty of God is a foundational theological truth. It asserts that God totally controls what happens in the world, the universe, and human life. Nothing occurs outside of God's direct or permissive will.

Although this truth permeates all of Scripture, it is most clear in Revelation, where the culmination of history, the final judgment of all people, and the vindication of the righteous are vividly pictured. God is sovereign, greater than any power in the universe. God is incomparable, far above and beyond any religion, government, or leader, including Satan. God controls history for the purpose of uniting true believers in loving fellowship with him.

Importance for today. Assaulted with negative news from across the world and in our own communities, we can feel powerless and hopeless. Often it seems as though the forces of evil control life and will triumph. Revelation teaches the opposite. Though Satan's power may temporarily increase, we must not be led astray. God is all-powerful. He is in control and will bring his true family safely into eternal life. Because God cares for us, we can trust him with every aspect of our lives.

Christ's return (19:11-16; 20:4-6; 21:1-7; 22:6-21). When Christ came to earth as a man, he came as a perfect "Lamb," without blemish or spot, fulfilling God's requirement of a perfect sacrifice for sin. When Christ returns, he will come as the triumphant "Lion," the rightful ruler and conqueror. Christ will defeat Satan, settle accounts with all those who have rejected him, and usher his faithful followers into eternity. Because finite humans are limited by time and space, it can seem as though Christ will never return—twenty centuries have passed since his first coming. Yet to God those years are but a flicker as his plan unfolds in his eternal present. The clear message of Revelation is that Christ's coming is sure—he *will* return. And he could come at any moment. What a triumphant and glorious day that will be!

Importance for today. For centuries struggling and suffering Christians have been given hope and strength to endure in the knowledge that their Savior could return at any time. We know that God's timing is perfect. Thus, Christ will return at just the right moment (Ephesians 1:10). At that time, he will come as King and Judge. Since no one knows when Christ will appear (Matthew 24:36), we must always be ready. This means keeping our faith strong and living as God wants us to live.

God's faithful people (14:1-5; 20:4-6; 21:3-4). Soon after Revelation was written, the church came under tremendous pressure from without and from within. Believers were pressured by the government, with threats of violent persecution, to renounce their faith in Christ and to worship the emperor. At the same time, a number of heresies threatened to negatively influence believers and divide the church. John wrote to encourage believers to resist the demands to worship the Roman emperor and to be devoted only to Christ. Revelation identifies the faithful people and explains how they should live until Christ returns.

Importance for today. Christians today still face pressures to compromise or reject their faith. In many countries persecution is as violent as it was in ancient Rome. In more affluent and civilized areas, believers face more subtle pressure to worship "Caesar." And heresies have never been in short supply. God's message in Revelation is clear: stay focused on Christ and his Word; stay faithful and true to your calling. Regardless of the sources and strength of pressure and persecution, we must be faithful. Victory is sure for those who resist temptation and who make loyalty to Christ their top priority.

Judgment (6:10-17; 11:15-19; 15:1–16:21; 18:1–20:15; 22:10-15). As first-century believers looked at their world, they must have wondered at the seeming triumph of evil. The church was being persecuted, the government was corrupt, and pagan morality was the norm. Revelation clearly shows that God is just; eventually all evildoers will be punished. One day God's anger toward sin will be fully and completely unleashed. At that time Satan will be defeated with all of his agents, and false religion will be destroyed. God will reward the faithful with eternal life, and all who refuse to believe in him will face eternal punishment.

Importance for today. Because human nature is still sinful and because Satan still lives and works in the world, evil and injustice are prevalent. Living as a distinct minority in faith and morality, Christians can become discouraged and feel defeated. But the strong message of Revelation is that evil and injustice will not prevail forever; God's final judgment will put an end to them. We can take hope in this sure promise from God. But we also should spread this truth to others: no one who rejects Christ will escape God's punishment.

Hope (1:3, 7-8; 2:7, 11, 17, 26-29; 3:8-13, 20-22; 4:1-11; 7:9-17; 14:13; 19:1-10; 20:4-6; 21:1–22:7; 22:17-21). Surrounded by enemies, overwhelmed by pain and grief, or confronted by seemingly insurmountable obstacles, a person can lose hope. The first-century believers must have struggled with maintaining a hopeful perspective during those dark days of persecution and depravation. In contrast, Revelation presents the promise that one day God will create a new heaven and a new earth. All believers will live with him forever in perfect peace and security. Regardless of their present troubles, believers can look ahead with hope, trusting in their loving God.

Importance for today. Today people still struggle with discouragement, doubt, and defeat. Depression has become epidemic as men and women feel that they are trapped in hopeless circumstances. Even Christians can lose hope in the midst of trials. But the message of Revelation still rings hope through the night. We know that what God has promised will come true. And each day the Lord's appearing is one day closer. When we have confidence in this truth and in our ultimate destination, we can follow Christ with unwavering dedication, no matter what we must face.

VITAL STATISTICS

Purpose: To reveal the full identity of Christ and to give warning and hope to believers

Author: The apostle John

To Whom Written: The seven churches in Asia and all believers everywhere

Date Written: Approximately A.D. 95, from Patmos

Setting: Most scholars believe that the seven churches of Asia to whom John writes were experiencing the persecution that took place under Emperor Domitian (A.D. 90–95). It seems that the Roman authorities had exiled John to the island of Patmos (off the coast of Asia). John, who had been an eyewitness of the incarnate Christ, had a vision of the glorified, risen Christ. God also revealed to John what would take place in the future—judgment and the ultimate triumph of God over evil.

Key Verse: "God blesses the one who reads this prophecy to the church, and he blesses all who listen to it and obey what it says. For the time is near when these things will happen" (1:3 NLT).

Special Features: Revelation is written in "apocalyptic" form— a type of Jewish literature that uses symbolic imagery to communicate hope (in the ultimate triumph of God) to those in the midst of persecution. The events are ordered according to literary, rather than strictly chronological, patterns.

OUTLINE

A. Letters to the Churches (1:1–3:22)

B. Message for the Church (4:1–22:21)
  1. Worshiping God in heaven
  2. Opening the seven seals
  3. Sounding the seven trumpets
  4. Observing the great conflict
  5. Pouring out the seven plagues
  6. Seizing the final victory
  7. Making all things new

Revelation 1

The book of Revelation unveils Christ's full identity and God's plan for the end of the world, and it focuses on Jesus Christ, his second coming, his victory over evil, and the establishment of his kingdom. As you read and study Revelation, don't focus so much on the timetable of the events or the details of John's imagery that you miss the main message—the infinite love, power, and justice of the Lord Jesus Christ.

1:1 The revelation of Jesus Christ, which God gave him to show his servants what must soon take place. He made it known by sending his angel to his servant John.[NIV] The word "revelation" is the Greek word *apokalupsis,* from which the word "apocalypse" is derived. A "revelation" exposes what was formerly hidden or secret. The revelation recorded in this book will show God's servants (the believers) *what must soon take place.* That information had been formerly veiled but would now be disclosed.

A particular style of ancient literature was called "apocalyptic." Many Jewish apocalyptic works existed at the time Revelation was written. Written to describe the end of the world and God's final victory over evil, these works usually featured spectacular and mysterious imagery as well as hidden secrets that would be revealed. These Jewish works were largely pessimistic, for there was not much hope for the present. Such literature was often written under the name of an ancient hero.

The book of Revelation is apocalyptic but is different in several ways:

- It names John as the author rather than an ancient hero.
- It denounces evil and exhorts people to high Christian standards.
- It offers hope rather than gloom.

John was not a psychic attempting to predict the future; he was a prophet of God describing what God had shown him (this book is called "the prophecy," 1:3). Specifically, the apocalyptic literature in Scripture (Daniel 10–12; Mark 13; and the book of Revelation) includes fantastic imagery to remind the readers of their constant supernatural battle with evil.

Readers need to understand some characteristics of apocalyptic literature in the Bible. First, the Bible's apocalyptic sections are revelations from God. Revelation is God's giving his people a peek into the future. Second, apocalyptic literature emphasizes God's supernatural acts. Revelation highlights God's power by focusing on the end times, when God will interrupt human history and defeat evil once and for all. Third, apocalyptic literature is symbolic. It attempts to describe supernatural actions with graphic symbols of real events, things, or traits. For example, Christ is described in Revelation 5:6 as having "seven horns and seven eyes." The number seven represents perfection. A horn symbolizes power. So "seven horns" speak of Jesus' extraordinary power, and "seven eyes" speak of his ability to see all things.

This book is the revelation *of* (mediated by) *Jesus Christ. God* gave the revelation of his plan to Jesus Christ (see also John 1:18; 5:19-23; 12:49; 17:8). Jesus Christ, in turn, sent his *angel,* who revealed it *to his servant John* (see also 22:16). The angel will explain various scenes to John, acting as a guide. Angels are referred to sixty-seven times in Revelation. They are highly significant in this book; we see them worshiping God, revealing his Word, and carrying out his judgments. (For more on angels, see the commentary on 5:11-12.)

John, the servant, then passed the message along to the churches—God's *servants.* God's people are described as "servants" in Revelation (see, for example, 2:20; 7:3; 22:3). The word is used elsewhere in the New Testament to describe believers.

The phrase "what must soon take place" means imminence—it would happen "soon." This seems odd to today's readers because 1,900 years have passed since the time this was proclaimed. We must remember that in apocalyptic literature the future is imminent, without concern for intervening time. Recall the words of 2 Peter 3:8, "A day is like a thousand years to the Lord, and a thousand years is like a day" (NLT). God is timeless. In God's eyes the future is just around the corner, even though it may seem far away to us. No one knows when these events will happen, so believers should live at all times as though Christ will come in the next moment.

According to tradition, John, the author, was the only one of Jesus' original twelve disciples who was still alive at this time (that is, if the date of A.D. 90–95 is accepted; see the

Introduction). John wrote the Gospel of John and the letters of 1, 2, and 3 John. John's Gospel and letters show the great God of love, while the thunder of God's justice bursts from the pages of Revelation. John wrote Revelation in exile on the island of Patmos in the Aegean Sea, sent there by the Romans as punishment for his witness about Jesus Christ.

Jesus gave his message to John in a vision, allowing him to see and record certain future events so that they could be an encouragement to all believers. The vision includes many signs and symbols that convey the essence of what is to happen. What John saw, in most cases, was indescribable, so he used illustrations to show what it was like. Readers of this symbolic language don't have to understand every detail—John himself didn't. Instead, we must realize that John's imagery reveals that Christ is indeed the glorious and victorious Lord of all. Some of Revelation's original readers were being severely persecuted because of their faith. The awesome and sometimes frightening pictures of Jesus' ultimate victory over evil were intended to encourage them to persevere.

Jesus is the ruler of the universe! He will come to this earth in victory. For believers, this is Good News. For unbelievers, it's a sober call to repent of their evil ways and prepare for Christ's return. The same God who controlled the past, and who will be in control in the future, still controls the present—even if it seems as though evil is winning. This world is an illusion; the real world is the spiritual world. God is allowing evil to triumph for a time, but evil is ultimately doomed. The primary point of the book of Revelation is that God is sovereign. He has already determined the end of history. The secondary point is that Satan's rebellion is futile. Although Satan is the ultimate foe of God and God's people, he has already lost.

For information on the four main ways to interpret Revelation, see the Introduction, "Understanding Apocalyptic Literature."

1:2 John faithfully reported the word of God and the testimony of Jesus Christ—everything he saw.[NLT] John saw the vision and then *faithfully reported . . . everything he saw.* He saw *the word of God and the testimony of Jesus Christ.* Revelation, according to John, is God's Word—not simply John's narration of what he saw. It is an eternal message. The testimony "of" Jesus Christ could also be translated "from" Jesus Christ. The words of this book describe the promises and actions of God that have come true through Jesus. Revelation, as difficult as it may be to understand, should not be neglected. It should be read and studied, for it is the Word of God and the testimony of Christ to all believers, from the first century to today.

1:3 Blessed is the one who reads aloud the words of the prophecy, and blessed are those who hear and who keep what is written in it; for the time is near.NRSV "Blessed" means "God blesses those who" or "God's blessing is upon." This promise sets John's writing apart from other Jewish apocalyptic literature and points out that these words were inspired by God. This is the first of seven beatitudes in Revelation (see also 14:13; 16:15; 19:9; 20:6; 22:7, 14). See the chart at 14:13.

Who is blessed? *The one who reads aloud the words* of the prophecy. The public reading of Scripture was common in Jewish heritage (see, for example, Nehemiah 8:2-3; Luke 4:16; Acts 13:15). Christians also read Scripture aloud in public because copies of the Gospels and the letters of the apostles were not available to every believer. Someone—usually a scribe or someone trained in writing and reading texts—would be chosen to read aloud portions of the text. Later, the office of "reader" became a position in the church.

Scripture reading was an important event. In addition to the reader, *blessed* also *are those who hear and who keep what is written.* This echoes Jesus' words in Luke 11:28: "Blessed are those who hear the word of God and keep it" (NKJV). "Hear" and "keep" are important terms and major themes of the book. Used together, they mean "to persevere in faithful obedience." The blessed ones are those who come to church to hear God's Word and then keep (obey) it so that it changes their lives (Ephesians 4:13).

Revelation is a book of *prophecy* that is both prediction (foretelling future events) and proclamation (preaching about who God is and what he will do). Prophecy is more than telling the future. Behind the predictions are important principles about God's character and promises. These words will bless the hearers because through them they can get to know God better and be able to trust him more completely. The words are more than just predictions of the future; they include moral instruction that the listeners were to "hear" and "keep."

The phrase "the time is near" is like the phrase "what must soon take place" in 1:1 and refers to imminence. Believers must be ready for Christ's second coming. The Last Judgment and the establishment of God's kingdom are certainly near. No one knows when these events will occur, so all believers must be prepared. They will happen quickly, with no second chance to change minds or sides.

INSPIRING WORDS
The typical news reports—filled with violence, scandal, and political haggling—are depressing, and we may wonder where the world is heading. God's plan for the future, however, provides inspiration and encouragement because we know he will intervene in history to conquer evil. John encourages churches to read this book aloud so everyone can hear it, apply it ("keep what is written in it"), and be assured of the fact that God will triumph.

JOHN'S GREETINGS AND PRAISE TO GOD / 1:4-8

John began to address the recipients of this letter, a letter that would be sent along the roads through the various cities with the churches to whom John was writing. After this brief greeting comes a doxology of praise to God.

1:4-5a **This letter is from John to the seven churches in the province of Asia. Grace and peace from the one who is, who always was, and who is still to come; from the sevenfold Spirit before his throne; and from Jesus Christ, who is the faithful witness to these things, the first to rise from the dead, and the commander of all the rulers of the world.**ᴺᴸᵀ Jesus told *John* to write to *seven churches* that knew and trusted John and had read his earlier letters (see 1:9, 11). These were literal churches in literal cities. The letter was addressed so that it could be read and passed on in a systematic fashion, following the main Roman road clockwise around *the province of Asia* (now called Turkey).

These were not the only churches in Asia at the time. For example, Troas (Acts 20:5ff), Colosse (Colossians 1:2), and Hierapolis (Colossians 4:13) also had churches. Why did the Lord direct John to write to these seven in particular? It is possible that the number seven, as with the other sevens in the book, signifies completeness. While the seven churches were actual churches, they also represented all churches throughout the ages.

. *Grace and peace* were standard greetings in the ancient world. "Grace" was the Greek greeting *(charis)*; "peace" was the Hebrew greeting *(shalom)*. The early church took these two greetings and used them together as a way of declaring that God had given these realities to his people.

The Trinity—the Father *(the one who is, who always was, and who is still to come)*, the Holy Spirit *(the sevenfold Spirit)*, and the Son *(Jesus Christ)*—is the source of all truth (John 14:6-17; 1 John 2:27; Revelation 19:11).

All of time is encompassed in the Father—he is, was, and will be. This title is used only in Revelation (see also 11:17; 16:5). God is eternally present and therefore able to help his people in any age, in any situation. Note that the present tense is first, stressing that the God of the Old Testament and the God of the future is still in control of the present, even though it doesn't seem like it. The pressures and stresses that the early Christians faced made the truth of God's control over all history that much more meaningful.

The "sevenfold Spirit" has been identified by some to mean the seven angelic beings or messengers for the churches (see a further discussion at 1:20). Others have interpreted this to refer to those angels that accompany Christ at his return (Luke 9:26; 1 Timothy 5:21). But the reference to the Trinity here gives more weight to the interpretation that the sevenfold Spirit is the Holy Spirit. The "sevenfold Spirit" refers to the fullness of the Holy Spirit. The number seven is used throughout Revelation to symbolize completeness and perfection (see also 3:1; 4:5; 5:6). This also pictures the sevenfold ministry of the Holy Spirit as recorded in Isaiah 11:2 and the seven lamps in Zechariah, which also describe the Holy Spirit (Zechariah 4:1-10).

Jesus is seen in all his sovereignty. He is the *faithful witness* of the truth from God, who sent him to earth to die for sins. Both Jesus and the believers are called "witnesses." The word "martyr" comes from the Greek word for witness. Jesus was a "witness" as the first to die. This would have comforted believers who were suffering for their faith. Those who would die for their faith in Christ, the martyrs, would "witness" through their deaths. Jesus Christ is the preeminent "faithful witness" because he died and because he was *the first to rise from the dead* (see also Colossians 1:18). Christ's resurrection assures the same for all the believers. He shows us all how to stand firm for the faith even when faced with persecution. Others had risen from the dead—people whom the prophets, Jesus, and the apostles had brought back to life during their ministries—but later those people had died again. Jesus was the first to rise from the dead in an imperishable body (1 Corinthians 15:20), never to die again. He is the firstborn from the dead.

Jesus is also portrayed as *the commander of all the rulers of the world*—an all-powerful King, victorious in battle, glorious in peace. Satan had tried to tempt Jesus with an offer of ruling all the nations of the world if Jesus would bow and worship him (Matthew 4:8-9). Jesus refused and, through obedience to God through death on the cross, gained ultimate leadership. Psalm 89:27 says, "I will make him my firstborn son, the mightiest king

on earth" (NLT). Jesus was not just a humble earthly teacher; he is
the glorious God. When he returns, he will be recognized for who
he really is. Then, "at the name of Jesus every knee will bow, in
heaven and on earth and under the earth, and every tongue will
confess that Jesus Christ is Lord, to the glory of God the Father"
(Philippians 2:10-11 NLT).

WORDS OF TRUTH
We live in a day of conflicting claims for various religions (they
can't all be true), and the desire to be tolerant of all others (if
it's true for you, it's true). Yet how do we as Christians determine what we believe? We regard Jesus Christ as our faithful
witness (1:4-5). He is the only religious leader who has risen
from the dead.
   So when you read John's description of the vision, keep in
mind that his words are not just good advice; they are truth from
the King of kings. Don't just read his words for their interesting
and amazing portrayal of the future. Let the truth about Christ
penetrate your life, deepen your faith in him, and strengthen your
commitment to follow him—no matter what the cost.

**1:5b-6 To him who loves us and has freed us from our sins by his
blood, and has made us to be a kingdom and priests to serve
his God and Father—to him be glory and power for ever and
ever! Amen.**[NIV] This doxology concludes the prologue to this
book. John was writing to believers experiencing persecution; yet
he assured them that Jesus not only continuously cared for and
loved them but also had set them free, no matter how they might
feel. Jesus had set them free from their sins *by his blood,* that is,
through his death on the cross. Through that blood, he had made
his people *to be a kingdom and priests to serve his God and
Father.* Israel had been called to be "a kingdom of priests, [a]
holy nation" (Exodus 19:6 NLT). This saying describes the Christians as the continuation of the Old Testament people of God—
his kingdom and priests (see also Hebrews 13:15; 1 Peter 2:5, 9).
Together believers make up a kingdom of which Christ is their
King; individually they are priests because each has direct access
to God because of the sacrifice of Christ on the cross. Their
whole purpose, of course, is to serve God.
   The doxology ends with words of praise: *to him be glory and
power for ever and ever!* "Amen" means "let it be so."

**1:7 Look! He comes with the clouds of heaven. And everyone will
see him—even those who pierced him. And all the nations of
the earth will weep because of him. Yes! Amen!**[NLT] Jesus will
indeed have "glory and power for ever and ever" (1:6 NIV)—the

STAR WITNESS
Many hesitate to witness about their faith in Christ because
they don't think the change in their lives has been spectacular
enough. But you qualify as a witness for Jesus because of
what he has done for you, not because of what you have done
for him. Christ is seen through the whole book of Revelation as
the Lamb who was slain. He demonstrated his great love by
setting his people free from their sins through his death on the
cross ("freed us from our sins by his blood"), guaranteeing
them a place in his kingdom, and making them priests to admin-
ister God's love to others. The fact that the all-powerful God
has offered eternal life to you is nothing short of spectacular.
Testify about his wonderful gift!

book of Revelation describes that day when he will return to
earth. That Jesus will come *with the clouds of heaven* summarizes the message of Revelation. When Jesus ascended into
heaven, "he was taken up into the sky . . . and he disappeared into
a cloud" (Acts 1:9 NLT; see also Luke 24:50-51). An angel had
told the astonished disciples, "Jesus has been taken away from
you into heaven. And someday, just as you saw him go, he will
return" (Acts 1:11 NLT). The imagery of coming in the clouds is
probably a military picture, alluding to the clouds of dust kicked
up by the war chariots, the ultimate war machines in ancient
times. When Christ is pictured this way, he is coming as the ultimate Victor and conquering King (see also Daniel 7:13).

Jesus' second coming will be visible and victorious. *Everyone
will see him* arrive (Mark 13:26), and they will know it is Jesus.
When Christ returns, he will conquer evil and will judge all
people according to their deeds (Revelation 20:11-15).

Even those who pierced him will see him. "Those who pierced
him" could refer to the Roman soldiers who pierced Jesus' side as
he hung on the cross, but it probably refers to the Jews who were
responsible for his death (see Acts 2:22-23; 3:14-15). John saw
Jesus' death with his own eyes, and he never forgot the horror of
it (see John 19:34-35). Zechariah had written, "Then I will pour
out a spirit of grace and prayer on the family of David and on all
the people of Jerusalem. They will look on me whom they have
pierced and mourn for him as for an only son. They will grieve
bitterly for him as for a firstborn son who has died" (Zechariah
12:10 NLT). In Zechariah the twelve tribes mourned because of
their sin. Here, however, all people across the ages who have
rejected Christ have themselves "pierced" him through their indifference to his sacrifice on their behalf. *All the nations of the
earth*—both Jews and Gentiles—*will weep because of him.* They

will mourn because they know they will be facing God and his judgment and will be destroyed.

1:8 "I am the Alpha and the Omega," says the Lord God, "who is, and who was, and who is to come, the Almighty."[NIV] *Alpha* and *Omega* are the first and last letters of the Greek alphabet. The Lord God is the beginning and the end. God the Father is the eternal Lord and Ruler of the past, present, and future (see also 4:8; Isaiah 44:6; 48:12-15). God is sovereign over history and is in control of everything.

The one *who is, and who was, and who is to come* is also described in 1:4, the *Lord God,* who controls present, past, and future.

The phrase "the Almighty" comes out of the Old Testament and conveys military imagery, referring to God as a mighty warrior. The military imagery helped the people in the churches to whom this book was written understand that they had the ultimate Warrior fighting on their side. God rules over all.

> God is an infinite circle whose center is everywhere and whose circumference is nowhere.
>
> *Augustine of Hippo*

THE VISION OF CHRIST / 1:9-20

John again gave his name as the author of the letter and described his whereabouts and why he was there. Next he explained his commissioning to write this letter to the churches. Then he described his vision of the exalted Christ, leaving no mistake as to Christ's true identity. The vision has much in common with Isaiah 6 and Ezekiel 1.

1:9 I am John, your brother. In Jesus we are partners in suffering and in the Kingdom and in patient endurance. I was exiled to the island of Patmos for preaching the word of God and speaking about Jesus.[NLT] John had been one of Jesus' twelve disciples. (For more on John, see commentary on 1:1 above.) Although John was an apostle and an elder of the church, he described himself as their *brother* in Christ because he and the persecuted believers were *partners in suffering,* partners in God's coming *Kingdom,* and partners in *patient endurance* of their suffering. They were partners in suffering for Christ, as persecution against believers began to escalate at the end of the century. They shared in God's kingdom because, as believers, they were already its citizens. As believers faced persecution, they were awaiting the arrival of God's coming kingdom.

The Christian church was facing severe persecution. Almost all believers were socially, politically, or economically suffering because of this Empire-wide persecution, and some were even being killed for their faith. The word "Kingdom" is surrounded by "suffering" and "patient endurance." Although the North American churches are not facing the kind of oppression John referred to here, two-thirds of all Christians in the world face persecution today.

John had paid for his faithfulness to the message of Jesus by being *exiled to the island of Patmos,* a small rocky island about ten miles long and six miles wide in the Aegean Sea, about fifty miles offshore from the city of Ephesus on the Asia Minor seacoast (see map). The Romans used Patmos for banishing political prisoners. John, like Paul, was caught in a time when Rome turned against Christianity. There are two possible dates for Revelation. One is under the reign of Nero in the mid-60s, toward the time when Paul and Peter were both martyred. The other date is the mid-90s, when John was at the end of his life and the ruler was Domitian, a man who was far more anti-Christian than even Nero. Domitian issued an edict (under threat of death) demanding that all peoples in the Empire worship the reigning emperor. The date of the 90s is more likely. Eusebius wrote that John was exiled to the island by the emperor Domitian in A.D. 95 and released about eighteen months later.

John was exiled for *preaching the word of God and speaking about Jesus.* Although John was away from the churches and unable to travel, his exile did not stop what God would do through John, nor did it stop God's message from getting to his churches.

HE WHO HESITATES
John described himself as a partner in suffering (1:9). Early Christians faced imprisonment, economic injustice, slanderous accusations by Jews, and attacks from government soldiers or mobs. We may not face persecution for our faith as the early Christians did, but even with our freedom, few of us have the courage to share God's Word with others. If we hesitate to share our faith during easy times, how will we do it during times of persecution?

1:10-11 On the Lord's Day I was in the Spirit, and I heard behind me a loud voice like a trumpet, which said: "Write on a scroll what you see and send it to the seven churches: to Ephesus, Smyrna, Pergamum, Thyatira, Sardis, Philadelphia and Laodicea."^{NIV}
On the Lord's Day (Sunday), John *was in the Spirit,* which refers to a visionary experience given to John by the Holy Spirit. There are four "in-the-Spirit" passages in Revelation, which probably refer to

the actual visions John received (see 4:2; 17:3; 21:10; see also Eze-kiel 3:12, 14; 37:1; Acts 10:10; 11:5; 22:17). This is the first.

In this vision John *heard . . . a loud voice like a trumpet.* The trumpet heralds the return of Christ (1 Corinthians 15; 1 Thessalo-nians 4). The voice commands John to *write on a scroll* every-thing he would see in the visions. John's record then became this book, which he would *send* to the *seven churches.* The names of these churches are presented, as noted earlier, in a circular fash-ion, following the Roman road from one church to the next—starting at the church in the port city of Ephesus. Presumably, this letter was taken from John on Patmos by a messenger who crossed the water and landed at Ephesus, where he began his route. The contents of specific messages to these churches are in chapters 2 and 3.

1:12-14 When I turned to see who was speaking to me, I saw seven gold lampstands. And standing in the middle of the lamp-stands was the Son of Man. He was wearing a long robe with a gold sash across his chest. His head and his hair were white like wool, as white as snow. And his eyes were bright like flames of fire.[NLT] The *seven gold lampstands* are the seven churches in Asia to whom this letter is addressed (Revelation 1:11, 20). (See also Zechariah 4:1-10 for his vision of seven lamps.) Jesus, *the Son of Man,* stands among them. No matter what the churches face, Jesus is in control and protects them with his all-encompassing love and reassuring power. Through his Spirit, Jesus is still among the churches today. When a church faces persecution, it should remember Christ's deep love and compassion. When a church is wracked by internal strife and conflict, it should remember Christ's concern for purity and his intolerance of sin. Jesus is sovereign over the church.

The title "Son of Man" occurs many times in the New Testa-ment in reference to Jesus as the Messiah. John recognized Jesus because he had lived with him for three years and had seen him both as the Galilean preacher and as the glorified Son of God at the Transfiguration (Matthew 17:1-8). Here Jesus appears as the mighty Son of Man.

The *long robe* pictures Jesus as a leader. The *gold sash across his chest* reveals him as the high priest who goes into God's pres-ence to obtain forgiveness of sin for those who have believed in him. In the first century, wearing a sash, especially across the chest, indicated leadership and authority. Hebrews 2:17 identifies Jesus as the final high priest. His glowing white hair indicates his wisdom and divine nature (see also Daniel 7:9). His blazing eyes symbolize judgment of all evil (see Daniel 10:6) and deep insight, not only over the churches and the believers but over the entire course of history (see also 2:18; 19:12).

1:15 His feet were like bronze glowing in a furnace, and his voice was like the sound of rushing waters.[NIV] The *feet* like *bronze* picture an exalted person with great power (also from Daniel). Bronze usually symbolized the might of Rome—bronze shields and breastplates were used by the Roman army. In addition, the altar of burnt offering was covered with bronze (Exodus 38:1-7). Again, this is a picture of an all-powerful Victor. The description of *glowing* metal used to describe this Son of Man is also found in Ezekiel 1:13, 27; 8:2; and Daniel 10:6.

The *voice* like *rushing waters* (see also 19:6) evokes the image of a huge waterfall roaring over a high cliff. Thus, the voice is powerful and awesome. When this man speaks with authority, nothing else can be heard.

TO SEE JESUS
Revelation will probably challenge and change your mental picture of Jesus Christ. That is its purpose—to reveal Jesus Christ. What forms your impression of Jesus right now—famous paintings, movies, Sunday school art? To what degree do you picture Jesus with gold sash and snow white, woolly hair? Do his eyes flash fire and his feet glow like bronze? When you imagine Jesus speaking to you, does his voice sound like a trumpet or rushing waters? Reevaluate the way you think of Jesus as you read and study Revelation. Allow his awesome presence to transform your life.

1:16 He held seven stars in his right hand, and a sharp two-edged sword came from his mouth. And his face was as bright as the sun in all its brilliance.[NLT] In his *right hand,* Christ holds *seven stars,* explained in 1:20 as "the angels of the seven churches," referring to the seven churches, listed in 1:11, to whom this letter is addressed. That Christ is holding the stars implies his protection of these churches as he walks among them.

There are two swords in Revelation. Chapter 19 has the "great sword." The sword here is the *sharp two-edged sword.* This type of sword, invented by the Romans, represents invincible might. Only two to two and a half feet long, these swords were quite possibly the greatest military invention of the ancient world. Previously, swords were about three feet long and made of an inferior metal. They could not be sharp on both edges because the metal wasn't strong enough. The double-edged sword was lighter and sharp on both edges. With the older swords, fighting was done by drawing back and hacking, but when the Romans used their double-edged swords, they could slice and cut both ways. These swords gave such a great advantage in hand-to-hand combat that the Roman army was called "the short swords." It made them virtually invincible.

This sharp two-edged sword is coming *from* Jesus' *mouth,* symbolizing the power and force of his message. Jesus' words of judgment are as sharp as swords; he is completely invincible (2:16; 19:15, 21; Isaiah 49:2; Ephesians 6:17; Hebrews 4:12).

His face was as bright as the sun in all its brilliance. This shining brilliance probably describes Christ's entire being. The same sort of picture is described in the Transfiguration, an event that John himself had witnessed (10:1; Matthew 17:2).

1:17-18 **When I saw him, I fell at his feet as though dead. Then he placed his right hand on me and said: "Do not be afraid. I am the First and the Last. I am the Living One; I was dead, and behold I am alive for ever and ever! And I hold the keys of death and Hades."**NIV John's response to the awesome sight of the glorious Son of Man was to fall *at his feet as though dead.* Most likely this was not a trance; rather, it was in response to having seen a spectacular vision. (Other such responses are recorded in Joshua 5:14; Ezekiel 1:28; Daniel 8:17; 10:8-9; Matthew 17:6; and Acts 26:14.)

The message given by this glorious figure—Christ—is the same one that had been given to the women at the tomb (Matthew 28:5): *"Do not be afraid."* Jesus had also told his followers not to be afraid when he had walked over to them across the water (Matthew 14:27) and when the three who had witnessed his Transfiguration had fallen terrified to the ground (Matthew 17:7). For those who believe, there is no need to fear. This Christ is *the First and the Last*—essentially the same as the Alpha and the Omega in 1:8. In Isaiah 44:6, God says, "I am the First and the Last; there is no other God" (NLT). Christ is *the Living One*—not a dead idol but alive and always with his people, every moment, in control of all things. He is the same one who was resurrected. He *was dead;* that is, he experienced physical death on the cross. But now he is *alive for ever and ever.* Because Jesus rose from the dead, he can promise the same for his people.

Jesus holds *the keys of death and Hades,* which give him complete control over that domain. Keys open doors, thus revealing what is behind them. In ancient days the key holders had high status in the community. Christ alone has absolute authority over people's lives and deaths—and even when they are raised from the dead. He alone can free people from the ultimate enemy,

death. He alone can say who will die and who will live, because
he has the keys. The word "Hades" is the Greek word for the
underworld, the realm of the dead; a different word describes
"hell," the place of torment. Hades is the word used in the New
Testament for "Sheol"—the Old Testament word describing the
place of the dead. The word "Hades" occurs here, in 20:13-14,
and in Matthew 16:18. Believers need not fear death and Hades,
because Christ holds the keys to both (see Luke 16:23).

NO FEAR
Jesus told John not to be afraid (1:17). As the Roman government stepped up its persecution of Christians, John must have
wondered if the church could survive and stand against the
fearful opposition. But Jesus appeared in glory and splendor,
touched John with his right hand as if commissioning him, and
reassured him that he and his fellow believers had access to
God's strength to face these trials. Believers and churches of
any age who face difficult problems should remember that the
power available to John and the early church is also available
to them (see 1 John 4:4). Because Christ has such wonderful
power, we need not fear death or judgment.

**1:19 "Write down what you have seen—both the things that are
now happening and the things that will happen later."**NLT
The command to *write down* what John had seen is repeated
(see also 1:11). The phrase "what you have seen" is a general
statement referring to *both the things that are now happening
and the things that will happen later.* The vision that will
unfold in the following chapters will include present and future
events intertwined—events that both are and will be. Every
future revelation has relevance for the present—the churches
to whom this letter was written. The revelation also applies to
churches and believers even today, two thousand years later.

**1:20 "The mystery of the seven stars that you saw in my right
hand and of the seven golden lampstands is this: The seven
stars are the angels of the seven churches, and the seven
lampstands are the seven churches."**NIV Christ first reveals to
John *the mystery of the seven stars* that he was holding in his
right hand (1:16). In the New Testament, the word "mystery"
describes something formerly hidden but now revealed. Christ
explains that *the seven stars are the angels of the seven
churches.* But just who are the "angels of the seven churches"?
Because the Greek word *angeloi* can mean angels or messengers, some believe that they are angels designated to guard the
churches; others believe that they are elders or pastors of the

churches. The case for angels as the correct interpretation comes from the fact that every other use of "angels" in Revelation refers to heavenly beings. However, because the seven letters in Revelation 2–3 contain reprimands against the messengers, and angels are not ever considered to be heads of churches, it is doubtful that these angels are heavenly messengers. If these are earthly leaders or messengers, they are accountable to God for the churches they represent.

The *seven golden lampstands* among which Christ had been standing (1:13) represent *the seven churches* to whom this letter would be circulated (1:11). The churches may have been facing difficulties and persecution, but they must never forget that Christ was standing among them, totally in control.

Revelation 2

In a sense, the letters to the seven churches are like form letters. Each letter is formulated with seven elements:

1. They all begin by stating the addressee—"To the angel of the church in . . ."
2. The speaker, Christ, is mentioned—"These are the words of him who . . ."
3. Christ's knowledge about each church is noted.
4. Christ's evaluation of each church's condition is declared.
5. Christ's command to the congregation is noted.
6. Christ's call is given: "Anyone who is willing to hear should listen."
7. Finally, Christ's promise is given: "To the victorious, I will give."

Two letters have no commendation; two letters have no rebukes.

The letters comprise a literary unit tied to the vision of Christ in chapter 1, for each letter includes a distinct portion from the description of Christ. For example, in one letter Christ is described as the one who is the First and the Last (2:8), and in another he is described as the one who has the sharp two-edged sword (2:12).

"Classical dispensationalism" contends that these letters picture different periods in the history of the church and do not refer to actual churches. Dispensationalism understands these letters to describe seven "ages" of the church. Scholars acknowledge that these seven churches existed in John's time; the messages to the churches, however, apply to the church through the ages. Each letter calls believers to listen to what the Spirit says to the "churches" (plural). The commendations and rebukes recorded in each letter were to be applied by each of the churches (see 2:7, 11, 17, 23, 29) as well as by churches today. Although each letter describes an actual situation in an individual church, the letters serve as warnings to all churches through the ages.

A chart at the end of chapter 3 summarizes the letters to these seven churches.

CHAIN LETTER
Christians reading these opening chapters of Revelation invariably ask, "Which church is ours like?" Actually, a particular church may share positive and negative traits with several of the Asian churches. This is probably why Jesus had John write one letter to seven churches. They all got to read each other's mail. What a neighboring church was struggling with today, they might face tomorrow. Taken together, the letters give us a good picture of what Jesus expects from his church—faithful gatherings made up of believers who overcome. Jesus still expects us to overcome, and he promises his help along the way. Rather than trying to decide which church yours resembles, focus on faithful obedience to Christ.

THE LOVELESS CHURCH / 2:1-7

The first letter is addressed to the church in Ephesus—the crossroads of civilization—considered to be a city of great political importance. Aquila, Priscilla, and Paul had planted the church in Ephesus (see Acts 19); Timothy had ministered there (1 Timothy 1:3); John, the writer of this letter, was closely associated with the church. The carrier of this letter to the churches would have landed

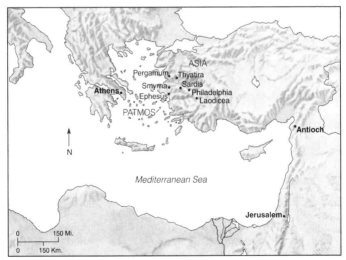

THE SEVEN CHURCHES
The seven churches were located on a major Roman road. A letter carrier would leave the island of Patmos (where John was exiled), arriving first at Ephesus. He would travel north to Smyrna and Pergamum, turn southeast to Thyatira, and continue on to Sardis, Philadelphia, and Laodicea—in the exact order in which the letters were dictated.

at the port of Ephesus and begun his journey by visiting the church there.

The basic problem with the church in Ephesus is that even though church members had stood fast against evil and false teaching, they had left their "first love"—their basic love for Christ and for one another.

2:1 "To the angel of the church in Ephesus write: These are the words of him who holds the seven stars in his right hand and walks among the seven golden lampstands."[NIV] *Ephesus* was a center of land and sea trade, for three major land-trade routes converged in the city, and a large port sat on its coast on the Aegean Sea. Along with Alexandria in Egypt and Antioch in Syria, Ephesus was one of the three most influential cities in the eastern part of the Roman Empire. Ephesus had been accorded an advantage given to a few cities in the Empire—it was a "free" city, meaning that it enjoyed a certain amount of self-rule. The city boasted a huge stadium, marketplace, and theater. The theater, built on the slope of a mountain that overlooked the harbor, seated twenty-five thousand people.

The temple to Artemis (the Roman name is Diana), one of the ancient wonders of the world, was located in Ephesus. According to Pliny, the temple was 425 feet long, 220 feet wide, and 60 feet high. There were 127 marble pillars, some of them overlaid with gold and jewels. The temple employed thousands of priests and priestesses; many of the priestesses were temple prostitutes, for Artemis was the goddess of fertility. A major industry was the manufacture of images of this goddess (see Acts 19:21-41). This city also was proud of its temples to the emperors—a growing cult, called the "imperial cult," viewed the _ruling caesar as a god, so the city had built temples to the succession of ruling caesars. In short, Ephesus was a city known for its idolatry.

In each of the seven letters Jesus Christ passes moral judgment upon the church concerned. To the church in Smyrna He gives unmixed praise, but to the church in Laodicea He expresses unrelieved condemnation. The Philadelphian church is more praised than blamed and the church in Sardis more blamed than praised, while in the letters to Pergamum and Thyatira and this first one to Ephesus, approval and disapproval are fairly evenly balanced.

John Stott

Paul had ministered in Ephesus for three years and had warned the Ephesian believers that false teachers would come and try to draw people away from the faith (see Acts 20:29-31). False teachers did indeed cause problems in the Ephesian church, but the church resisted them, as we can see from Paul's letters to Timothy, who stayed in Ephesus when Paul left for Macedonia. John spent

much of his ministry in this city and knew that these believers had
resisted false teaching (2:2).

Although John was writing, the words are clearly from Christ,
*the one who holds the seven stars in his right hand and walks
among the seven golden lampstands* (1:13, 16). Christ controls the
churches. Christ is described differently in every letter, mainly
because each description is tied to the problems of the specific
church. Ephesus, the mother church of all the other churches, was
filled with pride. That Christ held these churches in his hand shows
that he was in control over the churches. Ephesus had become a
large, proud church, and Christ's message would remind them that
he alone is the head of the body of believers.

YOUR CHURCH CAN CHANGE THE WORLD
Does God care about your church? If you are tempted to doubt
it, look more closely at these seven letters. The Lord of the universe knew each church and its precise situation. Jesus told
John to write about specific people, places, and events. He
praised believers for their successes and told them how to
correct their failures. Just as Jesus cared for each of these
churches, he cares for yours. He wants it to reach its greatest
potential. The group of believers with whom you worship and
serve is God's vehicle for changing the world. Take it seriously—God does.

2:2-3 **"I know your works, your toil and your patient endurance.
I know that you cannot tolerate evildoers; you have tested
those who claim to be apostles but are not, and have found
them to be false. I also know that you are enduring patiently
and bearing up for the sake of my name, and that you have
not grown weary."**NRSV The one who walks among the churches
(2:1) is able to say to this church in Ephesus, *I know your works.*
Over a long period of time, this church had steadfastly refused to
tolerate sin among its members. This was not easy in a city noted
for immoral sexual practices associated with the worship of the
goddess Artemis. The Ephesian church had been strong in its
orthodoxy and had resisted false teachers.

Christ commended the church at Ephesus for five things:

1. working hard *(toil)*
2. persevering *(patient endurance)*
3. resisting sin *(cannot tolerate evildoers)*
4. critically examining the claims of false apostles *(tested those
   who claim to be apostles)*
5. *enduring patiently and bearing up* without becoming weary.

All of these characteristics show a church busy with good works and suffering willingly for the cause of Christ. The Ephesian believers knew evil when they saw it and did not tolerate it.

The false apostles would be those who claimed to be believers but were not. The church had succeeded in weeding out those who falsely claimed apostleship. Generally, the word "apostle" in the New Testament refers first to the twelve disciples (Mark 3:13; Acts 1:2, 26) because of their special place in building the foundation of the church (Ephesians 2:20). The word was also expanded to include those such as Paul (Galatians 1:1), Barnabas (Acts 14:14), and James, the brother of Jesus (Galatians 1:19). The name referred to those who had been specially appointed by Christ. They were eyewitnesses to his ministry on earth. Miracles often accompanied apostolic authority; however, false prophets could often also do what appeared to be miracles. It was important, therefore, as John wrote in another letter, to "not believe everyone who claims to speak by the Spirit. [Believers] must test them to see if the spirit they have comes from God. For there are many false prophets in the world" (1 John 4:1 NLT). John went on to explain that the way to test if a person has the Spirit of God is to examine what he or she believes about Jesus Christ (1 John 4:2-3). That was probably the method that the Ephesian church had used to "test" those who claimed to be apostles but were not.

Paul had warned the Ephesian elders, "I know full well that false teachers, like vicious wolves, will come in among you after I leave, not sparing the flock. Even some of you will distort the truth in order to draw a following" (Acts 20:29-30 NLT). Jesus had told his disciples, "Beware of false prophets who come disguised as harmless sheep, but are really wolves that will tear you apart. You can detect them by the way they act" (Matthew 7:15-16 NLT). The message to the church in Ephesus shows that false teachers had indeed come in among the believers.

The damage that false teachers cause is not limited to cults, nor to past days in church history. Some of the characteristics of false teachers show up today in churches and ministries professing to be faithful to the true gospel. Many leaders and authorities today demand allegiance. Because they seem to know the Bible, their influence can be dangerously subtle. How can believers recognize false teaching?

- It promotes controversies instead of helping people come to Jesus.
- It is often initiated by those whose motivation is to make a name for themselves.
- It will be contrary to the true teaching of the Scriptures.

To protect the church from the deception of false teachers, church leaders must not avoid theology but should teach clearly what the Bible says about key doctrines. This will help believers identify false teachers and false doctrines.

TOLERANCE
The church at Ephesus faced a culture characterized by immorality. We, too, live in a culture tolerant of sexual immorality. It is popular to be open-minded toward many types of sin, calling them personal choices or alternative lifestyles. But when the body of believers begins to tolerate sin in the church, it is lowering the church's standards and compromising its witness. Remember that God's approval is infinitely more important than the world's. Use God's Word, not what people around you are willing to accept, to set the standards for what is right or wrong.

2:4 "Yet I hold this against you: You have forsaken your first love."[NIV] Despite the commendations, Christ had something against this church—they had *forsaken* their *first love*. This "first love" probably refers to the maxim "Love the Lord your God . . . and your neighbor as yourself" (see Acts 20:35; Ephesians 1:15). The Ephesians, though commended for their zeal in protecting the faith, had fallen into caring more about orthodoxy than love.

Every church should have pure faith and root out heresy. But these good efforts should spring from their love for Jesus Christ and for other believers. Both Jesus and John stressed love for one another as an authentic proof of the gospel (John 13:34; 1 John 3:18-19). In the battle to maintain sound teaching and moral and doctrinal purity, it is possible to lose a charitable spirit. Yet we need both. Prolonged conflict can weaken or destroy patience and affection. In defending the faith, believers must guard against any structure or rigidity that weakens love.

FIRST LOVE
Christ told the Ephesian believers that they had forsaken their first love (2:4). Just as when a man and woman fall in love, so also new believers rejoice at their newfound forgiveness. But when we lose sight of the seriousness of sin, we begin to lose the thrill of our forgiveness (see 2 Peter 1:9). In the first steps of your Christian life, you may have had enthusiasm without knowledge. Do you now have knowledge without enthusiasm? Both are necessary if we are to keep our love for God intense and untarnished (see Hebrews 10:32, 35).

2:5 **"Remember the height from which you have fallen! Repent and do the things you did at first. If you do not repent, I will come to you and remove your lampstand from its place."**^{NIV} Paul had once commended the church at Ephesus for its love for God and for others (Ephesians 1:15). That love is pictured at *the height from which* the church had *fallen.* Jesus called this church back to love. They needed to *repent* of their lack of love and *do the things* they *did at first*—love as they had originally loved, with enthusiasm and devotion.

If they refused to repent, however, Christ said that he would come and *remove* the church's *lampstand from its place.* For Jesus to remove a church's lampstand from its place would mean the church would cease to be a church. Just as the seven-branched candlestick in the temple gave light for the priests to see, the churches were to give light to their surrounding communities. But Jesus warned them that their lights could go out. In fact, Jesus himself would extinguish any light that did not fulfill its purpose. The church had to repent of its sins.

2:6 **"Yet this is to your credit: you hate the works of the Nicolaitans, which I also hate."**^{NRSV} Christ added a further commendation to this church in Ephesus—he credited them for hating *the works of the Nicolaitans,* which Christ also hated. The Nicolaitans were believers who had compromised their faith in order to enjoy some of the sinful practices of Ephesian society, including idolatry and sexual immorality. The name "Nicolaitans" is roughly the Greek equivalent of the Hebrew word for "Balaamites." Balaam was a prophet who induced the Israelites to carry out their lustful desires (see 2:14; Numbers 31:16). These Nicolaitans had amalgamated some Greek, some Christian, and some Jewish practices to form a sort of civil religion. It may have been that they were willing to worship in the imperial cult, worshiping the emperor, justifying it as a civil duty. They were probably advocates of freedom and compromise, but the Ephesian church had taken a strong stand against these heretics.

INTOLERANT
Through John, Jesus commended the church at Ephesus for hating the wicked practices ("the works") of the Nicolaitans (2:6). Note that they didn't hate the people, just their sinful actions. Believers should accept and love all people and refuse to tolerate all evil. God cannot tolerate sin, and he expects us to stand against it. The world needs Christians who will stand for God's truth and point people toward right living.

2:7 **"Anyone who is willing to hear should listen to the Spirit and understand what the Spirit is saying to the churches. Everyone who is victorious will eat from the tree of life in the paradise of God."**NLT Each of the seven letters ends with the exhortation, *Anyone who is willing to hear should listen to the Spirit and understand what the Spirit is saying to the churches.* The words of the Spirit are the words of Christ. Note that all the letters were to be read to all the churches. Those who "hear" what is read should then "listen to the Spirit" in order to understand what the Spirit is saying and to know what should be done. Those who listen and do what the Spirit leads them to do will be *victorious* (also translated "overcome"). These who are victorious will remain faithful to Christ no matter what the cost.

Those victorious ones will *eat from the tree of life in the paradise of God.* The Garden of Eden contained the tree of life and the tree of the knowledge of good and evil (see Genesis 2:9). Eating from the tree of life brought eternal life with God; eating from the tree of knowledge brought the ability to discern good and evil and, therefore, to choose evil. When Adam and Eve ate from the tree of knowledge, they disobeyed God's command. So they were excluded from Eden and barred from eating from the tree of life. Eventually, evil will be destroyed, and believers will be brought into a restored paradise. In the new earth, everyone will eat from the tree of life and will live forever (22:2, 19). Eating from the tree of life pictures the gift of eternal life. In paradise God will restore the perfect fellowship that existed in the Garden of Eden before sin entered and ruined the relationship between people and God.

THE PERSECUTED CHURCH / 2:8-11

The port city of Smyrna lay thirty-five miles up the coast, north of Ephesus. It also had an excellent harbor on the Aegean Sea and rivaled Ephesus in the export business. This is the only one of the seven cities that is still in existence; its modern name is Izmir. The church in Smyrna was one of the two churches that received no rebukes from Christ.

2:8 **"To the angel of the church in Smyrna write: These are the words of him who is the First and the Last, who died and came to life again."**NIV Smyrna, like Ephesus, was a proud and beautiful city. Smyrna also had earned the right to be self-governing. It had a large library, stadium, and the largest public theater in Asia. Mount Pagus rose above the harbor with an acropolis built on it that was considered the city's "crown." A famous "Golden Street" traversed the city with a temple to Zeus at one end and a temple to a local goddess Sipylene (Cybele) at the other. Other temples to Apollo, Asclepius, and Aphrodite lined the way.

Perhaps even more important, the city had become a center for the cult of emperor worship. Smyrna received permission (over several other cities who requested) to build a temple to the emperor Tiberius in 23 B.C.. Under the emperor Domitian (who ruled from A.D. 81 to 96), emperor worship was required for all Roman citizens. Those who refused could receive the death penalty. Once a year, all citizens were required to burn incense on an altar to Caesar, after which they would receive a certificate proving that they had done their civil duty. While this was more an act of political loyalty than a religious act, the citizen had to say, while burning the incense, "Caesar is lord." Many Christians considered this act blasphemous and refused to do it.

In addition to being a center for the imperial cult, Smyrna also had a large Jewish population that actively opposed the Christians. Thus, the church in this city struggled against two hostile forces: a Gentile population that was loyal to Rome and supported emperor worship and a large Jewish population strongly opposed to Christianity. Persecution and suffering were inevitable in that kind of environment. Years later, in A.D. 156, the eighty-six-year-old church father, Polycarp, was burned alive as "the twelfth martyr of Smyrna." Obviously, the church in Smyrna was persecuted.

The description of Christ given to this small church on the verge of being snuffed out by persecution is that Christ is the *First and the Last, who died and came to life again* (see 1:17-18). Although this church was almost dead due to persecution, Christ was reminding them that he was sovereign and eternal. No matter what they faced, Christ already knew about it; as the "First and the Last," nothing could take him by surprise. Christ identified himself as the one who died and came back to life again. Even if believers have to suffer to the point of death, Christ, the one who "came to life again," would raise them to eternal life with him.

2:9 **"I know about your suffering and your poverty—but you are rich! I know the slander of those opposing you. They say they are Jews, but they really aren't because theirs is a synagogue of Satan."**[NLT] The church in Smyrna was *suffering* because of persecution, and believers faced *poverty* even in this wealthy city. This probably refers to material poverty because Christ immediately assured them that despite their poverty, they were *rich*—referring to their heavenly riches (see James 2:5). These Christians' poverty may have come from sanctions against them as part of the persecution they faced.

Much of the persecution seems to have been coming from the Jews who, as noted above, were actively opposing Christianity. Christ identified them as those who claimed to be Jews but *really* weren't. They may have claimed to have descended from Abraham, but true Jews (God's people) are those who have accepted Jesus as Messiah and Savior. Paul had written to the Christians in Galatia, "Now that you belong to Christ, you are the true children of Abraham. You are his heirs, and now all the promises God gave to him belong to you" (Galatians 3:29 NLT). Because these Jews had rejected the Messiah, they were, in reality, no more than *a synagogue of Satan* (John 8:31-47). The phrase "synagogue of Satan" means that these Jews were serving Satan's purposes, not God's, when they gathered to worship, because they hated and persecuted the true people of God, the Christians.

2:10 **"Don't be afraid of what you are about to suffer. The Devil will throw some of you into prison and put you to the test. You will be persecuted for 'ten days.'" Remain faithful even when facing death, and I will give you the crown of life."**[NLT] Christ told the believers in Smyrna, who had already been facing persecution and suffering, that they ought not to be afraid of what they were *about to suffer.* More was coming, yet they should remember that although the Jews and Roman authorities were carrying out the persecution, behind any actions against them was *the Devil* himself. Satan would cause some of the believers to be thrown *into prison* and even be killed. He would put the believers *to the test*—that is, he would test their faith. Jesus had told his disciples, "Don't be afraid of those who want to kill you. They can only kill your body; they cannot touch your soul" (Matthew 10:28 NLT). The persecution would continue for *"ten days"*—probably symbolizing that although persecution would be intense, it would be relatively short and have a definite beginning and end. God was in complete control. The church was challenged to *remain faithful* to Christ even when *facing death.*

Believers need not fear death because it will only result in their receiving *the crown of life.* Smyrna was famous for its athletic games. Each champion would receive a crown, a victory wreath. In ancient Rome this was the most sought-after prize. To have gained this wreath meant that one had done special acts for Rome and would be considered a patron of the Empire. This can be compared to being knighted in England. In contrast, those who have suffered for their faith will receive "the crown of life" in God's kingdom.

The message to the Smyrna church was to remain faithful during their suffering because God is in control and because his promises are reliable. Jesus never taught that by being faithful to him, believers would avoid troubles, suffering, and persecution. Rather, believers must be faithful to Christ *even when* suffering. Only then will their faith prove genuine. Believers remain faithful by keeping their eyes on Christ and on what he promises for now and for the future (see Philippians 3:13-14; 2 Timothy 4:8).

OUT OF SUFFERING
John predicted that the church in Smyrna would be persecuted (2:10). Pain is part of life, but it is never easy to suffer, regardless of the reason. Jesus commended the church at Smyrna for its faith in suffering. He then encouraged the believers that they did not need to fear the future—if they remained faithful. Don't let difficult times turn you away from God. Remember that when you suffer, Christ suffers with you because you belong to him (Philippians 3:10). Allow your suffering to draw you toward greater faithfulness. Trust God, and remember your heavenly reward (see also 22:12-14). Out of suffering will come the crown of life.

2:11 **"Anyone who is willing to hear should listen to the Spirit and understand what the Spirit is saying to the churches. Whoever is victorious will not be hurt by the second death."**[NLT]
The call for *anyone who is willing to hear* to *listen to the Spirit* is repeated at the end of each letter. *Whoever is victorious*—that is, whoever stands strong for the faith despite persecution and suffering—*will not be hurt by the second death.* The Greek negative is emphatic—they will not in any way be hurt. Believers and unbelievers alike experience physical death. The first death for those in Smyrna might well be martyrdom. But even then they would be victorious because they would not face the second death. All people will be resurrected, but believers will be resurrected to eternal life with God, while unbelievers will be resurrected to be punished with a second death—eternal separation from God (see also 20:14; 21:8, 27; 22:15).

THE LENIENT CHURCH / 2:12-17

After leaving Smyrna, a letter carrier traveled along the coast of the Aegean Sea for about forty miles. Then the road turned northeast along the Caicus River. About ten miles inland stood the impressive city of Pergamum, built on a hill one thousand feet above the surrounding countryside, creating a natural fortress. Rivaling Ephesus as the leading city in the region, Pergamum had become the capital of the province of Asia and the center of Asian culture. It was proud of its links with Rome.

The problem in Pergamum was leniency toward those in the church who were compromising their faith with the idol worship and sexual immorality of pagan worship. Compromise can be good and is often needed, but the church must never compromise the basic tenets of the Christian faith.

2:12 "To the angel of the church in Pergamum write: These are the words of him who has the sharp, double-edged sword."NIV *Pergamum,* a sophisticated city and center of Greek culture and education, boasted a 200,000-volume library that was second only to the famous library in Alexandria in Egypt. According to legend, when Pergamum tried to lure away from Alexandria one of its librarians, the king in Alexandria stopped exporting papyrus to Pergamum. This embargo resulted in Pergamum's development of what became known as parchment, a writing material made from animal skins.

Pergamum was the center of four of the most important gods of the day—Zeus, Athene, Dionysus, and Asclepius. The city's chief god was Asclepius, whose symbol was a serpent and who was considered the god of healing. People came to Pergamum from all over the world to seek healing from this god.

The city was also a center for the imperial cult. While Smyrna had built temples to the emperor, Pergamum was the first city to receive permission to build a temple dedicated to a governing emperor, Augustus, whose temple was built in 29 B.C.

The proconsul of Pergamum had been granted the rare power known as "the right of the sword," meaning that he could perform executions. To the church in this city, Christ described himself as *him who has the sharp, doubled-edged sword* (1:16). Just as the sword was a symbol of Rome's authority and judgment, Jesus' sharp, double-edged sword represents God's ultimate authority and judgment. Only Christ has ultimate power over life and death.

2:13 "I know where you are living, where Satan's throne is. Yet you are holding fast to my name, and you did not deny your faith in me even in the days of Antipas my witness, my faithful one, who was killed among you, where Satan lives."NRSV As the center for four idolatrous cults (those of Zeus, Athene, Dionysius, and Asclepius), Pergamum was called the city *where Satan's throne is.* Idolatry is satanic. Surrounded by the worship of idols and of the Roman emperor as god, the church at Pergamum refused to renounce its faith. The believers held *fast to* the name of Christ, even after Satan's worshipers had killed one of their members.

It was not easy to be a Christian in Pergamum. Believers experienced great pressure to compromise or leave the faith. Nothing is known about *Antipas* except that he did not compromise. He was *faithful* as a *witness* for Christ (see 1:5), and he *was killed* for his faith.

2:14-15 **"And yet I have a few complaints against you. You tolerate some among you who are like Balaam, who showed Balak how to trip up the people of Israel. He taught them to worship idols by eating food offered to idols and by committing sexual sin. In the same way, you have some Nicolaitans among you—people who follow the same teaching and commit the same sins."**[NLT] Despite commending believers for holding fast to the faith (2:13), Christ had *a few complaints* against this church in Pergamum. Apparently, some in the church were tolerating those who were teaching or practicing what Christ opposed. Christ described the church as tolerating some believers who were *like Balaam, who showed Balak how to trip up the people of Israel.* Balaam had done that, in a roundabout way, by influencing some in Israel *to worship idols by eating food offered to idols and by committing sexual sin.*

The complete story of Balak and Balaam is recorded in Numbers 22–25. In brief, Balak was a king who feared the large number of Israelites traveling through his country, so he hired Balaam, a sorcerer, and told him to pronounce a curse on them. Balaam had refused at first, but an offer of money had changed his mind. Numbers 25:1-3 describes the Israelite men getting involved with pagan women and then worshiping the gods of Moab. While these verses do not mention Balaam, Numbers 31:16 explains that Balaam knew he could undermine Israel's worship and power by sending the Moabite women to entice the men of Israel. Balaam's influence caused great disaster for Israel, and he has earned the station as one who led people astray (see 2 Peter 2:15; Jude 11).

The church in Pergamum had stood strong against persecution, but what Satan could not accomplish from without he was trying to do from within—through Balaam-like deceit. Christ rebuked the church for tolerating those who, like Balaam, were undermining people's faith. Apparently some in the church were corrupting others in their attempt to justify idol worship—perhaps by joining in with civic ceremonies where idols were worshiped. Eating food offered to idols probably refers to these people's taking part in pagan feasts. Sexual sin may also be understood as being part of certain pagan festivities.

The church also had *some Nicolaitans among* them—*people who follow the same teaching and commit the same sins* as those

who were like Balaam. These two groups were essentially the
same in their practices. The Nicolaitans are described in 2:6 as
those whose actions Christ hates. The believers in Ephesus had
recognized the error of these people, but apparently the believers
in Pergamum were being deceived by it. The Nicolaitans were
Christians who had compromised their faith in order to enjoy the
sinful pleasures of their society and perhaps to be able to burn
incense on the altar to the emperor to avoid the penalty for not
doing so. Their sin was in compromising their faith for the world.
They thought that the best policy was to peacefully coexist and
go along with what they could of Roman society in order to be
left alone. But such compromise could only dilute their faith;
thus, Christ said it could not be tolerated.

NO COMPROMISE
Christ rebuked the church at Pergamum for toleration and compromise (2:14-15). Compromise involves blending the qualities
of two different things or conceding principle. While believers
should cooperate in society as much as they can, they must
avoid any alliance, partnership, or participation that may lead to
immoral practices. There can be no compromise between loyalty to Christ and the sinful pleasures of idol worship or sexual
immorality. Christians may differ in some areas, but there is no
room for heresy and moral impurity. Don't tolerate sin by bow-
ing to the pressure to be open-minded.

2:16 **"Repent, or I will come to you suddenly and fight against
them with the sword of my mouth."**[NLT] Christ was not only telling the "Balaams" and Nicolaitans to repent; he also wanted the
church to repent of its leniency toward these sinners. The church
should get rid of those who were attempting to compromise
where there could be no compromise. A church who tolerates
such people will find that Christ will come *suddenly and fight
against them with the sword of [his] mouth.* This sword represents God's judgment against rebellious nations (19:15, 21) and
all forms of sin. If the church did not repent of its sin and deal
with the compromisers, then God would come and do it—and
that would be disastrous.

2:17 **"Anyone who is willing to hear should listen to the Spirit and
understand what the Spirit is saying to the churches. Everyone who is victorious will eat of the manna that has been hidden away in heaven. And I will give to each one a white stone,
and on the stone will be engraved a new name that no one
knows except the one who receives it."**[NLT] This closing calls
upon readers to *listen to the Spirit and understand.* Those who

are *victorious* (faithful against compromise) will be given a reward that here includes three symbols: hidden manna, a white stone, and a new name.

Being able to *eat of the manna that has been hidden away in heaven* suggests spiritual nourishment that faithful believers will receive for keeping their churches doctrinally pure. On the journey toward the promised land, God provided manna from heaven to the Israelites for their physical nourishment (Exodus 16:13-18). Then God told Moses to place a jar of the manna in the ark of the covenant as a reminder of God's provision (Exodus 16:32-34; Hebrews 9:4). Jewish tradition held that this golden pot of manna still existed somewhere; hidden by Jeremiah at the destruction of Jerusalem, it would be restored at the messianic age. The hidden manna symbolizes the promises and blessings that will come with the arrival of the Messiah. Jesus, the bread of life (John 6:51), provides spiritual nourishment that satisfies our deepest hunger. Those who were refusing to revel in the pagan feasts of Pergamum were promised the manna that would satisfy hunger and bring blessing.

It is unclear what the white stones represent or what the names on each will be. Because these stones seem to relate to the hidden manna, they may be symbols of the believer's eternal nourishment, or eternal life. Small stones served many purposes in ancient times. Some were given to the poor to help them obtain food, like food stamps. Some were used as invitations to a banquet. The invited person would bring along the stone in order to be admitted. Each stone would have an invited person's name on it. For those who refused to go to the pagan banquets, a place was reserved at the Messiah's banquet in heaven. The stones may be significant because each will bear the new name of every person who truly believes in Christ. Alternately, the new name may be Christ's name as it will be fully revealed (19:12). Or perhaps, because a person's name represented his or her character, it may be that the new name signifies the believer's transformed life and character because of Christ's saving work. The new name may be the evidence that a person has been accepted by God and declared worthy to receive eternal life. In any case, we know that God will give believers new names and new hearts.

THE COMPROMISING CHURCH / 2:18-29

A letter carrier, upon leaving Pergamum, would travel southeast about forty miles, over a range of small hills, and finally into the fertile plain of Lycus. There he would find Thyatira, a city known for its manufacturing.

The problem in Thyatira was a woman, called Jezebel, who

was teaching compromise with the pagan world. Christ condemned such teaching. There can be no compromise with evil. Believers must be discerning in order to see evil for what it is.

2:18 "To the angel of the church in Thyatira write: These are the words of the Son of God, whose eyes are like blazing fire and whose feet are like burnished bronze."NIV *Thyatira* was a working person's town, a center for manufacturing. The city was filled with many trade guilds for commerce such as cloth making, dyeing, leatherworking, bronzeworking, and pottery making. Lydia, Paul's first convert in Philippi, was a merchant from Thyatira (Acts 16:14). The city was not important as a center for any temples to particular gods, although Apollo was worshiped as a guardian of the city. This was combined with the required worship of the emperor, considered an incarnation of Apollo and thus a son of Zeus himself. Besides Apollo, each guild appears to have had its own patron deity with its own festivals.

Christ's description of himself as the speaker to this church is that he is *the Son of God.* This sets him against Apollo and the emperor, who were said to be sons of the chief god, Zeus. This title is used nowhere else in Revelation. This Son of God has *eyes* of *blazing fire* and *feet* of *burnished bronze* (see 1:14-15; see also Daniel 10:6). The blazing eyes indicate the penetrating power of his vision; the feet of bronze indicate strength for executing judgment.

2:19 "I know all the things you do—your love, your faith, your service, and your patient endurance. And I can see your constant improvement in all these things."NLT The believers in Thyatira were commended for their good deeds. Christ sees all good deeds. He knew of the believers' *love* for one another (love that the Ephesian church had lost—2:4-5), their *faith,* their *service,* and their *patient endurance.* Christ was pleased to see their *constant improvement* in all of these things.

2:20 "Nevertheless, I have this against you: You tolerate that woman Jezebel, who calls herself a prophetess. By her teaching she misleads my servants into sexual immorality and the eating of food sacrificed to idols."NIV Thyatira had the opposite problem that Ephesus had. Whereas the Ephesian church had been good at dealing with false teachers but had lacked love, the church in Thyatira had lots of love but had become tolerant of false teachers. And, as was happening in Pergamum, the church in Thyatira was tolerating false teaching that was attempting to compromise with the pagan society.

In this case, the problem was *Jezebel, who calls herself a*

prophetess, a woman from among the believers, who claimed to
have the gift of prophecy. She may indeed have had unusual
gifts, but she was using her influence to teach positions that were
contrary to God's Word, misleading the believers. Like Balaam,
she was leading the people into sexual immorality and idolatry
(2:14-15), probably by teaching that immorality was not a serious
matter for believers. Her name may have been Jezebel, or John
may have used the name Jezebel to symbolize the kind of evil
she was promoting. Jezebel, a pagan Philistine queen of Israel,
was considered the most evil woman who ever lived. She had led
Israel's king, Ahab, into Baal worship and eventually had spread
that idolatry throughout all of Israel (see 1 Kings 16:31-33;
19:1-2; 21:1-15; 2 Kings 9:7-10, 30-37).

"Jezebel" was being tolerated in the Thyatiran church—perhaps her manner was so manipulative and persuasive that many
did not notice, or perhaps no one realized the severe danger into
which she was placing the entire church.

Jezebel was somehow misleading the believers by her teaching, which seems to have had much in common with the
Nicolaitans and the followers of Balaam (2:6, 14-15). The teaching was misleading about *sexual immorality* and the *eating of
food sacrificed to idols.* She had been able to give convincing
teaching about compromising with society. The two issues probably tied in with the guilds in Thyatira. Most of the people in the
city were tradesmen, so they belonged to various guilds. These
guilds (such as potters, tentmakers, etc.) each had an area in the
city and a guild hall, which functioned as a center for the guild's
religious and civic activities. Usually the guild would hold a banquet at the hall once a week, and these banquets would often be
centered on idolatry—featuring meat sacrificed to idols and, most
likely, some form of sexual license as part of the revelry. Jezebel
was probably encouraging the believers, mostly tradespeople
themselves, to continue to take part in their guilds' activities as
their civic duty. A refusal to join the guilds and take part in their
activities would mean certain economic hardship. Jezebel suggested a way of compromise. Christ was pleased neither with this
woman's teaching nor with the fact that the church tolerated her.

2:21-22 **"I gave her time to repent, but she would not turn away from
her immorality. Therefore, I will throw her upon a sickbed,
and she will suffer greatly with all who commit adultery with
her, unless they turn away from all their evil deeds."**NLT God
in his mercy had given Jezebel *time to repent* of her wicked
ways, *but she would not turn away from her immorality.* Conse-
quently, God was going to punish her with sickness and suffering.

The reference to those who *commit adultery with her* may refer
to both involvement in sexual immorality and in idolatry by way
of her teaching. Those involved would also be punished *unless*
they turned *away from all their evil deeds.*

STAY AWAY
Jezebel was promoting sexual immorality (2:20). Sexual immorality is serious because sex outside marriage always hurts
someone. It hurts God because it shows that we prefer to satisfy our own way instead of according to God's
Word. It hurts others because it violates the commitment so
necessary to a relationship. It hurts us because it often brings
disease to our bodies and adversely affects our personalities.
Sexual immorality can destroy families, churches, and communities because it destroys the integrity on which these relationships are built. God wants to protect us from hurting ourselves
and others; thus, we are to have no part in sexual immorality,
even if our culture accepts it.

2:23 **"I will strike her children dead. And all the churches will
know that I am the one who searches out the thoughts and
intentions of every person. And I will give to each of you whatever you deserve."**NLT The phrase "I will strike her children
dead" most likely refers to Jezebel's followers, her spiritual *children,* those whom she had convinced to compromise with the
pagan world. God wanted the church to deal with Jezebel. This
judgment would be an example so that *all the churches* would
know that God can see (with his "blazing eyes," 2:18) *the
thoughts and intentions of every person.* No matter how a person
appears on the outside, God alone knows what is going on in that
person's heart. No one can hide from Christ; he knows what is in
every person's heart and mind. Those who work against Christ
will be found out and will receive *whatever* they *deserve.*

2:24-25 **"But to the rest of you in Thyatira, who do not hold this teaching, who have not learned what some call 'the deep things of
Satan,' to you I say, I do not lay on you any other burden; only
hold fast to what you have until I come."**NRSV Many in the church
in Thyatira had not followed Jezebel and had seen through her
deception. After the church would repent and get rid of Jezebel
and her teaching, Christ would not place any other responsibilities
on them other than simply to *hold fast* to what they had until his
return. All they needed was their pure faith, not the *deep things of
Satan* that Jezebel had been teaching.

This teaching of "deep things" probably involved so-called
secret insights that were guaranteed to promote deeper spiritual

life. Jezebel may have considered her insights to be deeper knowledge of God, but Christ explained that these "insights" were really the teachings of Satan. It is also possible that Jezebel may have been saying exactly what she meant; that is, she may have been teaching that in order to stand strong for the faith, a person had to plumb the depths of Satan to prove one's spiritual strength. In either case, Christ condemned her teaching.

DEADLY ATTRACTION
There is great danger when we try to accomodate and integrate nonbiblical ideas into our faith. Christ warned against seeking "the deep things of Satan." What was the appeal of such knowledge? Christians were being led astray by the teaching that what happened in the body was inconsequential; therefore, it was not sin. So one appeal was that sexual desires could be fulfilled outside of marriage without consequences. An even more deadly appeal to the "deep things" was the sense of pride that such knowledge stimulated in those seeking it.
   Believers should hold tightly to the basics of the Christian faith and view with caution and counsel any new teaching that turns them away from the Bible and the basics of its moral teaching, from the fellowship of the church, or from the basic confession of faith.

2:26-27 **"To all who are victorious, who obey me to the very end, I will give authority over all the nations. They will rule the nations with an iron rod and smash them like clay pots."**^{NLT} Christ says that those who *are victorious* (over Jezebel, etc.) and *who obey* to *the very end* will rule over Christ's enemies and reign with him as he judges evil. Earlier, Christ had given this promise concerning those who obey to the very end: "Those who endure to the end will be saved" (Matthew 24:13 NLT). The "end" refers to Christ's second coming.

The promised *authority over all the nations* fulfills Psalm 2, a messianic psalm describing how God will hand the nations of the world over to Christ: "Only ask, and I will give you the nations as your inheritance, the ends of the earth as your possession. You will break them with an iron rod and smash them like clay pots" (Psalm 2:8-9 NLT). Christ applies this psalm to the readers by showing that the future reign of the Messiah will be shared with those who remain faithful (see 1:6; 3:21; 20:6; 1 Corinthians 6:2).

The iron rod symbolizes total judgment. In Isaiah 30:12-14, God had warned his rebellious people, "Because you despise what I tell you . . . you will be smashed like a piece of pottery" (NLT). Jeremiah issued a similar warning: "As this jar lies shattered, so I will shatter the people of Judah and Jerusalem beyond all hope of repair"(Jeremiah 19:11 NLT). This warning was being given to the cults. Believers dare not take a light view of heresy, because heresy will destroy people for eternity. Those who stay true, however, will rule with Christ. This promise must have been a great encouragement to the believers in Thyatira who were facing difficulties because of their faith in Christ.

2:28 "They will have the same authority I received from my Father, and I will also give them the morning star!"NLT Those who are victorious in Thyatira were promised the *same authority* that Christ had received from the Father; they would also receive *the morning star.* Christ is called the morning star in 2:28; 22:16; and 2 Peter 1:19. A morning star appears just before dawn, when the night is coldest and darkest. When the world is at its bleakest point, Christ will burst onto the scene, exposing evil with his light of truth and bringing his promised reward. The morning star may also picture the authority given to the saints because of their faithfulness (see Numbers 24:17).

2:29 "Anyone who is willing to hear should listen to the Spirit and understand what the Spirit is saying to the churches."NLT The conclusion that marks each of these messages to the churches implores everyone to *listen* and *understand what the Spirit is saying to the churches.* All these letters would be read to all the churches. The message included in each letter was for more than just the church to whom it had been written. The others churches should listen and hear, as should churches of the present day. We, too, are called to listen and understand what the Spirit is saying to us.

Revelation 3

The letter carrier continued south from Thyatira for about thirty miles to reach the city of Sardis.

The problem in this church was not heresy but spiritual death. Despite its reputation for being active, Sardis was infested with sin. The church's deeds were evil, and its clothes were soiled. The Spirit had no words of commendation for this church that looked so good on the outside but was so corrupt on the inside.

3:1 **"Write this letter to the angel of the church in Sardis. This is the message from the one who has the sevenfold Spirit of God and the seven stars: 'I know all the things you do, and that you have a reputation for being alive—but you are dead.'"**NLT The wealthy city of *Sardis* was actually in two locations. The city had been built on a mountain. When its population outgrew that spot, a newer section had been built in the valley below. The newer section of the city boasted a theater, a stadium, and a huge temple to Artemis that had been started but never finished. The older city on the mountain had an acropolis and had become an emergency refuge for the city's inhabitants when under attack. Sardis was also known for its impressive necropolis, or cemetery, with hundreds of burial mounds.

Sardis had been one of the most powerful cities in the ancient world due to heavy trade among the Aegean islands. Gold and silver coins were first minted at Sardis. The city also claimed to have discovered the art of dyeing wool. A devastating earthquake in A.D. 17 had destroyed the city and several others in the area (including Philadelphia and Laodicea).

The original city had been virtually impregnable because of its natural rock walls that were nearly vertical on three sides. Sardis had only been sacked twice in its history, although it had been attacked several times because of its strategic location. The city was first defeated by the Persian general Cyrus in the sixth century B.C. One of the Persian soldiers had observed a soldier from Sardis making his way up the winding road into the city. The people of Sardis thought they were safe in the upper city on the mountain, but Cyrus's soldiers climbed the cliffs. After Cyrus's victory, Sardis became the capital of Persia. Later, in the third century B.C., the city was conquered again the same way by Antiochus the Great. A few of his soldiers climbed the mountain, entered the city, and opened its gates to the invading army.

Sardis had declined, however, by the time of the Roman Empire. Sardis had requested the honor of building a temple to Caesar, but they were refused, and the honor went to Smyrna instead. The wealth of the city eventually led to moral decadence. The city had become lethargic, its past splendor a decaying memory.

Christ had no words of commendation for this church. It seems to have been untroubled by heresy from within or persecution from without. Yet this church had compromised with its pagan surroundings. Thus, Christ's words to the church paralleled the city's history—*you have a reputation for being alive—but you are dead.*

YOU ARE DEAD
While Christ's description of the church in Sardis appears the harshest, he does not promise the kind of judgment he predicts for the church of Laodicea. The church in Sardis wasn't lukewarm (like the church in Laodicea); it was dead.

Even though Christ called Sardis a dead church, he also affirmed the handful that were faithful believers. Christ loves to defeat death. If you find yourself in a dead church, make sure you preserve your own faithfulness. Ask God to intervene. Ask God to help you find other believers, and pray together with them for an awakening of your church.

Christ described himself as *the one who has the sevenfold Spirit of God and the seven stars* (see 1:4, 16). The "sevenfold Spirit of God" is another name for the Holy Spirit. The seven stars are the messengers, or leaders, of the churches (see 2:1). Knowing this church's deeds, Christ had no good words to say. The believers may have thought they were a living and active church, but according to Christ they were dead. Like the city itself, the church in Sardis may have been trying to live on past glory. They had compromised with the surrounding society to the point that they had become lethargic. They were as good as asleep, so Jesus told them to wake up and repent.

3:2 "Wake up! Strengthen what remains and is about to die, for I have not found your deeds complete in the sight of my God."^{NIV} The following verses record five commands focusing on watchfulness. The city had been sacked twice because the watchmen on the walls had not seen the enemies scaling the cliffs. Thinking that they were impregnable on the mountaintop led to a deadly complacence. What had happened to the city was happening to the church, and it needed to *wake up.* The situation was not completely hopeless—if they caught themselves in time, they could *strengthen what remains* even though it, too, was *about to die.* Christ knew all their deeds, and condemned them as *not . . . complete in the sight of my God.* The church may have looked impressive from the outside, but like the unfinished temple to Artemis, the church's deeds were incomplete; there was no spiritual motivation or power behind them. In letters to the other churches, Christ commended deeds of love, faithfulness, obedience, and perseverance. Sardis, however, had none of these qualities.

RESTING ON THEIR LAURELS
When Christ gave the message for the believers in Sardis, he rebuked them because they were not living up to their reputation (3:1). Sardis was a wealthy and secure city, but the believers were lethargic—unwilling to fulfill their Christian responsibilities.
Today many church members are known as Christians. They want to be known as caring for the poor or supporting evangelism and missions but are nowhere to be found when the work must be done. They vote for all the proper initiatives but disappear when service or money are required. To merely keep up the appearance of Christian dedication without any intent to serve or support amounts to hypocrisy. Make sure your own deeds back up your words.

3:3 "Remember then what you received and heard; obey it, and repent. If you do not wake up, I will come like a thief, and you will not know at what hour I will come to you."[NRSV] Christ commanded the church at Sardis to obey the Christian truth they had heard when they had first believed in Christ—to get back to the basics of the faith and *remember . . . what you received and heard.* They needed to return to the apostolic teaching that had changed their lives and once again make it their central focus. These believers had slipped away from that teaching into compromise with the world, so they would need to *obey* and *repent.* Only a change of heart could save them from punishment. That would mean taking God's Word seriously and purposefully obeying it. If they refused to *wake up* and see what was happening to them, Christ would come *like a thief,* unexpectedly, as had the soldiers who had climbed the walls to capture the city. The soldiers had brought destruction; Christ would bring punishment, giving them what they deserved. In this context, the phrase "like a thief" refers not to the Second Coming (1 Thessalonians 5:2; 2 Peter 3:10) but to judgment.

WAKE UP!
Sardis needed to wake up (3:2). Their wealth and comfort had lulled them to sleep. Their self-satisfaction caused them to die spiritually. Not only had they wandered from the apostles' teachings, but they were no longer growing in faith or evangelism. They lacked compassionate service to others and had no unity or love. Are you watchful and alert? If God has given you a place of responsibility to teach, lead, or serve, use that position to encourage those around you to be spiritually awake and morally prepared.

3:4-5 **"Yet even in Sardis there are some who have not soiled their garments with evil deeds. They will walk with me in white, for they are worthy. All who are victorious will be clothed in white. I will never erase their names from the Book of Life, but I will announce before my Father and his angels that they are mine."**NLT Not every believer in Sardis was being condemned for complacency and compromise with the world. Christ pointed out that *some* had *not soiled their garments with evil deeds.* These believers were being faithful. It must have been encouraging to those few who had been attempting to live for Christ in this dead church that Christ was commending them as worthy of his name. Christ promises a threefold reward for these faithful few:

1. They *will be clothed in white.*
2. *I will never erase their names from the Book of Life.*
3. *I will announce before my Father and his angels that they are mine.*

To be "clothed in white" means to be set apart for God, cleansed from sin, and made morally and spiritually pure. Revelation mentions white robes several times. The believers in Laodicea are told to buy white robes to cover their shame (3:18); the martyrs awaiting justice wear white robes (6:11); the twenty-four elders in heaven wear white robes (4:4) as do the people in the great multitude who have washed their robes in the blood of the Lamb and made them white (7:9, 13). The armies of heaven are also clothed in white (19:14). The white of these garments symbolizes the purity that comes when one has been "washed" in Christ's blood.

Evil deeds soil garments, but Christ can clean those sins away. Isaiah had said, "No matter how deep the stain of your sins, I can remove it. I can make you as clean as freshly fallen snow. Even if you are stained as red as crimson, I can make you as white as wool" (Isaiah 1:18 NLT). Only those who have allowed Christ to cleanse them from their sins and clothe them in white will be able to reign with him (2:27). In pagan religions it was forbidden to approach a god with soiled garments, so a person had to be clean in order to come into a temple. Christ, however, invites soiled, sinful people to come; *he* will give them clean clothing.

"The Book of Life" refers to the heavenly registry of those who have accepted salvation in Christ. This expression appears elsewhere in the Bible. The picture of God's "book" first appears in Exodus 32:32-33. Also, the psalmist had cried out against his enemies, "Erase their names from the Book of Life; don't let them be counted among the righteous"(Psalm 69:28 NLT). Daniel had prophesied, "At that time every one of your people whose name is written in the book will be rescued"(Daniel 12:1 NLT). This "book" symbolizes God's knowledge of who belongs to him. At that time cities had registry books, so having one's name removed meant losing citizenship. A city would also erase a person's name from the registry when he or she died. For the citizens of heaven, however, death is not a cause for one's name to be removed; instead, it is the way of entrance.

> I desire to have both heaven and hell ever in my eye, while I stand on this isthmus of life, between these two boundless oceans; and I verily think the daily consideration of both highly becomes all men of reason and religion.
>
> *John Wesley*

Some have suggested that Christ's statement that he will "never erase" certain names leaves open the possibility that he might erase some name, and may imply that people can lose their salvation. In other words, can a name be written in the book and then later erased? It would be shaky to base one's theology of salvation on this symbol, so it is best to take Christ's statement at face value. Those who remain faithful to him are promised future honor and eternal life—they are guaranteed citizenship in heaven.

The names of all believers are registered in the Book of Life, and Christ will introduce them to the hosts of heaven ("my Father and his angels") as belonging to him. Christ had stated, "If anyone acknowledges me publicly here on earth, I will openly acknowledge that person before my Father in heaven"(Matthew 10:32 NLT). Believers can have no greater reward than to stand in heaven with Christ and have him announce to the entire assembled host, "They are mine."

3:6 "Anyone who is willing to hear should listen to the Spirit and understand what the Spirit is saying to the churches."^{NLT} Again Christ emphasizes the importance for the readers of Revelation to *listen* and *understand.* The message in this letter is also for you.

THE OBEDIENT CHURCH / 3:7-13

About twenty-five miles southeast of Sardis on a high plateau sat the city of Philadelphia. The city was also about one hundred miles due east of Smyrna (another city on the letter carrier's route).

Christ had no words of rebuke for this church. Though small and struggling, the church in Philadelphia had stayed true to Christ, and he told them simply to hold on to what they had.

3:7 **"To the angel of the church in Philadelphia write: These are the words of him who is holy and true, who holds the key of David. What he opens no one can shut, and what he shuts no one can open."**[NIV] *Philadelphia* had been founded by the citizens of Pergamum in a frontier area as a gateway to the central plateau of Asia Minor. Trade routes leading to Mysia, Lydia, and Phrygia merged in Philadelphia. Rome's imperial postal route also went through Philadelphia, earning the city the name Gateway to the East. Plains to the north were suitable for growing grapes, so Philadelphia's economy was based on agriculture and industry. The earthquake of A.D.17 that had destroyed Sardis had also been particularly devastating to Philadelphia because the city was near a fault line, and it had suffered many aftershocks. This kept the people worried, causing most of them to live outside the city limits.

After the earthquake, Philadelphia received help for rebuilding from Rome. In appreciation, the citizens changed the name of the city to Neocaesarea. Later, the name became Flavia, and then Little Athens because of its many temples and religious festivals. Grapes were an important crop for Philadelphia, and wine-making was an important industry. Worship of Dionysus may have been the main religion.

Philadelphia was a small church in a difficult area with no prestige and no wealth, discouraged because it hadn't grown. But Christ had no words of rebuke for this small, seemingly insignificant church, and he described himself to the church in Philadelphia as *him who is holy and true.* This title (also translated "Holy One") was a familiar title for God (see Isaiah 40:25; Habakkuk 3:3; Mark 1:24; John 6:69).

For Christ to hold *the key of David* means that he has the authority to open the door to his future kingdom. This alludes to an event recorded in Isaiah 22:15-25 when the official position of secretary of state in Judah was taken from Shebna and given to Eliakim. God through Isaiah said to Eliakim: "I will give him the key to the house of David—the highest position in the royal court. He will open doors, and no one will be able to shut them; he will close doors, and no one will be able to open them" (Isaiah 22:22 NLT). Christ holds absolute power and authority over

entrance into his future kingdom. After the door is opened, no
one can shut it—salvation is assured. Once it is shut, no one can
open it—judgment is certain.

**3:8 "I know all the things you do, and I have opened a door for
you that no one can shut. You have little strength, yet you
obeyed my word and did not deny me."**NLT As in the letters to
the other churches, Christ here stated that he knew their deeds—
all the things you do—yet he had no words of rebuke for the
believers. The church may have been small *(you have little
strength)* and may have had little impact upon the city, but it had
obeyed and had not denied God. They had been faithful in a difficult area.

The phrase "I have opened a door for you that no one can
shut" may mean that the church had a prime location for missionary activity—they had an open door that no one could shut. The
meaning, however, may refer to the Jewish believers who had
been excommunicated from the synagogue for their faith in
Christ (see 3:9). While the door to the synagogue may have been
closed to them, Christ had *opened a door . . . that no one can
shut.* The door to eternal life stood open to them, and Christ held
the keys. No one could keep them out if they trusted in Christ.

**3:9 "Look! I will force those who belong to Satan—those liars who
say they are Jews but are not—to come and bow down at your
feet. They will acknowledge that you are the ones I love."**NLT
Apparently there was significant conflict between the Christians
and the Jews in Philadelphia. As in the letter to the church in
Smyrna (2:9), Christ referred to those who called themselves Jews
but who were really *liars* and *those who belong to Satan* (literally,
"of the synagogue of Satan"). These people, descended from Abraham and Jews by birth, vehemently opposed and persecuted the
Christians for their belief that Jesus was the Messiah. Because of
their opposition, Christ considered them as belonging to Satan.
True Jews (God's people) have accepted Jesus as Messiah and Savior (see Romans 2:28-29; Galatians 3:29; 6:16). These Jews who
had rejected the Messiah truly belonged to Satan, not to God. They
had shut the Christians out of their synagogues, but Christ says that
he *will force* these people to *come and bow down at* the feet of his
faithful people. Then *they will acknowledge* that the Christians are
indeed the ones whom Christ loves. At Christ's return, true believers will be vindicated.

**3:10 "Since you have kept my command to endure patiently, I will
also keep you from the hour of trial that is going to come
upon the whole world to test those who live on the earth."**NIV

The believers had endured patiently, as Christ had commanded, so Christ promised to keep them *from the hour of trial* that would *come upon the whole world to test those who live on the earth.* Some believe that the phrase "I will also keep you from the hour of trial" means there will be a future time of great tribulation from which true believers will be spared. This is a key verse for those who subscribe to the pre-Tribulation-Rapture theory—that believers will be kept from the hour of trial because they will not be on the earth during that time of great tribulation. Christians will have been taken to heaven in what is called the "Rapture" (based on 1 Corinthians 15:51-53; 1 Thessalonians 4:15-17). Others believe that the verse refers to times of great distress in general, the church's suffering through the ages. Others interpret "keep from" to mean that the church will go through the time of tribulation and that God will keep them strong during it, providing spiritual protection from the forces of evil (7:3). The verb "keep from" is the same Greek verb in the Lord's prayer ("Deliver us from the evil one," Matthew 6:13 NLT). As Jesus said before his death, "I'm not asking you to take them out of the world, but to keep them safe from the evil one" (John 17:15 NLT). See the chart at 3:13, page 47.

This "hour of trial" is also described as the Great Tribulation or Day of the Lord, mentioned also in Daniel 12:2; Mark 13:19; and 2 Thessalonians 2:1-12. All the judgments recorded in the remainder of the book of Revelation take place during this time of tribulation. While believers may have to face difficulty and suffering, they will certainly be protected from God's wrath and judgment.

NOT A HAIR WILL PERISH
Jesus promised protection for the obedient church at Philadelphia (3:10). We cannot interpret from this verse when or for how long Christians will experience the "hour of trial." Today, millions of Christians are suffering and dying at the hands of godless tyrants throughout the world. To them, the "hour of trial" has already begun. But whenever Christians suffer, Christ promises protection of their eternal souls. Jesus said, "Everyone will hate you because of your allegiance to me. But not a hair of your head will perish! By standing firm, you will win your souls" (Luke 21:17-19 NLT).

3:11 **"Look, I am coming quickly. Hold on to what you have, so that no one will take away your crown."**[NLT] For the churches in Ephesus (2:5), Pergamum (2:16), and Sardis (3:3), Christ's *coming* would be a time for them to fear if they did not repent, for he would come as their judge. To the church in Philadelphia, however, Christ's words "I am coming quickly" would not be threatening. Rather, they would be a promise to the believers of his imminent return. The word "quickly" should be taken as "soon" or "without warning" (see 1:1, 3). In the meantime, they should *hold on to what [they] have,* referring to obedience and refusal to deny Christ (3:8). Their reward would be a *crown*—referring to the wreath awarded to winners of athletic contests (see 1 Corinthians 9:25; 2 Timothy 4:8). Philadelphia was known for its games and festivals, so the picture of the eternal crown awaiting believers was especially meaningful (see also 2:10).

HOLD ON
Christians have differing gifts, abilities, experience, and maturity. God doesn't expect believers to all be and act the same, but he does expect us to "hold on" to what we have, to persevere in using our resources for him. The Philadelphians were commended for their effort to obey (3:8) and encouraged to hold tightly to whatever strength they had. If you are a new believer, you may feel that your faith and spiritual strength are small. Use what you have (even if it's small) to live for Christ, and God will commend you.

3:12 **"All who are victorious will become pillars in the Temple of my God, and they will never have to leave it. And I will write my God's name on them, and they will be citizens in the city of my God—the new Jerusalem that comes down from heaven from my God. And they will have my new name inscribed upon them."**[NLT] The believers *who are victorious* and remain faithful to the end receive the promise to *become pillars in the Temple of my God.* The word "pillars" symbolizes permanence and stability. Philadelphia was constantly threatened by earthquakes. Often experiencing tremors, the people would evacuate the city and stay in temporary dwellings in the rural areas. Sometimes the pillars would be the only part of a building left standing after an earthquake. This permanence is further stressed in the next phrase, "they will never have to leave it."

Christ also gives these victorious believers three further promises:

1. He will *write . . . God's name on them.*
2. *They will be citizens in . . . the new Jerusalem.*
3. *They will have* Christ's *new name inscribed upon them.*

This "new name" of Christ has not been revealed, but those who are victorious and persevere will have this new name inscribed upon them. For more on the new Jerusalem, see 21:2.

This threefold promise pictures believers belonging to God, having citizenship in heaven, and having a special relationship with Christ. The new Jerusalem is the future dwelling of the people of God (21:2). They will be citizens in God's future kingdom. Everything will be new, pure, and secure.

3:13 "Anyone who is willing to hear should listen to the Spirit and understand what the Spirit is saying to the churches."NLT This closing is the same as for the letters to the other churches: all should *listen to the Spirit and understand* what is being said.

THE LUKEWARM CHURCH / 3:14-22

At the end of the route was Laodicea, about forty-five miles southeast of Philadelphia. The problem in this church was self-sufficiency, which caused believers to forget their need of pure love and faith in the Savior.

3:14 "To the angel of the church in Laodicea write: These are the words of the Amen, the faithful and true witness, the ruler of God's creation."NIV Laodicea was the wealthiest of the seven cities. The city was known for its banks, its manufacture of a rare black wool, and a medical school that produced eye salve. Laodicea lay at the juncture of two major trade routes between Rome and the Orient. The main road from Ephesus on the coast into Asia ran through Laodicea, as did the route from the capital of the province in Pergamum to the Mediterranean coast.

The great earthquake of A.D.17 that had destroyed Philadelphia and Sardis also destroyed Laodicea. But while the other cities had accepted financial help from Rome for rebuilding, Laodicea had enough wealth to rebuild on its own. Unfortunately, the city had a poor water supply. A six-mile long aqueduct brought water to the city from the south, so by the time it reached the city, the water was lukewarm. The city was a center for the imperial cult as well as for the worship of Asclepius (god of healing) and Zeus (chief of the gods). The city also had a fairly large Jewish population.

The church may have been founded by Epaphras (see Colossians 4:12). It is not known whether Paul ever visited the city, although he did write them a letter, and the letter to the Colossians was read by the Laodiceans (Colossians 4:16).

To this church, Christ is described as *the Amen, the faithful and true witness.* The word "amen" signals an acknowledgment of something true and binding. Christ was true and faithful, but the Laodiceans were not. They were rich and powerful, but they were not "faithful and true."

THEORIES REGARDING THE TRIBULATION

According to the premillennial view, the Tribulation is a seven-year period right before Christ returns when the Antichrist will rule. The premillennial position believes in a literal 1000-year reign of Christ (for more about the millennial positions, see the chart in chapter 20, page 240). All of these theories hold that Christ will return to judge those who have been the enemies of God and his people. (See also the chart located at 7:2-3, page 82.)

Pre-Tribulation
Christ will come at the beginning of the seven-year period of tribulation and take the church. Then he will return again at the end to defeat his enemies. Some Christians go so far as to divide the tribulation into specific sections. They base these divisions on the prophetic writings of Daniel 9:24-27. According to this view, the first half of the tribulation— three-and-a-half years—will include the seven seal judgments (chapter 6), the seven trumpet judgments (chapters 8–9), the ministry of the two witnesses (11:3-6), and the rise of the Antichrist and his forces (12:3; 13:1; 17:12). The middle of the tribulation will be marked by the death and resurrection of the two witnesses (11:7-13), the persecution of the Jewish nation (12:1-6), the death and resurrection of the Antichrist (13:3-4), and the Antichrist's defilement of the temple (Daniel 9:27; 2 Thessalonians 2:3-4). The last part of the tribulation will include the seven bowl judgments (chapter 16), the battle of Armageddon (19:11–21), and the conversion of Israel (Romans 11:25-27).

Mid-Tribulation
Christians will be removed from the earth ("raptured") halfway through the Tribulation (after three and a half years), when the Antichrist defiles the temple. At this time, Christ will return to take the church back, and then he will return again at the end of three and a half years to defeat his enemies.

Post-Tribulation
Christians must endure the catastrophes of the entire Tribulation period. Then, Christ will return at the end of the Tribulation to take all believers to heaven and immediately fight the forces of evil.

3:15-16 **"I know your works; you are neither cold nor hot. I wish that you were either cold or hot. So, because you are lukewarm, and neither cold nor hot, I am about to spit you out of my mouth."**NRSV This allusion to the Laodicean water supply is a fitting metaphor for the activities of this church. Laodicea had always had a problem with its water supply. The city of Hierapolis, to the northwest, was famous for its hot mineral springs. An aqueduct had been built to bring water to the city from the hot springs. But by the time the water reached the city, it was neither hot nor refreshingly cool—only lukewarm and filled with minerals (impure), so it tasted terrible. According to Christ, these believers were *neither cold nor hot;* instead, they were merely *lukewarm,* as bland as the tepid water that came into the city.

Many have thought that this cold and hot refers to spirituality—
and that Christ would rather have "cold" people (without faith at
all, or without any sort of growth) than "lukewarm" believers
(who believe some). They take the word "cold" to be negative
and "hot" to be positive, with "lukewarm" in between. Instead,
both "cold" and "hot" should be taken as positive. Christ wished
that the church had cold, refreshing purity or hot, therapeutic
value, but it had neither. They were lukewarm.

HALFWAY
The Laodiceans were "lukewarm" (3:16). The church had become
distasteful and unusable like the city's water. Lukewarm water
makes a disgusting drink. The church in Laodicea had become
lukewarm, and thus distasteful and repugnant. The believers
didn't take a stand for anything; indifference had led to idleness.
By neglecting to do anything for Christ, the church had become
hardened and self-satisfied, and it was destroying itself. As a
result, Christ was about to *spit* them out of his mouth.
    There is nothing more disgusting than a halfhearted, in-name-
only Christian who is self-sufficient. Don't settle for following God
halfway. Let Christ fire up your faith and get you into the action.

**3:17 "You say, 'I am rich; I have acquired wealth and do not need a
thing.' But you do not realize that you are wretched, pitiful,
poor, blind and naked."**[NIV] Laodicea was a wealthy city, and
apparently the church was also a wealthy church. It is unclear
whether the Laodiceans were claiming spiritual or material wealth.
They may have been materially rich and assuming that riches were
a sign of God's blessing on them. With their wealth came an
attitude of self-sufficiency—feeling that they did *not need a thing.*
They were materially secure and felt spiritually safe—with no need
for further growth. Unfortunately, that attitude made them blind to
their own true condition—*wretched, pitiful, poor, blind and naked.*
Contrast this with the church in Smyrna; they were poor, but Christ
called them rich (2:9). The Laodicean believers may have been
wealthy, but spiritually they were impoverished. While the city
prided itself on extreme financial wealth, a productive textile industry, and the special healing eye salve, the church's true spiritual
condition left it poor, naked, and blind (see 3:18).

**3:18 "Therefore I counsel you to buy from me gold refined by fire
so that you may be rich; and white robes to clothe you and to
keep the shame of your nakedness from being seen; and salve
to anoint your eyes so that you may see."**[NRSV] Laodicea was
known for its great wealth, but Christ told the Laodiceans to buy
their *gold* from him; then they would have real spiritual treasures

(see 1 Timothy 6). They had fool's gold in their bank accounts, gold from this world with no spiritual or eternal value. Only with Christ's gold would they *be rich.*

The city was proud of its cloth and dyeing industries. They had developed a black wool that had become famous all over the Roman Empire and was bringing huge prices. Although they had wealth in their clothing, they were naked before God. They were self-centered. But Christ told them to purchase *white robes* (his righteousness) from him. That alone would *keep the shame of [their] nakedness from being seen.*

Laodicea prided itself on its precious eye salve that healed many eye problems, but they were spiritually blind. Christ told them to get *salve* from him to heal their eyes so they could *see* the truth (John 9:39).

Christ was showing the Laodiceans that true value is not in material possessions but in a right relationship with God. Their possessions and achievements were valueless compared with the everlasting future of Christ's kingdom.

TRUE RICHES
Some believers falsely assume that numerous material posses-sions are a sign of God's spiritual blessing. Laodicea was a wealthy city, and the church was also wealthy (3:17). But what the Laodiceans could see and buy had become more valuable to them than what is unseen and eternal. Wealth, luxury, and ease can make people feel confident, satisfied, and complacent. No matter how much you possess or how much money you make, however, you have nothing if you don't have a vital relationship with Christ. How does your current level of wealth affect your spiritual desire? Instead of centering your life around comfort and luxury, find your true riches in Christ.

3:19 **"Those whom I love I rebuke and discipline. So be earnest, and repent."**^{NIV} There was a second chance for this church; Christ offered them the opportunity to *repent.* His *rebuke and dis-cipline* came because of his *love* for the church. "For the Lord corrects those he loves, just as a father corrects a child in whom he delights" (Proverbs 3:12 NLT). Christ will "spit out" those who disobey (3:16), but he will discipline those he loves. "When we are judged and disciplined by the Lord, we will not be con-demned with the world" (1 Corinthians 11:32 NLT). Because of such mercy, believers should willingly repent, realizing their need for Christ in every part of their lives and ministry. Then they will be effective for him.

THE LETTERS TO THE SEVEN CHURCHES

This summary of the letters to the seven churches shows us the qualities our churches should seek and those we should avoid. Jesus' words of commendation and rebuke should cause us to think carefully of our own lives and what Jesus would have us do in order to be completely focused on him.

Church/ Reference	Commendation	Rebuke	Action (quoted from NLT)
Ephesus (2:1-7)	Worked hard, persevered, did not tolerate evil	Had forsaken first love	"Turn back to me again"
Smyrna (2:8-11)	Suffered persecution and poverty	None	"Don't be afraid"
Pergamum (2:12-17)	Remained true to the faith	Had compromised with unbelievers and false teachers	"Repent"
Thyatira (2:18-29)	Acted in love, faith, service	Had allowed immorality and false teaching	"Hold tightly to what you have"
Sardis (3:1-6)	None	Were superficial	"Go back to what you heard and believed at first"
Philadelphia (3:7-13)	Remained faithful	None	"Hold on to what you have"
Laodicea (3:14-22)	None	Were lukewarm	"Turn from your indifference"

REKINDLED
God would discipline this lukewarm church unless it turned from its indifference toward him (3:19). God's purpose in discipline is not to punish but to bring people back to him. Are you lukewarm in your devotion to God? God may discipline you to help you out of your uncaring attitude, but he uses only loving discipline. You can avoid God's discipline by drawing near to him again through confession, service, worship, and studying his Word. Just as the spark of love can be rekindled in marriage, so the Holy Spirit can reignite our zeal for God when we allow him to work in our hearts.

3:20 "Listen! I am standing at the door, knocking; if you hear my voice and open the door, I will come in to you and eat with you, and you with me."[NRSV] The Laodicean church was complacent and rich. They felt self-satisfied, but they didn't have Christ's presence among them. Christ knocked at the door of their hearts, but they were so busy enjoying worldly pleasures that they didn't notice him trying to enter. The pleasures of this world—money, security, material possessions—can be dangerous because their temporary satisfaction can make people—even believers—indifferent to God's offer of lasting satisfaction.

Many have taken this verse as a help in evangelism, picturing Christ wanting to enter an individual's heart. The context is actually Christ speaking to an entire church. The people in the church in Laodicea needed to accept Christ for the first time, for some of them had never made that commitment. Others needed to return to wholehearted faith in him. Christ is knocking on their door, desiring that the Laodicean church remember its need for him and open the door. He would *come in* and *eat* with the believers, picturing table fellowship. In Oriental fashion, this "eating" referred to the main meal of the day in which intimate friends would share together. Such a meal portrays the kind of fellowship that will exist in the coming kingdom of the Messiah (19:9; Isaiah 25:6-8; Luke 22:30). The church needed to repent of its self-sufficiency and compromise and return to Christ.

OPEN THE DOOR
Jesus is knocking on the door of our hearts (3:20) every time we sense we should turn to him. Jesus wants to have fellowship with us, and he wants us to open up to him. He is patient and persistent in trying to get through to us—not breaking and entering but knocking. He allows us to decide whether or not to open our lives to him. Do you intentionally keep his life-changing presence and power on the other side of the door?

3:21 **"I will invite everyone who is victorious to sit with me on my throne, just as I was victorious and sat with my Father on his throne."**ᴺᴸᵀ This promise that *everyone who is victorious* will sit with Christ on his throne refers to the heavenly kingdom (see also 1:6, 9; 2:26-27). Believers' reign with Christ is mentioned in several places in Scripture (see, for example, Matthew 19:28; Luke 22:28-30; Romans 8:17; 2 Timothy 2:12). This promise is certain because Christ won that right for believers through his own victory on the cross. *Victorious* over sin and death when he rose again, he *sat with* his *Father on his throne.* The Gospel of Mark records, "When the Lord Jesus had finished talking with them, he was taken up into heaven and sat down in the place of honor at God's right hand" (Mark 16:19 ɴʟᴛ).

3:22 **"Anyone who is willing to hear should listen to the Spirit and understand what the Spirit is saying to the churches."**NLT
At the end of each message to these churches, believers were urged to listen and take to heart what had been written to them. Although a different message was addressed to each church, all the messages contain warnings and principles for everyone. Which letter speaks most directly to your church? Which has the greatest bearing on your own spiritual condition at this time? How will you respond?

Revelation 4

The book now shifts from the seven churches in Asia to the future of the worldwide church. John saw the course of coming events similar to the way Daniel and Ezekiel had seen them. Many of these passages contain clear spiritual teachings, but others seem beyond our ability to understand. The clear teaching of this book is that God will defeat all evil in the end. Meanwhile, we must live in obedience to Jesus Christ, the coming Conqueror and Judge.

Revelation 4–5 provide glimpses into Christ's glory. Chapter 4 is John's vision into the throne room of heaven, and chapter 5 is John's vision of the Lamb and the scroll. The events described in chapters 6 and 7 occur as the seals on the scroll are broken. Therefore, chapters 4–8 contain one continuous vision.

God is on the throne, orchestrating all the events that John recorded. The world is under his control, and he will carry out his plans as Christ initiates the final battle with the forces of evil.

4:1 After this I looked, and there in heaven a door stood open! And the first voice, which I had heard speaking to me like a trumpet, said, "Come up here, and I will show you what must take place after this."NRSV After writing the letters to the seven churches, John *looked* and saw a door standing open *in heaven.* Ezekiel said, "The heavens were opened to me, and I saw visions of God" (Ezekiel 1:1 NLT). It is God who opens the door, so this is God revealing these visions to John and to us. This first *voice* that sounded *like a trumpet* was the voice of Christ (see 1:10-11). The voice spoke again and told John to *"come up here."* From there, Christ would show John *what must take place after this*—that is, after the time of the letters to the churches in chapters 2 and 3. These would be visions of the end of the world and the beginning of Christ's kingdom.

Some who subscribe to the pre-Tribulation theory see a veiled reference to the rapture of the church in the words of Christ to "come up." But the text indicates that John alone was commanded to be transported in the Spirit to heaven. The Rapture is not mentioned specifically in the book of Revelation. For more on the Rapture, see 1 Thessalonians 4:13-17 and the chart in 3:13.

4:2-3 **And instantly I was in the Spirit, and I saw a throne in heaven and someone sitting on it! The one sitting on the throne was as brilliant as gemstones—jasper and carnelian. And the glow of an emerald circled his throne like a rainbow.**^{NLT} Four times in the book of Revelation, John wrote that he was in the Spirit (1:10; 4:2; 17:3; 21:10). This expression means that the Holy Spirit was giving him a vision—showing him situations and events that he could not have seen with mere human eyesight. All true prophecy comes from God through the Holy Spirit (1:10; 2 Peter 1:20-21).

John *saw a throne in heaven and someone sitting on it* (compare with 1 Kings 22:19; Isaiah 6:1; Ezekiel 1:1). The throne of God is mentioned forty times in the book of Revelation. In Jewish mysticism God was pictured as ruling all of creation from a celestial throne. The throne symbolizes God's absolute authority. For the first-century readers, the most powerful throne in the world would have been Caesar's throne. Caesar sat on the most glorious throne in the world and had control of one-half of the gross national product of the Roman Empire. His glory and wealth, however, were nothing compared to God's. God's throne *was as brilliant as gemstones. Jasper and carnelian* were semiprecious stones. Caesar's pomp and splendor were nothing compared to the *glow of an emerald* that *circled* God's throne *like a rainbow.* The stones symbolize great wealth—God owns all the riches of the entire world. These gemstones were the most pure elements known at that time—and God transcends even these. John did not describe this person on the throne, other than to mention the brilliant light around him. God alone is sovereign; Caesar is not a god. Only God is God.

PRAISE THE LORD!
John describes the majestic throne room of God and all those who were praising him there. Praise is saying thank you to God for each aspect of his divine nature. Our inward attitude becomes outward expression. When we praise God, we help ourselves by expanding our awareness of who he is. As you read Revelation, look for names and attributes or characteristics of God for which you can praise him.

4:4 **"Twenty-four thrones surrounded him, and twenty-four elders sat on them. They were all clothed in white and had gold crowns on their heads."**^{NLT} Surrounding God's throne were *twenty-four thrones* with *twenty-four elders* sitting on them. These elders fell before God in worship (see 5:14; 11:16; 19:4), continually praising him (4:11; 5:9-10; 11:17-18; 19:4). One of them served as a spokesman (5:5; 7:13). The elders joined with the four living creatures to present the prayers of the saints to God (5:8).

John did not identify these twenty-four elders. Evidently, the worship they were providing was more significant than who they were. Scholars have proposed several possibilities for the identity of these twenty-four elders:

> God . . . is eternal, infinite, immeasurable, incomprehensible, omnipotent, invisible.
> *The Scots Confession*

- Because there were twelve tribes of Israel in the Old Testament and twelve apostles in the New Testament, the twenty-four elders (twelve plus twelve) in this vision represent all the redeemed of God for all time (both before and after Christ's death and resurrection). They symbolize all those—both Jews and Gentiles—who are now part of God's family. The twenty-four elders show us that *all* the redeemed of the Lord are worshiping him.
- The twenty-four elders are the heavenly counterpart of the twenty-four priestly ranks who served the temple (1 Chronicles 23:6; 24:7-18).
- Most likely, the elders are an angelic group providing this worship, and the reference to twenty-four remains speculative. Their continuous praise supports this view and the fact that they serve with, but are distinguished from, the four living creatures (4:11; 5:9-10; 11:17-18; 19:4). The twenty-four elders are beings who live in heaven and worship God at his throne (see also 14:3). Though they are crowned and dressed in white, they clearly do not represent the church. These leaders sing of human believers, not about themselves (5:9). In view of their actions, such as worshiping and offering bowls of incense, they seem to be a special order of angels.

4:5 From the throne came flashes of lightning, rumblings and peals of thunder. Before the throne, seven lamps were blazing. These are the seven spirits of God.[NIV] In Revelation, *lightning* and *thunder* are associated with significant events in heaven. Lightning and thunder had filled the sky at Mount Sinai when God had given the people his laws (Exodus 19:16). The Old Testament often uses such imagery to reflect God's power and majesty (see Psalm 77:18). God's throne is the final "Sinai." In Revelation, thunder and lightning always form part of the scene in God's throne room and highlight a significant coming event—for example, they mark the seventh seal (8:5), the seventh trumpet (11:19), and the seventh bowl (16:18).

The *seven lamps* (also translated "torches") represent the Holy Spirit (see also comments on 1:4 and Ezekiel 1:13; Zechariah 4:2-6). *The seven spirits of God* is another name for the Holy Spirit.

4:6 Also before the throne there was what looked like a sea of glass, clear as crystal.^{NIV} Glass was very rare in New Testament times, and crystal-clear glass was virtually impossible to find. The *sea of glass* serves as the magnificent floor of God's throne room and highlights both the magnificence and holiness of God. It is probably not a literal "sea"; rather, it is a metaphor for the scene. No earthly ruler can compare with the awesomeness of God. See also Job 37:18 and Ezekiel 1:22.

In the center, around the throne, were four living creatures, and they were covered with eyes, in front and in back.^{NIV} These *four living creatures* are angelic beings of high order, serving as part of the worship and government in heaven (see Isaiah 6:1-4; Ezekiel 1:5-25). Isaiah 6:2 refers to these creatures (or "beings") as "seraphim." The seraphim surround God's throne, lead others in worship, and proclaim God's holiness. The *eyes* picture knowledge and alertness. They see and scrutinize everything. These are powerful figures, as noted by the wings (4:8). These four living creatures also appear throughout Revelation (see also 5:6, 8, 14; 6:1; 7:11; 14:3; 15:7; 19:4).

WORSHIP
John describes these scenes in such detail because Christians in the first century came from many backgrounds. Not all of them understood Jewish history or knew the glory of the Temple. Revelation instructs us in worship. It shows us where, why, and how to praise God. What does worship do? Worship takes our minds off our problems and focuses them on God. Worship leads us from individual meditation to corporate worship. Worship causes us to consider and appreciate God's character. Worship lifts our perspective from the earthly to the heavenly.

4:7 The first living creature was like a lion, the second was like an ox, the third had a face like a man, the fourth was like a flying eagle.^{NIV} The Old Testament prophet Ezekiel saw four similar creatures in one of his visions (Ezekiel 1:5-10; 10:14). In his vision, however, each cherub had four faces. In John's vision, each creature has only one face. In Ezekiel's vision, God called

Ezekiel to be a prophet. God showed Ezekiel that the coming
destruction of Jerusalem was punishment for Judah's sins. Ezekiel prophesied during the time when the Babylonians sacked
Jerusalem.

In John's vision, the living beings will show to John the final
destruction of the world as punishment for sin. The appearance
of these creatures symbolizes the highest expression of God's
attributes. The animallike appearances of these four creatures
include majesty and power (the *lion*), faithfulness (the *ox*),
intelligence (the *man*), and sovereignty (the *eagle*).

**4:8 Each of the four living creatures had six wings and was covered
with eyes all around, even under his wings. Day and night they
never stop saying: "Holy, holy, holy is the Lord God Almighty,
who was, and is, and is to come."**^{NIV} A further description of these
four living creatures indicates that each had *six wings,* indicating
power and swiftness (see Isaiah 6:2). The
eyes all around are mentioned again (4:6) and
indicate complete knowledge—that is, they
could perceive and understand everything
that was happening. *Day and night they never
stop saying* praises to God, meaning that
these creatures continuously worship.

> He that sees the beauty
> of holiness, or true moral
> good, sees the greatest
> and most important thing
> in the world.
>
> *Jonathan Edwards*

The four living creatures sing about God's
holiness. The repetition three times of the word "holy" means ultimate holiness (see also Isaiah 6:3). "Lord God Almighty" pictures
the ultimate, divine Warrior (see commentary on 1:8). Churches of
all ages facing persecution gain great comfort knowing that no matter what happens on earth, God is almighty. Those who are victorious will one day join in praise with the angels. The phrase "who
was, and is, and is to come" describes God's transcendence over
time—he is eternal (see also commentary on 1:4).

KNOWING GOD
God cannot be known apart from his holiness. The key to
God's eternal reign is his holiness. His glory is not only his
strength but also his perfect moral character. God will never do
anything that is not perfect. This reassures us that we can trust
him, yet it places a demand on us. Our desire to be holy (dedicated to God and morally clean) is the only suitable response.
To be prepared for Christ's return, we must renounce sin and
desire God's holiness.

**4:9-10a Whenever the living beings give glory and honor and thanks
to the one sitting on the throne, the one who lives forever and**

ever, the twenty-four elders fall down and worship the one who lives forever and ever.^{NLT} The actions of these living beings picture complete worship and submission to God. *The one who lives forever and ever* emphasizes God's eternality (see 5:14; 10:6; 15:7). God is far more worthy of worship than any person because he lives forever (see Psalms 45:6; 102:27). His *throne* symbolizes his power and authority (see also 4:2-3). As the *living beings* (the four living creatures) praise God, the *twenty-four elders fall down and worship.* That they "fall down" refers to lying prostrate in a position of submission and adoration. Their worship means giving God all *glory and honor and thanks.*

4:10b-11 **And they lay their crowns before the throne and say, "You are worthy, O Lord our God, to receive glory and honor and power. For you created everything, and it is for your pleasure that they exist and were created."**^{NLT} These verses are the second hymn sung in Revelation (see 4:8), a hymn of praise to God for his work in creation. The point of this chapter is summed up in this verse: All creatures in heaven and earth will praise and honor God because he is the Creator and Sustainer of *everything.* No king or emperor can make such a claim. No Roman emperor could ever be acknowledged for creating heaven and earth. This role belongs to God alone (14:7; 21:5; Romans 8:18-25).

The phrase "you are worthy" was used to herald the entrance of an emperor when he came in his triumphal procession. Later, the emperor Domitian added the phrase "our Lord and God" as a reference to himself, thereby promoting the cult of emperor worship. Christians, however, are to acknowledge only one Lord and God.

Earthly honor and power is to be laid before the throne, just as the living creatures *lay their crowns before the throne.* This demonstrates that all authority and honor belong to God. He delegates his authority to others, but it belongs to him.

Revelation 5

Revelation 5 continues the glimpse into heaven begun in chapter 4. The scene in Revelation 5 shows that only the Lamb, Jesus Christ, is worthy to open the scroll, which reveals the events of future history. Jesus, not Satan, holds the future. Jesus Christ is in control; he alone is worthy to set into motion the events of the last days of history. Verses 9, 12, and 13 contain three hymns. The first two worship the Lamb; the third one worships God and the Lamb.

5:1 And I saw a scroll in the right hand of the one who was sitting on the throne. There was writing on the inside and the outside of the scroll, and it was sealed with seven seals.^{NLT} The phrase "the one who was sitting on the throne" refers to 4:2-3, where John had been taken "in the Spirit" to the throne room of heaven. This *one* on the throne is God himself. In his *right hand* God is holding *a scroll.* In John's day some books were written on scrolls—pieces of papyrus or vellum up to thirty feet long, rolled up and sealed with clay or wax. Other books were written in codex form—much like our modern book. The *seven seals* indicate the importance of the scroll's contents, and they guaranteed the secrecy of the document. The book had writing *on both sides.* John does not tell us the exact contents of the book, but it seems that, from what follows in chapters 5-8, it is none other than the content of the rest of the book of Revelation. As each seal is broken, another part of the book is revealed. The final seal, the seventh one, opens the way to the seven trumpets, and so on through the rest of Revelation.

5:2-3 And I saw a mighty angel proclaiming in a loud voice, "Who is worthy to break the seals and open the scroll?" But no one in heaven or on earth or under the earth could open the scroll or even look inside it.^{NIV} As God was holding the scroll, *a mighty angel* asked, *"Who is worthy to break the seals and open the scroll?"* The identity of this angel is unknown. Some suggest Gabriel because Gabriel's name means "strength of God" (Daniel 8:16; see also Revelation 10:1; 18:2). The question, proclaimed

in a loud voice, went out across all of creation to find someone
worthy to bring history to its appointed end. But *no one in
heaven or on earth or under the earth* could be found who had
the authority and purity to *open the scroll or even look inside it.*
This emphasizes the sovereignty and centrality of Christ. He
alone was able to open the scroll.

THE ONE
John recorded his vision of God holding a scroll containing all
that would happen to the world (5:1). Such a vision pictures
God in complete control. He is the one with authority over all rulers, historical events, and hostile forces. Those who trust in
God's power and love have nothing to fear in the future. We will
never know enough about the future to predict our own personal future or to manipulate God in any way. But we can trust
him for the outcome. If you have believed in Christ, you can
rejoice that God knows you and loves you. Trust him to guide
you and protect your soul forever.

5:4-5 **And I began to weep bitterly because no one was found worthy to open the scroll or to look into it. Then one of the elders
said to me, "Do not weep. See, the Lion of the tribe of Judah,
the Root of David, has conquered, so that he can open the
scroll and its seven seals."**NRSV John *wept bitterly* that *no one*
could be found who was worthy to open or look into the scroll.
John wept because he knew that the unopened scroll would mean
that the closing scene of history could not begin; thus, evil would
continue unabated on the earth, and there would be no future for
God's people. But *one of the elders* (4:4, 10) told John not to
weep any longer, because someone was worthy to open the
scroll—*the Lion of the tribe of Judah, the Root of David.* This
phrase, "Lion of the tribe of Judah," comes from the prophecy
that Jacob gave to his son Judah in Genesis 49:9-10; Judah was
described as "a young lion" (NLT). The prophecy said, "The scepter will not depart from Judah, nor the ruler's staff from his
descendants, until the coming of the one to whom it belongs, the
one whom all nations will obey" (NLT). This is considered to be
a prophecy of the Messiah, born in the line of Judah, who would
be the only one whom all nations would one day obey. From
Judah's line had been born King David, hence the phrase, "the
Root of David," which alludes to Isaiah, chapter 11.

*Out of the stump of David's family will grow a shoot—yes,
a new Branch bearing fruit from the old root. And the Spirit
of the Lord will rest on him—the Spirit of wisdom and
understanding, the Spirit of counsel and might, the Spirit of*

*knowledge and the fear of the Lord. He will delight in obeying
the Lord. He will never judge by appearance, false evidence,
or hearsay. He will defend the poor and the exploited. He will
rule against the wicked and destroy them with the breath of his
mouth. He will be clothed with fairness and truth.* (Isaiah
11:1-5 NLT)

Isaiah predicted that Judah (the royal line of David) would be
like a tree chopped down to a stump, but from that stump a new
shoot would grow—the Messiah. He would be greater than the
original tree and would bear much fruit.
Christ, the Messiah, is the fulfillment of
God's promise that a descendant of David
would rule forever (2 Samuel 7:16; see also
Romans 15:12).

The Messiah, Jesus Christ, *has conquered, so that he can open the scroll and
its seven seals.* Christ proved himself worthy by living a perfect life of obedience to
God, dying on the cross to pay the penalty
for the sins of the world, and rising from the
dead to demonstrate his power and authority
over evil and death. Only Christ conquered
sin, death, hell, and Satan himself, so only he can set in motion
the forces that will bring about the final destruction of all evil.

> I should be ashamed
> to acknowledge him as
> my Savior if I could
> comprehend him—he
> would be no greater than
> I. Such is my sense of
> sin, and consciousness
> of my inability to save
> myself, that I feel I need
> a superhuman Savior.
> *Noah Webster*

5:6 **Then I saw a Lamb, looking as if it had been slain, standing
in the center of the throne, encircled by the four living creatures and the elders. He had seven horns and seven eyes,
which are the seven spirits of God sent out into all the
earth.**[NIV] While the previous verse pictured Jesus Christ as a Lion
(symbolizing his authority and power), this verse pictures him
as a Lamb (symbolizing his submission to God's will) that looks
as though it has been killed (perhaps a reference to the slaughter
of a Passover lamb). One of the elders called John to look at the
Lion (5:5), but when John looked, he saw a Lamb. Christ the
Lamb was the perfect sacrifice for the sins of all mankind; therefore, only he can save his people from the terrible events that will
be revealed by the scroll. This is a beautiful picture: the Lion of
the tribe of Judah became a slain Lamb, who is here seen as a
conquering Lamb at the center of the throne of God.

This Lamb is different from a dead Passover lamb, however.
This Lamb is standing upright, conquering and triumphant,
like a strong ram. This Lamb has *seven horns and seven eyes,*
symbolizing perfect (the number seven) power and wisdom.
The horns symbolize strength and power (see 1 Kings 22:11;

EVENTS IN REVELATION DESCRIBED ELSEWHERE IN THE BIBLE

Other Reference	Revelation Reference	Event
Ezekiel 1:22-28	4:2-3; 10:1-3	Glowing rainbow around God's throne
Isaiah 53:7	5:6-8	Christ pictured as a Lamb
Psalm 96	5:9-14	New song
Zechariah 1:7-11; 6:1-8	6:1-8	Horses and riders
Isaiah 2:19-22	6:12; 8:5; 11:13	Earthquake
Joel 2:28-32; Acts 2:14-21	6:12	Moon turning blood red
Mark 13:21-25	6:13	Stars falling from the sky
Isaiah 34:1-4	6:14	Sky rolling up like a scroll
Zephaniah 1:14-18; 1 Thessalonians 5:1-3	6:15-17	God's inescapable wrath
Jeremiah 49:35-39	7:1	Four winds of judgment
Luke 8:26-34	9:1-2; 17:3-8	Bottomless pit
Joel 1:2–2:11	9:3-11	Plague of locusts
Luke 21:20-24	11:1-2	Trampling of the holy city of Jerusalem
Zechariah 4	11:3-6	Two olive trees as witnesses
Daniel 7	13:1-10	A beast coming out of the sea
2 Thessalonians 2:7-14	13:11-15	Wondrous signs and miracles being done by the evil beast
Jeremiah 25:15-29	14:9-12	Drinking the cup of God's wrath
Isaiah 21:1-10	18:2-3	"Babylon" falling
Matthew 22:1-14	19:5-8	Wedding feast of the Lamb
Ezekiel 38; 39	20:7-10	Conflict with Gog and Magog
John 5:19-30	20:11-15	Judging of all people
Ezekiel 37:21-28	21:3	God living among his people
Isaiah 25:1-8	21:4	Tears being wiped away forever
Genesis 2:8-14	22:1-2	Tree of life
1 Corinthians 13:11-12	22:3-5	Seeing God face to face
Daniel 7:18-28	22:5	Believers reigning with God forever

Zechariah 1:18). Although Christ is a sacrificial lamb, he is
not weak. The eyes are further described as *the seven spirits
of God sent out into all the earth,* most likely referring to the
Holy Spirit (see 1:4; Zechariah 4:2-10; John 14:26; 15:26;
16:7-15).

John saw the Lamb *looking as if it had been slain;* the
wounds inflicted on Jesus' body during his trial and crucifixion
could still be seen (see John 20:24-31). During Old Testament
times, lambs would be sacrificed to atone for sins; the Lamb of
God died as the final sacrifice for all sins (see Isaiah 53:7;
Hebrews 10:1-12, 18). The Lamb had conquered because he
had been slain. When Christ died on the cross, he defeated all
the forces of evil. Christ the Lion will lead the battle in which
Satan will be finally defeated (19:19-21). Christ the Lion is
victorious because of what Christ the Lamb has already done.

The Lamb was *standing in the center of the throne,* near God,
and was the object of adoration by all those present, including *the
four living creatures and the elders* (see 4:4, 6).

WHAT DO YOU EXPECT?
One of the elders alerted John that the conquering Lion of
Judah was present (5:5). Yet when John looked, he saw a
Lamb that had been killed. The Lamb was a creature of power
and knowledge. Certainly this scene in heaven was meant to
evoke worship and praise for Christ. It also reveals how Christ
differs from the expectations of him. Some Jews expected a
conquering hero in the Messiah, only to be disappointed by his
death. Others saw a powerless Jesus; they will be surprised
when he reigns in power. As you study Revelation, see the
whole picture of Christ—his love, power, humility, and sacrifice.
Don't limit him by your present understanding.

5:7-8 **He stepped forward and took the scroll from the right hand
of the one sitting on the throne. And as he took the scroll, the
four living beings and the twenty-four elders fell down before
the Lamb. Each one had a harp, and they held gold bowls
filled with incense—the prayers of God's people!**[NLT] Christ
stepped forward and took the scroll from his Father, who was
seated *on the throne.* Christ was worthy to take the scroll because
of his sacrifice on the cross, by which salvation was won for all
who believe. In this vision the time had come for God to unleash
the final acts of history before setting up his kingdom. Christ
would open the scroll and begin the process that would bring
about the end of this fallen world.

As Christ took the scroll, *the four living beings and the twenty-four elders fell down before the Lamb.* This pictures all of the heavenly beings worshiping the Son, just as they had done for the one on the throne (4:10), thereby acknowledging Christ's deity. The *harp* that each held would be used as music for the "new song" they would sing (5:9; see also Psalm 33:2-3). The *gold bowls filled with incense* are described as *the prayers of God's people* (see Psalm 141:2). These prayers from the believers on earth were for God to bring his justice to the earth, as later chapters will describe (see 6:10; 8:3-4). The administration of God's righteous justice will mean deliverance for God's faithful people and punishment on those who have rejected God and persecuted his people.

 GOD'S JUSTICE
The prayers of God's people are for God's justice to be carried out. Why is justice so important in the Bible?

- Justice is part of God's nature; it is the way he runs the universe.
- Justice is a natural desire in every person. Even as sinners, we all want justice.
- When government and church leaders are unjust, the poor and powerless suffer.
- God holds the poor in high regard. They are the ones most likely to turn to him for help and comfort.

Injustice, then, attacks God's children. When we do nothing to help the oppressed, we are in fact joining with the oppressor. Because we follow a just God, we must desire and uphold justice. Let your prayer be the prayer of our Lord: "Our Father in heaven, may your name be honored. May your kingdom come soon. May your will be done here on earth, just as it is in heaven" (Matthew 6:9 NLT).

5:9-10 **And they sang a new song with these words: "You are worthy to take the scroll and break its seals and open it. For you were killed, and your blood has ransomed people for God from every tribe and language and people and nation. And you have caused them to become God's kingdom and his priests. And they will reign on the earth."**ᴺᴸᵀ The remainder of this chapter contains three hymns of praise. This first *new song* was sung by the twenty-four elders and the four living creatures ("they" refers to 5:7-8). In 5:11-12, the singing group will grow to include countless angels in heaven. Finally, in 5:13, "every creature in heaven and on earth and under the earth" begins to sing. This is a celebration of salvation. Jesus' worthiness comes from his self-sacrifice. Because he is *worthy,* he is able to *take the scroll and break its seals and open it.*

The song of the twenty-four elders and the four living creatures praises Christ's work. (See Psalm 96 for a similar song.) He is worthy because:

- he was *killed*
- he *ransomed people* with his blood
- he gathered people from *every tribe and language and people and nation* into his *kingdom*
- he made them *priests*
- he appointed them to *reign on the earth.*

The twenty-four elders and the four living beings praise Christ for bringing people of every race and nation into the kingdom and for making them kings and priests. Believers may be despised and mocked for their faith (John 15:18-27), but in the future they will reign over all the earth (Luke 22:29-30). Christ's death made all believers priests of God—the channels of blessing between God and mankind (1 Peter 2:5-9).

The fact that the Lamb was "killed" refers to Christ's death on the cross as recorded in the Gospels. Through his blood shed on the cross, he ransomed his people. A "ransom" was the price paid to release a slave from bondage. Jesus often told his disciples that he must die, but in a later discussion, he told them why: "For even I, the Son of Man, came here not to be served but to serve others, and to give my life as a ransom for many" (Matthew 20:28 NLT). Through his death Jesus would redeem his people from the bondage of sin and death. The disciples thought that as long as Jesus was alive, he could save them. But Jesus revealed that only his death would save them and all those who trust in him.

How did Christ's blood ransom people? In the Old Testament, the sacrifice of an animal and the blood shed from it made forgiveness of sin possible. Blood represented the sinner's life, infected by his sin and headed for death. Blood also represented the innocent life of the animal that was sacrificed in place of the guilty person making the offering. The death of the animal (of which the blood was proof) fulfilled the death penalty, and God granted forgiveness to the sinner making the sacrifice. God's forgiveness was based on the faith of the person doing the sacrificing. How does Jesus' blood relate to this? People under the old covenant (those who lived before Jesus) could approach God only through a priest and an animal sacrifice. The old covenant was a picture of the new, pointing forward to the day when Jesus himself would be the final and ultimate sacrifice for sin. Rather than an unblemished lamb slain on the altar, the perfect Lamb of God was slain on the cross. He was a sinless sacrifice, making it possible for people all over the world (every tribe, language, people, and nation) to have all their sins forgiven. Jesus' death satisfied God's penalty for sin (Galatians 3:28). "Under the system of Jewish laws, the high priest brought the blood of animals into the Holy Place as a sacrifice for sin. . . . So also Jesus suffered and died outside the city gates in order to make his people holy by shedding his own blood" (Hebrews 13:11-12 NLT).

Only then could sinful people "become God's kingdom and his priests." This had been promised to the nation of Israel at Mount Sinai (Exodus 19:6), but it was fulfilled in God's people, the church, through the death of Christ. Each believer is a priest, having access to God; all believers together form God's kingdom (see also 1:6; 5:10; 20:6). That these believers "will reign on the earth" pictures their reign in God's future kingdom.

God has ransomed people from every tribe, language, people, and nation. God's message of salvation and eternal life is not limited to a specific culture, race, or country. Anyone who comes to God in repentance and faith is accepted by him and will be part of his kingdom. We must not allow prejudice or bias to keep us from sharing Christ with others. Christ welcomes all people into his kingdom.

BARRIER BREAKER
Christianity is the only religion in the world that can truly be described as an equal-opportunity faith. All Christians stand on level ground before the cross of Christ: young and old, male and female, Jew and Gentile, rich and poor, and black, white, and every other color. We are all sinners in need of salvation. Other religions set up barriers between people. Hindus believe in a caste system; Muslim men will not worship with Muslim women; until very recently, black people could not join the Mormon church. Christ alone abolishes all these barriers. Are there barriers in your church (or in your heart) based on race, economics, or sex? Check your attitudes and actions against Scripture. If you find yourself out of accord with God's Word, repent, and ask God to help you. Don't put up walls where Christ has torn them down.

5:11-12 Then I looked and heard the voice of many angels, numbering thousands upon thousands, and ten thousand times ten thousand. They encircled the throne and the living creatures and the elders. In a loud voice they sang: "Worthy is the Lamb, who was slain, to receive power and wealth and wisdom and strength and honor and glory and praise!"NIV The worship that had begun with the four living creatures and twenty-four elders here spreads to all of heaven with all of the angels. In 5:13-14, all creation will join in the praise.

The phrase "thousands upon thousands" is more literally "myriad upon myriad." The word "myriad" was used by the Greeks to describe something too great to count. We might think of "billions upon billions." This is the entire angelic host. Daniel saw a similar vision: "Millions of angels ministered to him, and a hundred million stood to attend him" (Daniel 7:10 NLT).

Created by God, angels are spiritual beings who help carry out his work on earth. They bring messages (Luke 1:26-28), protect God's people (Daniel 6:22), offer encouragement (Genesis 16:7ff), give guidance (Exodus 14:19), bring punishment (2 Samuel 24:16), patrol the earth (Ezekiel 1:9-14), and fight the forces of evil (2 Kings 6:16-18; Revelation 20:1). There are both good and evil angels (12:7), but because evil angels are allied with Satan, they have considerably less power and authority than good angels. Eventually, the main role of the good angels will be to offer continuous praise to God (see also 19:1-3).

The angels sang a hymn of praise. This sevenfold praise may have been a chant that was antiphonal to the elders' hymn of 5:9-10. Each word describes a quality of God that was bestowed upon Christ, making him worthy. *Power* and *strength* are synonyms (see also Luke 11:22; 1 Corinthians 1:24). *Wealth* is associated with kingship (see also 2 Corinthians 8:9; Ephesians 3:8). *Wisdom* is often regarded as a gift received from God (1 Corinthians 1:24). *Honor* is used to describe God (4:11; 7:12) and the Lamb (5:13), denoting the status and respect that is due him (see also Philippians 2:11). *Glory* is also used of God (4:11; 7:12; 19:1) and of God and the Lamb (5:13; see also John 1:14). *Praise* is also used in 4:11 and 7:12 and describes what all creation can give to him who already possesses everything.

5:13-14 **Then I heard every creature in heaven and on earth and under the earth and in the sea, and all that is in them, singing, "To the one seated on the throne and to the Lamb be blessing and honor and glory and might forever and ever!" And the four living creatures said, "Amen!" And the elders fell down and worshiped.**NRSV Finally, the choir grew to *every creature in heaven and on earth and under the earth and in the sea.* They sang both to the *one seated on the throne* as well as *to the Lamb*—both God and his Son. This pictures the unity of the Father and the Son because for them all creation sings of *blessing and honor and glory and might forever and ever.* The unity of the Father and the Son is a strong emphasis in Revelation.

In response to the song of creation, the *four living creatures said, "Amen!"* in agreement. The twenty-four *elders* responded by falling and worshiping the one on the throne (God) and the Lamb (Christ). Everything created, both in heaven and in earth, will one day worship God and his Son: "At the name of Jesus every knee will bow, in heaven and on earth and under the earth, and every tongue will confess that Jesus Christ is Lord, to the glory of God the Father" (Philippians 2:10-11 NLT).

Revelation 6

This is the first of three seven-part judgments. Chapters 6–16 form the core of Revelation. Chapters 1–5 are introductory, and chapters 17–22 conclude this section; chapters 6–16 describe the seal judgments (chapter 6), the trumpet judgments (chapters 8–9), and the bowl judgments (chapters 15–16), with interludes between them. In chapter 5, a scroll with seven seals had been handed to Christ, who is the only one worthy to break the seals and open the scroll, setting into motion the events of the end of the world (5:1-5). In chapter 6, the scroll is opened as each seal is broken. This scroll is not completely opened until the seventh seal is broken (8:1). The contents of the scroll reveal mankind's depravity and portray God's authority over the events of human history.

Each of the judgments (seals, trumpets, bowls) includes seven parts. The first four judgments involve natural disasters on the earth; the last three are cosmic disasters. There are three views about how to understand this series of judgments—seals, trumpets, bowls:

1. *Recapitulation View.* According to this view, the three sets of judgments repeat each other (are cyclical); they present three ways of viewing the same judgments. Because the trumpets and the bowls have the same order, many have concluded that the three sets are repetitive. In addition, in all three sets, the first four of the seven judgments are very similar, as are the last three of each set of seven. Exact repetition, however, occurs only in the trumpets and bowls.

2. *Consecutive View.* This view holds that judgments will follow in the order described in Revelation: first the seals, then the trumpets, then the bowls—in other words, Revelation is describing twenty-one separate events. Thus, chapters 6–16 in Revelation would be chronological.

3. *Progressive Intensification View.* The key to this view is understanding the results of the judgments. The seals destroy one-fourth of the earth; the trumpets destroy one-third; the

bowls affect everything. The picture seems to be one of progressive intensity, with each of these sets of judgments ending in the same place—that is, the end of history.

These views are helpful as you consider and study the book of Revelation. While many will feel very strongly about one view or another, only God knows the truth. He left much of Revelation unclear to his people for a reason, perhaps so we'll study it and be watchful and morally alert. One truth is sure: as God prepares to end history and usher in his kingdom, he *will* bring judgments.

In this chapter, four men on horses appear when the first four seals are opened; these are commonly known as the "four horsemen of the apocalypse." John describes these four horsemen as introducing God's judgment on the world. The first rides a white horse; the second, a bright red horse; the third, a black horse; the fourth, a pale horse. Each one has a mission related to the Lamb's breaking of the first four seals of judgment (Revelation 6:1-8). This series of judgments will affect one-fourth of the earth (6:8); in other words, these are not judgments of the entire earth, but are partial.

The horses represent God's judgment of people's sin and rebellion. God is directing human history—even using his enemies to accomplish his purposes. The four horses provide a foretaste of the final judgments yet to come. Some view this chapter as a parallel to Jesus' words about the end times (see Matthew 24:4-8; Mark 13:5-13; Luke 21:8-19). The imagery of colored horses and riders comes from Zechariah 1:8-17; 6:1-8. In Zechariah, the colors of the horses have no special significance; in Revelation, the colors of the horses do have symbolic meaning, as described below. In Zechariah, the horses and riders went out to patrol the earth; in Revelation, they are sent out to bring disaster.

Why does Christ break the scroll's seals and permit such devastation? Today's readers of Revelation must remember that this message was first for the persecuted early Christians. In breaking these seals, Christ does not send disaster because the mechanism for evil already exists in the hearts of sinful humanity. Rather, Christ breaking the seals demonstrates his lordship over history—even the evil that occurs in history is under his control. While evil people and evil systems appear to dominate, Christ unfolds a future in which he will triumph over every enemy (17:14). For the first-century believers who were facing persecution, Revelation revealed that Christ had seen their suffering and controlled human events. Thus, they could put their trust in him and stand up for their faith in times of difficulty.

6:1-2 I watched as the Lamb opened the first of the seven seals. Then I heard one of the four living creatures say in a voice like thunder, "Come!" I looked, and there before me was a white horse! Its rider held a bow, and he was given a crown, and he rode out as a conqueror bent on conquest.^{NIV} *The Lamb*, Christ, *opened the first of the seven seals.* (For more on the Lamb, see commentary on 5:6.) As each seal was opened, events signaling the end of the world took place. With the breaking of the first seal came four riders on horseback, the first of which John saw in this verse. *One of the four living creatures* said in a *voice like thunder, "Come!"* The creature was probably beckoning the rider on the horse to come forward because, when John looked, he saw *a white horse* with a rider holding *a bow.* As John watched, the rider *was given a crown, and he rode out as a conqueror bent on conquest.*

> If your own sin and mortality do not drive you to seriously consider Jesus Christ, no interpretation of Revelation will likely breach your defenses.
> *Neil Wilson*

This is the only rider who didn't bring catastrophe (the others initiated warfare, famine, and death); this rider was "bent on conquest." There is much debate over who or what this horseman represents. Some have suggested that this rider symbolizes the proclamation of the Good News of Christ. They see the white horse as being "good" and therefore the rider on a good mission. Others believe that the rider on the white horse is Christ himself, for Christ later appears on a white horse (19:11). Jesus is closely associated with the color white in Revelation (see 1:14; 6:11; 14:14).

The fact that this white horse and its rider precede three other horsemen who wreak havoc on the earth, however, suggests that the white horseman might represent the lust for conquest. When mankind is bent on conquest, the result is warfare, famine, and death. The color white could correspond, then, to conquest.

The picture behind this for the first-century readers may have been the powerful Roman legions and their greatest foes—the Parthians who lived east of the Euphrates River, which became the eastern boundary of the Roman Empire. The Parthians had defeated the Roman army twice with their cavalry (the rider on horseback) and their archery (his bow). This had caused much fear of an invasion by the Parthians, so Rome eventually had made a treaty with them.

Most likely, the rider on the white horse represents sinful mankind's desire for conquest; when this occurs, many suffer.

6:3-4 When he opened the second seal, I heard the second living creature call out, "Come!" And out came another horse, bright red; its rider was permitted to take peace from the

THE SEVEN SEALS

Seal	Reference	Description	Possible meanings
1. Rider on the white horse	6:1-2	A rider on a white horse has a bow and a crown and rides out as a conqueror bent on conquest.	Some believe that this rider symbolizes the spread of the Good News or that the rider is Christ himself. Others suggest that this symbolizes mankind's lust for conquest.
2. Rider on the red horse	6:3-4	A rider on a red horse has a great sword and is permitted to take peace from the earth so that people will kill one another.	This rider symbolizes coming warfare, even civil warfare, with great bloodshed.
3. Rider on the black horse	6:5-6	A rider on a black horse has a pair of scales and brings famine and pestilence on the earth.	This rider symbolizes famine and pestilence.
4. Rider on the pale horse	6:7-8	A rider on a pale horse is called Death and has Hades with him.	This rider is called Death, and Hades (the grave) is his inseparable companion. Together they are given power to kill a fourth of the earth.
5. Souls of the martyrs under the altar	6:9-11	The souls of the martyrs who were killed for being faithful in their witness are under the altar crying out for vengeance for their blood.	The breaking of this seal announces God's plan to judge those who persecuted believers.
6. Great earthquake	6:12-17	People on the earth face calamities: a huge earthquake and strange occurrences in the sky.	The wrath and power of the Lamb are seen in the cataclysmic earthquake and the supernatural events in the sky.
7. Silence in heaven	8:1	When the last seal is opened, there is complete silence in heaven.	The seventh seal either begins the next cycle of judgments, or it signals the end and Christ's return.

earth, so that people would slaughter one another; and he was given a great sword.NRSV At the opening of the *second seal,* the second of the four living creatures called out, *"Come!,"* and a rider on a *bright red* horse appeared. He was *given a great sword* and was sent out *to take peace from the earth.* The Greek word for "sword" here is different from the sharp two-edged sword (1:16). This sword probably would have been about five feet long and would have weighed about twenty-five pounds. Strong warriors would swing it while on horseback to kill foot soldiers.

The picture here is of warfare—even civil war because people *would slaughter one another.* Throughout history, conquest has led to civil war. For example, after Alexander the Great conquered the world, he died in his early thirties. For the next two hundred years, his generals fought each other in an attempt to gain superiority. The conquests of Alexander led to two centuries of civil war. In addition, Rome was nearly destroyed by a civil war in A.D. 68–69, after the death of Nero. In that one year, there were three contenders to the imperial throne. The rider on the white horse went out as a "conqueror bent on conquest," and in his wake came warfare. The color of this horse, red, symbolizes great bloodshed upon the earth.

JUSTICE AND PEACE
Complete peace will only come when Christ returns. The picture in Revelation of the coming persecutions and natural disasters is gloomy, but ultimately it is cause for great joy. When believers see these events happening, they will know that their Messiah's return is coming soon, and they can look forward to his reign of justice and peace. Rather than being terrified by what is happening in our world, we should confidently await Christ's return to bring justice and restoration to his people.

6:5-6 **When he opened the third seal, I heard the third living creature call out, "Come!" I looked, and there was a black horse! Its rider held a pair of scales in his hand, and I heard what seemed to be a voice in the midst of the four living creatures saying, "A quart of wheat for a day's pay, and three quarts of barley for a day's pay, but do not damage the olive oil and the wine!"**NRSV Christ opened the *third seal* and this time *the third living creature called out, "Come!,"* beckoning the rider of another horse. This time, when John looked, he saw a *black horse.* This rider is holding *a pair of scales* for weighing food. The words of the four living creatures regarding the amount of food for *a day's pay* pictures wartime inflation. First-century readers would have interpreted this amount as twelve to fifteen times what they were used to paying. What a person would earn in a day would buy only enough food to feed that person, no one else, not even his or her family. This then would lead to widespread famine, another devastating result of warfare.

Following on the heels of the red horse of warfare, therefore, comes a black horse, which represents the sorrow and desolation of warfare that leaves people without money or food. The phrase "Do not damage the olive oil and the wine" could be a warning to conserve two staples. It could mean that these items would be hoarded and thus unavailable in the marketplace. Most likely, it may be that although this famine would be severe, it would not destroy the olive trees and the vineyards. Worse calamity was still to come.

6:7-8 When the Lamb opened the fourth seal, I heard the voice of the fourth living creature say, "Come!" I looked, and there before me was a pale horse! Its rider was named Death, and Hades was following close behind him. They were given power over a fourth of the earth to kill by sword, famine and plague, and by the wild beasts of the earth.NIV The Lamb opened *the fourth seal,* and the fourth living creature said, *"Come!,"* calling a rider on *a pale horse.* The rider's name was *Death.* Following close behind was *Hades.* This does not refer to Hell but, instead, to the grave. The drive for conquest (white horse), had led to warfare and bloodshed (red horse), which had brought famine and pestilence (black horse), resulting in death and the grave (pale horse). The "pale" color indicates the color of death. The four riders were given power over *a fourth of the earth* to kill people *by sword, famine and plague, and by the wild beasts.* Death by wild beasts would be expected when millions of people have died through war, famine, and plague. The number of one-fourth of the earth, working from present-day numbers, would mean over a billion people would die in this first wave of judgment were it to happen today. Nothing that cataclysmic has occurred in all of history.

STILL TIME
That one-fourth of the people (and not all of the people) will die indicates that God is still limiting his judgment—it is not yet complete. This means that there is still time for unbelievers to turn to Christ and away from their sin. In this case, the limited punishment not only demonstrates God's wrath on sin but also his merciful love in giving people yet another opportunity to turn to him before he brings final judgment. We must not presume upon God's patience. Our repentance must be visible and authentic. In what ways does your life reflect new and different behavior?

6:9 **And when the Lamb broke the fifth seal, I saw under the altar the souls of all who had been martyred for the word of God and for being faithful in their witness.**^{NLT} After the four horses had ridden off, the Lamb broke *the fifth seal. It* reveals an altar in heaven, under which are *the souls of all who had been martyred* for faithfully proclaiming *the word of God.* They had been killed for standing up for Christ and for his word (see also 13:15; 18:24; 20:4).

> The greatest proof of Christianity for others is not how far a man can logically analyze his reasons for believing, but how far in practice he will stake his life on his belief. *T. S. Eliot*

The altar represents the altar of sacrifice in the Temple, where animals would be sacrificed to atone for sins. Instead of the animals' blood at the base of the altar, John saw the souls of martyrs who had died for preaching the gospel. The word for "souls" *(psyche)* refers to the persons or to their lives. These martyrs were told that still more would lose their lives for believing in Christ (6:11). In the face of warfare, famine, persecution, and death, Christians need to stand firmly for what they believe. Only those who endure to the end will be rewarded by God (14:12; Mark 13:13).

PRESSURE COOKER
These martyrs stand out because they were faithful. Jesus had predicted (Matthew 10:22) that his followers would be severely persecuted by those who hated what he stood for. In times of terrible persecutions, however, they could have hope, knowing that salvation was theirs. Standing firm to the end is not a way to be saved but the evidence that a person is really committed to Jesus. Persistence is not a means to earn salvation; it is the by-product of a truly devoted life. Times of trial serve to sift true Christians from false or fair-weather Christians. When you are pressured to give up and turn your back on Christ, don't do it. Remember the benefits of standing firm, and continue to live for Christ.

6:10-11 **They called loudly to the Lord and said, "O Sovereign Lord, holy and true, how long will it be before you judge the people who belong to this world for what they have done to us? When will you avenge our blood against these people?" Then a white robe was given to each of them. And they were told to rest a little longer until the full number of the servants of Jesus had been martyred.**^{NLT} The souls of the martyrs beneath the altar were calling out for vengeance for their deaths, asking God how long it would be before he would judge the earth and avenge their blood. This is an imprecatory prayer—a prayer for vengeance against

God's enemies. Just as David had written psalms that called for vengeance against his enemies (for example, Psalms 35; 94:3; see also Habakkuk 1:2), so these martyrs asked for vengeance and vindication against *the people who belong to this world* (see also 3:10; 8:13; 11:10; 13:8, 12; 17:2, 8). These words may sound harsh when used in prayer, but the martyrs were calling for God's justice, and they were leaving the vengeance to God. God promises to help the persecuted and to bring judgment on unrepentant sinners.

This was not revenge that *they* would carry out on their enemies but an appeal for God to punish his enemies. Those who had killed these believers had mocked God by harming his witnesses. The martyrs' cry echoes the words of the imprecatory psalms. The martyrs were eager for God to bring justice to the earth (see also Romans 12:19).

The martyrs were told to *rest a little longer until the full number of the servants of Jesus had been martyred.* God is not waiting until a certain number are killed; rather, he is waiting for the appointed time to arrive. He promises, however, that those who suffer and die for their faith will not be forgotten. In fact, they will be rewarded and honored by God. Today, oppressed people may wish for justice immediately, as these martyrs did, but they must be patient. God works according to his own timetable, and he promises to act. No suffering for the sake of God's kingdom, however, is wasted. God will vindicate his people, but he will do it in his time, not ours.

The *white robe* that each martyr was wearing, as throughout the book of Revelation, symbolizes purity (see also 3:4; 7:11). White robes were worn for special ceremonies in Greek cities.

WHEN GOD SAYS TO WAIT
The martyred witnesses had prayed for God's justice. Yet God's answer to them was to wait. For a person of faith, it is good when God answers our prayers with a "Wait" or a "No." Too often, people think that the only good answer to prayer is an immediate and thunderous "Yes!" That is not biblical faith, however. God shows his great love when he says no or wait because he knows best and is sovereign. Remember that God loves you and that his answers may not be what you expect. Trust him and pray for strength to endure.

6:12-14 I watched as he opened the sixth seal. There was a great earthquake. The sun turned black like sackcloth made of goat hair, the whole moon turned blood red, and the stars in the sky fell to earth, as late figs drop from a fig tree when shaken by a strong wind. The sky receded like a scroll, rolling up, and every mountain and island was removed from its place.[NIV] The *sixth*

COSMIC DISTURBANCES AT THE DAY OF THE LORD

The images in Revelation are not that unusual when compared to the prophets' description of the coming day of the Lord. The Old Testament has many of the same images that John saw (verses quoted from NLT).

Isaiah 2:10-22	" . . . When the Lord rises to shake the earth, his enemies will crawl with fear into holes in the ground . . ."
Isaiah 13:10	"The heavens will be black above them. No light will shine from stars or sun or moon."
Isaiah 34:4	"The heavens above will melt away and disappear like a rolled-up scroll. The stars will fall from the sky, just as withered leaves and fruit fall from a tree."
Jeremiah 4:24-29	"I looked at the earth, and it was empty and formless. I looked at the heavens, and there was no light . . ."
Ezekiel 32:7-8	"When I blot you out, I will veil the heavens and darken the stars. I will cover the sun with a cloud, and the moon will not give you its light. Yes, I will bring darkness everywhere across your land . . ."
Hosea 10:8	" . . . They will beg the mountains to bury them and the hills to fall on them."
Joel 2:11, 31	" . . . The day of the Lord is an awesome, terrible thing. Who can endure it? . . . The sun will be turned into darkness, and the moon will turn bloodred . . ."
Joel 3:15	"The sun and moon will grow dark, and the stars will no longer shine."
Amos 8:8	"The earth will tremble for your deeds, and everyone will mourn. The land will rise up like the Nile River at floodtime, toss about, and sink again."
Nahum 1:5-6	"In his presence the mountains quake, and the hills melt away; the earth trembles, and its people are destroyed. Who can stand before his fierce anger? Who can survive his burning fury? His rage blazes forth like fire, and the mountains crumble to dust in his presence."
Zephaniah 1:14-18	"The terrible day of the Lord is near . . . It is a day when the Lord's anger will be poured out. It is a day of terrible distress and anguish, a day of ruin and desolation, a day of darkness and gloom, of clouds, blackness, trumpet calls, and battle cries . . . He will make a terrifying end of all the people on earth."
Malachi 3:2	"But who will be able to endure it when he comes? Who will be able to stand and face him when he appears? For he will be like a blazing fire that refines metal or like a strong soap that whitens clothes."

seal changed the scene back to the physical world. The first five judgments had been directed toward specific areas, but this judgment was over the whole world. The entire population would be afraid when the earth itself trembled. With the opening of the sixth seal, *there was a great earthquake,* followed by other cosmic disturbances. The *sun turned black,* the *moon turned blood red,* and the *stars . . . fell to the earth.* To properly understand these events, we must go beyond the literal meaning. These word pictures were common to many of John's readers and stood for the coming "day of the Lord" or "day of judgment." The earthquake in Scripture always pictures God's presence (see Exodus 19:18; Isaiah 2:19-21; Haggai 2:6—when he visits, the earth shakes). The color of the sun is described as "black like sackcloth made of goat hair." This rough cloth was made from the hair of a black goat; sackcloth was worn in times of mourning. The moon will appear red due to whatever in the atmosphere caused the sun to be darkened. The stars falling to earth could refer to a terrifying meteor shower with meteors striking the earth (see also Joel 2:30-31; Mark 13:21-25).

Finally, the sky will roll up *like a scroll* (see also Isaiah 34:4). Those who interpret this book as chronological will consider this to be the end of the first round of judgments. Those who picture the book as cyclical, or as showing varying intensity with all the judgments ending at the return of Christ, see the *rolling up* of the sky as the time when Christ opens heaven and returns to earth (19:11). There will be such upheaval on earth that *every mountain and island* will be removed from its place, probably as a result of the great earthquake (see Hebrews 12:26-27).

For the first-century believers, the picture of such cosmic disruption would signal the end of the world. Yet they could find comfort in knowing that God still was in control. Peter wrote to persecuted believers, "You should look forward to that day . . . when God will set the heavens on fire and the elements will melt away in the flames. But we are looking forward to the new heavens and new earth he has promised" (2 Peter 3:12-13 NLT). But the new heaven and earth can only come after the destruction of the old. Paul wrote of the earth and the sin that has infected it, "Against its will, everything on earth was subjected to God's curse. All creation anticipates the day when it will join God's children in glorious freedom from death and decay. For we know that all creation has been groaning as in the pains of childbirth right up to the present time" (Romans 8:20-22 NLT).

6:15-17 **Then the kings of the earth and the magnates and the generals and the rich and the powerful, and everyone, slave and free, hid in the caves and among the rocks of the mountains, calling to the mountains and rocks, "Fall on us and hide us from the face of the one seated on the throne and from the wrath of the Lamb; for the great day of their wrath has come,**

and who is able to stand?"^{NRSV} As the earthquake moved the mountains and the sky was filled with terrifying signs, everyone on the earth—from the rich and powerful to the "middle-class" citizens to the slaves—all hid from God. They recognized that the end of the world had come and they hoped to *hide . . . from the face of the one seated on the throne and from the wrath of the Lamb.* The people were so terrified of the one seated on the throne that they would prefer that an avalanche fall on them rather than have to face God. The evil people on the earth dread God more than they dread death. They do not realize that even death cannot help them to escape their judgment by God.

On that day, all people will be made equal before the Lamb, for all will bow before him (Philippians 2:10). The *kings* and *magnates* who had ultimate authority, the *generals* who were used to warfare and being in command, the *rich and the powerful* who felt secure in their possessions—they, like Adam and Eve in the garden, ran and hid from God (see Genesis 3:8). Everyone else, *slave and free,* also attempted to hide from God's wrath, for they knew that these signs could mean nothing else (see also Zephaniah 1:14-18; 1 Thessalonians 5:1-3).

The picture is a paradox. Lambs are gentle animals—but this Lamb was bringing great wrath upon a world that had refused his sacrifice, mocked his name, and persecuted his people (see Luke 12:49).

By listing the kings, magnates, generals, the rich, and the powerful as well as the slaves, John was emphasizing that those who had escaped previously would not escape this. Those who thought they were safe and secure would find that they had no place to hide from God.

NO FEAR
At the sight of God sitting on the throne, all human beings, great and small, will be terrified, calling for the mountains to fall on them so that they will not have to face the judgment of the Lamb. This vivid picture was not intended to frighten believers. For them, the Lamb is a gentle Savior. But those generals, emperors, or kings who previously showed no fear of God and arrogantly flaunted their unbelief will find that they were wrong, and in that day they will have to face God's wrath. No one who has rejected God can survive the day of his wrath, but those who belong to Christ will receive a reward rather than punishment. Do you belong to Christ? If so, you need not fear these final days.

Revelation 7

The sixth seal had been opened, and the people of the earth had tried to hide from God, asking who would be able to survive God's judgment (6:17). Just when destruction seemed sure, four angels held back the four winds of judgment until God's people were sealed as his own. This sealing occurred in this interlude between the sixth and seventh seals. An interlude also comes between the sixth and seventh trumpets (10:1–11:13) but not between the sixth and seventh bowls (16:12-21). God did not open the seventh seal until he had marked his people as his own (8:1). This chapter answers the question in 6:17, "Who is able to stand?" The faithful believers would be kept safe. This chapter contains two pictures: first, the sealing of the 144,000; second, the great multitude worshiping before God's throne.

7:1 Then I saw four angels standing at the four corners of the earth, holding back the four winds from blowing upon the earth. Not a leaf rustled in the trees, and the sea became as smooth as glass.^{NLT} John saw *four angels* who were *standing at the four corners of the earth* (referring to the whole earth, the four points of the compass). The sudden silence and the angels *holding back the four winds from blowing upon the earth* picture God's protection from harm; they contrast the peace and security of the believers with the terror of those hiding in the rocks (6:16). The winds described here picture harmful winds as agents of God bringing destruction (see Daniel 7:2). The four angels hold back the winds so that *not a leaf rustled in the trees, and the sea became as smooth as glass.* This scene contrasts with the earthquakes and meteor showers that had just occurred (6:12-13).

7:2-3 Then I saw another angel coming up from the east, having the seal of the living God. He called out in a loud voice to the four angels who had been given power to harm the land and the sea: "Do not harm the land or the sea or the trees until we put a seal on the foreheads of the servants of our God."^{NIV} *Another angel* came from the *east* who had *the seal of the living God.* The east probably indicates the direction of Jerusalem. This seal differs from

THE GREAT TRIBULATION

Most Christians acknowledge the reality of a time of tribulation, but there is considerable debate concerning when this time will occur and who will be affected by it. (See also the chart located at 3:13, page 47.)

Dispensational Premillennialism
Dispensational premillennialists believe that Jesus' prophecy of a future Tribulation will affect Israel but not the church. Prior to the tribulation, the church will be raptured out of the world when Christ suddenly descends from the clouds. The Antichrist is an integral part of Daniel's prophecy concerning the seventieth week of years, and, according to dispensationalists, this prophecy only deals with God's plans for Israel (Daniel 9:27; Matthew 24:15-22). The rise of the Antichrist begins a seven-year period of tribulation designed to bring Israel back to God. In Daniel's seventieth week, the Antichrist first befriends Israel. Then after three and a half years, the Antichrist blasphemes the all-powerful God and aggressively persecutes the Jews (Daniel 7:8, 20-27; 9:24-27; Matthew 24:15-22). During this period of unspeakable suffering, many Jews recognize Christ as the Messiah and begin to turn back to God. After these seven years of horror, Christ returns to defeat his enemies at Armageddon and begin his thousand-year reign of peace (Matthew 24:29-31).

Historic Premillennialism
Historic premillennialists view the Tribulation as the final manifestation of evil at the end of history. The Antichrist will proclaim himself to be god and launch a worldwide campaign of persecution of Christians (Matthew 24:15-22; 2 Thessalonians 2:3-12). Thus, according to historic premillennialists, Christians will experience this Tribulation and suffer for the cause of Christ. But Christ will sustain his people and protect them from God's dreadful judgments on the Antichrist and his followers. At the height of this period of persecution, Christ will return to defeat his enemies at Armageddon and establish his thousand-year reign.

Amillennialism
Amillennialists believe that the battle between good and evil will climax in a period of intense persecution of Christians at the end of this age, just prior to Christ's second coming. They believe that the Tribulation is not a specific time in the future but instead may refer to this present age as well. The Tribulation occurs anywhere the Good News is being opposed and Christians are being persecuted. Amillennialists point out that Scripture doesn't state that the Tribulation is confined to Israel (Revelation 7:13–14). They believe that all of God's people will be persecuted. When Christ returns, bringing judgment on evil, he will gather believers (Matthew 24:31).

Postmillennialism
Postmillennialists believe that the church itself will usher in the Millennium. As a result, they deny the idea of a future Tribulation period. They believe that Jesus' prophecy of the abomination being placed in the temple has already been fulfilled in Titus's destruction of Jerusalem and its Temple in A.D. 70 (Matthew 24:15-22). They don't believe Jesus' prophecy speaks of a future Antichrist.

the seven seals on the scroll that the Lamb had been opening. In ancient days, a king would push his signet ring into wax on a scroll or document as a seal to mark his ownership and to protect its contents. God places his own seal on his followers, identifying them as his own and guaranteeing his protection over their souls. Here, God's seal was placed *on the foreheads* of his servants. This seal would be counterfeited by Satan in 13:16 (a seal known as "the mark of the beast"). These two marks would separate the people into two distinct categories—those owned by God and those owned by Satan. Ezekiel 9:4-7 records God sending a divine messenger through Jerusalem to mark the foreheads of those who still worshiped the one true God. Here, the seal that the angel put on the believers' foreheads was the name of the Lamb and his Father's name (see 14:1).

> We shall see his face, and his name shall be on our foreheads. We are sons with him, heirs of God and fellow heirs with our Lord Jesus Christ. The acquired glory of our Lord is the glory which every saved sinner will share with him.
> *Arno C. Gaebelein*

Why did the believers need this seal of protection? Most likely, they needed protection from what would be a time of intense difficulty on the earth, for the angels at the four winds were told, *"Do not harm the land or the sea or the trees until . . ."* At the end of history, people will face a time that will be marked by unprecedented evil and persecution (see Daniel 12:1). In 9:3-4, for example, during the fifth trumpet, stinging locusts descend on the earth and are told "to attack all the people who did not have the seal of God on their foreheads" (NLT). In 16:2, "the first angel left the Temple and poured out his bowl over the earth, and horrible, malignant sores broke out on everyone who had the mark of the beast" (NLT). However, the seal would not protect the believers in all instances from the pain and suffering of these judgments, nor would it protect them from death. Ultimately, the seal was a sign of spiritual and eternal protection. Those sealed would be protected from God's punishment of an impenitent world. They would not face God's wrath, even though they would face the wrath of those who hate God. Jesus had said, "I assure you that everyone who has given up house or brothers or sisters or mother or father or children or property, for my sake and for the Good News, will receive now in return, a hundred times over, houses, brothers, sisters, mothers, children, and property—with persecutions. And in the world to come they will have eternal life" (Mark 10:29-30 NLT).

Pretribulationists believe that Christians will have been raptured—removed from this world to meet the Lord in the air—just before the Tribulation begins. They believe that this seal means that many others will become believers during the time of tribulation—these new believers will receive this seal. According to this verse, the only believers who will suffer through this terrible evil and persecution will be those who become Christians during the Tribulation, perhaps because they had witnessed the rapture of true believers.

Some Christians believe that the Tribulation described in the book of Revelation is not limited to a specific time period. Instead, they see the Tribulation as referring to the constant conflict between good and evil that has existed throughout history. These Christians don't believe that evil and persecution will increase in the last days. Rather, they believe that the church of Christ will gradually convert the world and usher in Jesus' kingdom. Others who believe that the Tribulation is not a specific period of time do believe that the suffering will intensify toward the end, just as Jesus promised.

Although Scripture isn't clear whether believers will have to go through the "great tribulation," the Bible clearly states that God looks after his people (Psalms 1:6; 145:20; Ezekiel 34:12). He promises to protect believers and give them the strength to endure any and all tribulation (Psalm 32:7; John 17:15).

Both those who think that the Christians will be raptured before the Tribulation, as well as those who think they will remain on earth throughout, agree that the seal put on believers' foreheads will protect them. Both groups also consider 3:10 to describe this: "Because you have obeyed my command to persevere, I will protect you from the great time of testing that will come upon the whole world to test those who belong to this world" (NLT).

MARKED PEOPLE
The angel foretold that a seal, a mark of ownership, would be placed on faithful believers. This shows how valuable God's people are to him. Our physical bodies may be beaten, maimed, or even destroyed, but *nothing* can harm our souls when we have been sealed by God. Ephesians 1:13-14 says, "And now you also have heard the truth, the Good News that God saves you. And when you believed in Christ, he identified you as his own by giving you the Holy Spirit, whom he promised long ago. The Spirit is God's guarantee that he will give us everything he promised and that he has purchased us to be his own people" (NLT). Having believed, we were marked in him with a seal, the promised Holy Spirit. In our daily lives, we bear this mark now, although others can't see it directly. Does your life reveal that you are God's possession? Do your words and actions convey that you are a marked person?

7:4-8 **Then I heard the number of those who were sealed: 144,000 from all the tribes of Israel. From the tribe of Judah 12,000 were sealed, from the tribe of Reuben 12,000, from the tribe of Gad 12,000, from the tribe of Asher 12,000, from the tribe of Naphtali 12,000, from the tribe of Manasseh 12,000, from the tribe of Simeon 12,000, from the tribe of Levi 12,000, from the tribe of Issachar 12,000, from the tribe of Zebulun 12,000, from the tribe of Joseph 12,000, from the tribe of Benjamin 12,000.**^{NIV} The *number of those who were sealed* is *144,000.* This does not mean that only 144,000 people alive on the earth at that time will be saved. Most likely, it is a symbolic number: 12 x 12 x 1,000, symbolizing completeness. A similar multiple appears in 21:16, when John was measuring the new Jerusalem (see also 14:1).

Some believe that this refers specifically to Jews—that there will be a great revival among the Jews and that many will be saved. Some say that there will be exactly 144,000 Jews saved—perhaps to be evangelists for the rest of the great multitude (7:9). This list differs slightly from the lists of the twelve tribes that occur in various places in the Old Testament. Some reasons for the differences could be: (1) Judah is mentioned first because Judah is both the tribe of David and of Jesus the Messiah (Genesis 49:8-12; Matthew 1:1). (2) Levi had no tribal allotment because of the Levites' work for God in the temple (Deuteronomy 18:1), but here the tribe is given a place as a reward for faithfulness. (3) Dan is not mentioned because it was known for rebellion and idolatry—traits unacceptable for God's followers (Genesis 49:17). (4) The two tribes representing Joseph (usually called Ephraim and Manasseh, after Joseph's sons) are here called Joseph and Manasseh because of Ephraim's rebellion. See Genesis 49 for the story of the beginning of these twelve tribes.

Most likely, however, this listing of the twelve tribes is symbolic of all of God's true followers—the "true Israel," which is the church (Romans 2:29; 9:6; Galatians 3:29; 6:16; 1 Peter 2:9). All of God's followers will be brought safely to him; not one will be overlooked or forgotten. God seals these believers either by withdrawing them from the earth (in the Rapture, see commentary on 7:2-3 above) or by giving them special strength and courage to make it through this time of great persecution. No matter what happens, they will be brought to their reward of eternal life. Their destiny is secure. These believers will not fall away from God, even though they may undergo intense persecution. This is not saying that 144,000 individuals must be sealed before the persecution comes, but that when persecution begins, the faithful will have already been sealed (marked by God), and they will remain true to him until the end.

THE GREAT CROWD / 7:9-17

This "vast crowd" is the huge redeemed multitude, the great international family of God, offering praise to him. These are the ones
who have been protected, redeemed, and purified.

**7:9-10 After this I saw a vast crowd, too great to count, from every
nation and tribe and people and language, standing in front
of the throne and before the Lamb. They were clothed in
white and held palm branches in their hands. And they were
shouting with a mighty shout, "Salvation comes from our
God on the throne and from the Lamb!"**[NLT] In 7:4, John had
heard the number of those sealed; here, he *saw a vast crowd, too
great to count.* This fulfilled God's promise to Abraham that he
would have descendants too numerous to count (Genesis 15:5;
32:12; Romans 9:6-8; Galatians 3:29).

Who is this great multitude? In 7:14, they are described as those
who have "come out of the great tribulation." Some interpreters
identify them as the martyrs described in 6:9, but they may also be
the same group as the 144,000 just mentioned (7:4-8), for that may
be a symbolic number indicating *all* believers who had been sealed.
In other words, John may have seen the final state of the believers
who survive the Tribulation. This interpretation seems to be supported by 7:15-17, where the believers are described as serving
God day and night—thereby picturing eternity.

This scene provides great comfort to all believers facing persecution. Those believers who will face the Tribulation have a
guaranteed future with God. In this vision, the 144,000 were
sealed by God before the great time of persecution and brought
to heaven. Before, they were being prepared; here, they were
victorious. This multitude in heaven is all of God's faithful followers throughout the generations. No true believer needs to
worry about his or her final destination. God includes and protects each one, and all are guaranteed eternal life in his presence.

The angels, elders, and living creatures of chapters 4 and 5 were
joined by this *vast crowd* of people *from every nation and tribe and
people and language.* No distinctions of race, ethnic background,
or gender exist in this worshiping community. These were the
redeemed people—those who had accepted Christ's sacrifice on
their behalf and had experienced God's forgiveness. Thus they say,
"Salvation comes from our God on the throne and from the Lamb!"
Only human beings can know the reality of salvation from sin—
the angels, elders, and living creatures had not fallen. So only the
redeemed could sing of the salvation they had received.

These were *clothed in white,* symbolizing their purity because of the salvation they had received (3:4-5; 4:4; 19:14). The martyrs in 6:11 had been given white robes—thus, some think this crowd that has come through the Tribulation is those who have been martyred for their faith. They were holding *palm branches in their hands,* symbolizing the joy of this occasion, as they stood before God and the Lamb (see also John 12:13).

THROUGH THE LAMB
The vast crowd was shouting that salvation comes from God and from the Lamb. People try many methods to remove the guilt of sin—good deeds, intellectual pursuits, and even casting blame on others. By contrast, the multitude in heaven praises God, saying that salvation comes from him and from the Lamb. Salvation from sin's penalty can come only through Jesus Christ and his sacrifice. Suffering, or even martyrdom, cannot save anyone. Have you had the guilt of sin removed in the only way possible? Turn to Christ for cleansing and forgiveness.

7:11-12 **And all the angels stood around the throne and around the elders and the four living creatures, and they fell on their faces before the throne and worshiped God, singing, "Amen! Blessing and glory and wisdom and thanksgiving and honor and power and might be to our God forever and ever! Amen."**NRSV
The *angels,* the *elders,* and *the four living creatures* had stood before the throne in John's earlier vision. For more information about the elders, see the commentary on 4:4. For more information on the four living creatures, see the commentary on 4:6-7.

After the redeemed sang their song (7:9-10), the angels, elders, and four living creatures *fell on their faces before the throne.* They worshiped God and sang to him seven words of praise: *blessing, glory, wisdom, thanksgiving, honor, power,* and *might.* Compare this to 5:11-13 where the words are explained. Six of the same words are used, but in different order; here "thanksgiving" replaces "riches" in 5:12. Perhaps this shows that to have used all the same words in the same order would have reduced this doxology into a formula. Instead, singing all these praises in different orders causes the singers to think about the importance of each item for which they are praising God.

> Every saint in heaven is as a flower in the garden of God, and every soul there is as a note in some concert of delightful music.
> *Jonathan Edwards*

They were offering praise to God and the Lamb because of the salvation he had given to all the redeemed. Jesus said, "There is joy in the presence of God's angels when even one sinner repents" (Luke 15:10 NLT). Imagine the great joy of the angels in heaven

when they stand with this countless crowd of believers who had
repented of sin and accepted the salvation of the Lamb.

Amen occurs both at the beginning and at the end of this hymn.
This word unites us with God's will and sovereignty. To say
"amen" means to say, "may this be according to you, God."

PRAISE THE LORD
The angels and the four living creatures praised God by using
this seven-part doxology or song of praise. It praises God's attributes. The song presents a complete and balanced picture of
the wonder and power of God. Today, take time to praise God
using these seven attributes:
1. *Blessing*—praise God for the profound happiness he gives.
2. *Glory*—praise God for his moral perfection and splendor.
3. *Wisdom*—praise God for the wisdom of his plan of
   redemption.
4. *Thanksgiving*—thank God for pardoning sin.
5. *Honor*—attribute worth to God publicly for saving people.
6. *Power*—praise God for his power to act.
7. *Might*—thank God for his presence in past history and
   in current events.

7:13-14 **Then one of the elders asked me, "These in white robes—who
are they, and where did they come from?" I answered, "Sir, you
know. " And he said, "These are they who have come out of the
great tribulation; they have washed their robes and made them
white in the blood of the Lamb."**[NIV] One of the twenty-four elders
turned to John and anticipated his question regarding the identity
of this great crowd in white robes, *"Where did they come from?"*

These people *have come out of the great tribulation.* They have
persevered, standing true for Christ. Some may have been martyred, but probably not all of them. They have been redeemed, for
they *have washed their robes and made them white in the blood of
the Lamb.*

DO THE WASH
How did those in the vast crowd of believers wash their robes?
The only part humans can play is to come to God for forgiveness, renounce all loyalty to sin and false gods, trust Christ for
total cleansing, and rely on the Holy Spirit's power to live a new
life. Have you presented your life to God for cleansing, or are
you still making your robes dirty by living in sinful rebellion?

These people had been dirty with sin, but Christ had cleansed
them with his blood (see commentary on 5:9-10 regarding how

the blood makes them clean). It is difficult to imagine how blood could make any cloth white, but the blood of Jesus Christ is the world's greatest purifier because it removes the stain of sin. "Just think how much more the blood of Christ will purify our hearts from deeds that lead to death so that we can worship the living God. For by the power of the eternal Spirit, Christ offered himself to God as a perfect sacrifice for our sins" (Hebrews 9:14 NLT). White symbolizes sinless perfection or holiness, which can be given to people only by the death of the sinless Lamb of God on their behalf. This is a picture of how believers are saved through faith (see Isaiah 1:18; Romans 3:21-26).

For explanation on the various views of the great tribulation, see commentary on 7:2-3 above.

7:15-17 **"Therefore they are before the throne of God, and serve Him day and night in His temple. And He who sits on the throne will dwell among them. They shall neither hunger anymore nor thirst anymore; the sun shall not strike them, nor any heat; for the Lamb who is in the midst of the throne will shepherd them and lead them to living fountains of waters. And God will wipe away every tear from their eyes."**NKJV According to 7:1-8, the believers receive a seal to protect them through a time of great tribulation and suffering; in 7:9-17, John receives a glimpse into the future—the believers finally with God in heaven. All who have been faithful through the ages were singing before God's throne. Their tribulations and sorrows were over: no more tears for sin, for all sins were forgiven; no more tears for suffering, for all suffering was over; no more tears for death, for all believers had been resurrected to die no more.

The phrase "day and night" means continuous, unceasing service to God—that "service" refers to worship and praise (22:3-5). The *temple* is not limited to some particular building in heaven, nor is it a reference to the temple in Jerusalem; instead, all of heaven is God's sanctuary.

In this vision, *the Lamb* is *in the midst of the throne.* The Lamb himself is God. He will be their *shepherd* and will *lead them to living fountains of waters.* As a shepherd, Jesus gives daily care, guidance, and provision. The living fountains picture eternal refreshment in God's presence (Psalm 36:8-9; John 4:14). He *will dwell among* his people. This fulfills the Old Testament promises (Psalm 23:1; Isaiah 40:11; Ezekiel 37:27; Zechariah 2:10).

God will satisfy every need. There will be no *hunger* or *thirst,* there will not be overwhelming *heat* from the *sun.* This echoes Isaiah's prophecy, "They will neither hunger nor thirst. The searing sun and scorching desert winds will not reach them anymore.

For the Lord in his mercy will lead them beside cool waters" (Isaiah 49:10 NLT). The reference to hunger and thirst refers not just to food but also to spiritual fulfillment (Matthew 5:6). The heat and sun refer to God's shelter and protection. God's care extends to every part of life—he *will wipe away every tear* from their eyes. These are the blessings that God will provide to his people.

RENEW YOUR HOPE

This beautiful scene describes how God will provide for his children's needs in their eternal home where there will be no hunger, thirst, or pain and where he will wipe away all tears. When you are suffering or torn apart by sorrow, take comfort in this promise of complete protection and relief. Go to Jesus for strength and patience. He can help you renew your hope.

Revelation 8

Chapter 7 was an interlude. At the end of chapter 6, the sixth seal had been opened (6:12). Here at the beginning of chapter 8, the Lamb opens the seventh and last seal.

8:1-2 **When the Lamb broke the seventh seal, there was silence throughout heaven for about half an hour. And I saw the seven angels who stand before God, and they were given seven trumpets.**^NLT The Lamb broke the *seventh seal,* which was the last on the scroll (5:1). When the seal was opened, *there was silence throughout heaven for about half an hour* (see Habakkuk 2:20; Zechariah 2:13). Some have suggested that this silence is so that the prayers of the suffering saints on earth can be heard. However, most likely, this is the silence of breathless expectancy, as all of heaven waited for the hand of God to move. The psalmist had written, "Be still in the presence of the Lord, and wait patiently for him to act. Don't worry about evil people who prosper or fret about their wicked schemes" (Psalm 37:7 NLT). When the seventh seal was opened, the seven trumpet judgments were revealed. In the same way, the seventh trumpet will announce the seven bowl judgments in 11:15 and 16:1-21.

Seven angels . . . were given seven trumpets. The trumpet judgments, like the seal judgments, are only partial. God's final and complete judgment had not yet come. The Lamb had opened the seven seals to set in motion events of judgment, but angels had been given the power to execute the trumpet and bowl judgments. The use of the definite article (*the* seven angels) may designate a specific group. Jewish literature names seven specific archangels, so these may be the ones referred to here (their names are Uriel, Raphael, Raguel, Michael, Saragael, Gabriel, and Remiel—see 1 Enoch 20:2-8). These angels *stand before God.* When the archangel Gabriel spoke to Zechariah the priest, he said, "I am Gabriel! I stand in the very presence of God" (Luke 1:19 NLT). Whether these same seven angels also pour out the bowl judgments (15:6) or "the seven" are different angels is unknown.

Throughout the Old Testament, trumpets had a variety of

meanings and purposes. Moses was instructed to make two
silver trumpets that would call the people together, move the
tribes forward on their journey, sound an alarm, or signify the
feast days (Numbers 10:3, 5-6, 9-10). The trumpets herald
the arrival of the day of God's wrath.

Apparently the events of 8:3-5 occur immediately following
this time of silence.

DISCIPLINE OF SILENCE
There was silence in heaven for half an hour. With all the activity, this dramatic pause must have seemed to last for an eternity. During this time, the only activity was the prayers of the
saints (8:3-4). We must seek God in times of silence. How
proper for us to be quiet and honor God for his power and
might. Take time each day to be silent and exalt God. Silence
also conveys trust and confidence in God (see Isaiah 30:15).
We can trust God that he will give us strength and provide the
justice against oppressors that we seek.

8:3-4 **Then another angel with a gold incense burner came and
stood at the altar. And a great quantity of incense was given
to him to mix with the prayers of God's people, to be offered
on the gold altar before the throne. The smoke of the incense,
mixed with the prayers of the saints, ascended up to God
from the altar where the angel had poured them out.**[NLT] Then
John saw *another angel,* not one of the seven, who performed
another task. This angel had *a gold incense burner* and came to
the *altar* (also mentioned in 6:9). This gold incense burner is also
called a censer, or fire pan (see also 1 Kings 7:50). Then the
angel was given *a great quantity of incense,* which was used *to
mix with the prayers of God's people.* The angel acted in the role
of a priest, presenting the prayers of the saints to God. The angel
was not an intermediary, as Christ is (Hebrews 7:25; 9:24), nor
did the angel make the prayers acceptable. The incense symbolized the offered prayers, and the angel was merely the agent. No
one should conclude from these verses that anyone should pray
to angels.

When the angel put the incense in the fire pan, *the smoke . . .
ascended up to God.* The cloud of fragrant smoke rose, much as
it did in the tabernacle and the temple. A censer filled with live
coals was used in temple worship. Incense would be poured on
the coals, and the sweet-smelling smoke would drift upward, symbolizing believers' prayers ascending to God (see Exodus 30:7-
9). This would be done twice a day, at the morning and evening
sacrifices. These prayers are most likely prayers for justice and

deliverance, as described in 6:10. God brings judgment in response to the prayers of his people. One of the reasons for the trumpet judgments is God's answer to the prayers of the saints.

8:5 Then the angel took the censer and filled it with fire from the altar and threw it on the earth; and there were peals of thunder, rumblings, flashes of lightning, and an earthquake.^{NRSV}
Then the angel *took the censer and filled it with fire from the altar and threw it on the earth.* Ezekiel described a similar scene when a man was told to "take a handful of glowing coals and scatter them over the city" (see Ezekiel 10:2-7), thereby picturing judgment on the city of Jerusalem as God's glory departed. The fire from the altar being thrown to the earth symbolizes the prayers

> Prayer is a shield to the soul, a sacrifice to God, and a scourge to Satan.
> *John Bunyan*

of the saints on earth being answered. God was about to act on their behalf. The *peals of thunder, rumblings, flashes of lightning, and an earthquake* are the beginning of his answer to their prayers. These indicate that God is about to take action and answer (Exodus 19:16-19).

PRAY FOR JUSTICE
The angel threw the censer to the earth. This symbolizes the judgment of God released on earth in answer to the prayers of the saints for justice for those who had oppressed and killed them. This shows that judgment, vindication, and revenge are in God's hands, not ours (see Matthew 5:38; Romans 12:9; 1 Peter 3:9). No matter how strong the desire to exact revenge and retaliate at our enemies, our work is to pray to God for his justice.

THE TRUMPETS / 8:6-13

The seven trumpet judgments call forth a series of God's plagues on his enemies. These judgments affected every part of the world: the earth, the sea, rivers and lakes, the sky, and the "people who did not have the seal of God on their foreheads" (9:4). Unlike the bowl judgments described in chapter 16, the first six trumpets were targeted on just a third of the cosmos and were intended to produce repentance (9:20-21).

The trumpet and the bowl judgments symbolically reenacted the plagues of Egypt recorded in Exodus 7–12. The plagues had two purposes:

(1) They were directed against the gods of Egypt. Every plague was directed at a force that the Egyptians thought was on

THE SEVEN TRUMPETS

Trumpet	Reference	Description	Results
1	8:7	Hail and fire, mixed with blood, are hurled to the earth.	A third of the earth, a third of the trees, and all green grass are burned up.
2	8:8-9	A great mountain of fire is thrown into the sea.	A third of the sea becomes blood, killing one-third of its living creatures. One-third of all ships on the sea are destroyed.
3	8:10-11	A flaming star falls out of the sky.	A third of the earth's water is turned bitter, or polluted, killing many people.
4	8:12-13	One third of the sun, moon, and stars are darkened.	There is less light from the sky, and people spend more time in darkness.
5	9:1-11	A star falls from the sky and opens the Abyss.	Poisonous locusts are let loose to attack people on the earth for five months.
6	9:13-21	A war with huge numbers of mounted troops begins.	A third of all the people on the earth are killed.
7	11:14–14:20	The final struggle between God and Satan—good and evil—takes place first in heaven, then on earth.	Satan acts against God's plan, causing more destruction before he is finally defeated.

their side because they worshiped that force. For example, the Egyptians worshiped the sun, so God sent a plague of darkness (Exodus 10:21-29); they worshiped the Nile River, so God sent a plague to turn the sacred river to blood (7:14-24). The first purpose of the plagues against Egypt was to prove the powerlessness of the Egyptian gods.

(2) The plagues were oriented to the cycle of nature. The Egyptians worshiped many gods representing the various forces of nature so that nature would feed and take care of them. The second purpose of the plagues was to show the Egyptians that God controlled nature and that Egypt's gods controlled nothing.

The plagues showed the helplessness of the people of Egypt, who worshiped false gods. In the same way, through these trumpet and bowl judgments, God will show the people of this world their helplessness and hopelessness without him. Many in this world worship false gods, and God will show the powerlessness of those gods. Many believe that there is no God, so, in reality, they worship themselves as gods. They believe in nothing but the world and what they see. But God will show that he is in control. In the trumpet and bowl judgments, the world that these people are worshiping will turn against them. Through these judgments, God will once again bring punishment upon those who oppress his people, just as he did in Egypt.

The first four seal judgments (the four horsemen) show the inevitable course of humanity's own sinfulness; the first four trumpet judgments reveal God's active involvement in bringing punishment upon a world that has opposed God. The final three trumpet judgments involve demonic attacks on people. These judgments will affect more of the world (one-third, in addition to the one-fourth destruction during the seal judgments), but they still will not be final. And even as God intervenes in these ways, many people stubbornly will refuse to turn to him.

8:6 Then the seven angels with the seven trumpets prepared to blow their mighty blasts.NLT Returning to the action of 8:2, the *seven angels* who had been given *the seven trumpets* got ready to *blow their mighty blasts.* The picture is of these mighty angels raising the trumpets to their lips and then awaiting the signal to blow at the appropriate time. The trumpet blasts have three purposes: (1) to warn that judgment is certain, (2) to call the forces of good and evil to battle, and (3) to announce the return of the King, the Messiah.

8:7 The first angel blew his trumpet, and there came hail and fire, mixed with blood, and they were hurled to the earth; and a third of the earth was burned up, and a third of the trees were burned up, and all green grass was burned up.
NRSV At the beginning of chapter 7, an angel had called for the angels holding back the four winds to not hurt "the land or the sea or the trees" until God's servants had been sealed (7:1-3). But after they had been sealed, God's fury was unleashed upon the earth.

As the first angel *blew his trumpet, there came hail and fire, mixed with blood.* This compares to the seventh plague on Egypt when hailstorms killed anything that was outside (people and animals) and destroyed much vegetation (Exodus 9:13-35). Some have suggested that this could refer to volcanic activity—volcanoes erupting as a result of the massive earthquake (6:12). Others say that this is a violent storm, with the fire representing lightning and the blood referring to the color of the sky. The reference to the blood could have its roots in Ezekiel 38:22 and

Joel 2:31. Jesus had said, "There will be strange events in the skies—signs in the sun, moon, and stars. And down here on earth the nations will be in turmoil, perplexed by the roaring seas and strange tides. The courage of many people will falter because of the fearful fate they see coming upon the earth, because the stability of the very heavens will be broken up" (Luke 21:25-26 NLT).

The result of this volcanic activity or massive thunderstorm is that *a third of the earth was burned up,* along with *a third of the trees,* and *all* the *green grass.* These trees may have been fruit trees; thus, all the olive oil would be cut off. With the grass gone, all the livestock would die. Since only one-third of the earth was destroyed by these trumpet judgments, this was only a partial judgment from God. His full wrath was yet to be unleashed. The purpose of this judgment was to warn people to repent.

8:8-9 **Then the second angel blew his trumpet, and a great mountain of fire was thrown into the sea. And one-third of the water in the sea became blood. And one-third of all things living in the sea died. And one-third of all the ships on the sea were destroyed.**[NLT] One-third of the land had been destroyed at the blowing of the first trumpet; when the *second angel blew his trumpet, one-third* of the sea was destroyed. The *great mountain of fire was thrown into the sea,* causing the disruption. Some suggest that this refers to a falling meteor or asteroid that, upon impact in the sea, disrupts the ecology of the sea and creates a tidal wave. The water is described as becoming *blood,* with the result that *one-third of all things living in the sea died.* This compares to the first plague when the Nile River was turned to blood (Exodus 7:14-24). This plague on the sea somehow also affected *one-third of all the ships on the sea* because they were *destroyed.* Perhaps this occurred from a tidal wave caused by the "great mountain of fire" that had been thrown into the sea.

For an economy centered around the sea for its trade and food, as was Rome's, this would be especially terrifying. Because travel by land was slow, Rome depended on the sea for most of its transport of goods. The key cities in the Roman Empire were the ports on the Mediterranean Sea. Rome's navy insured the safety of travel on the Mediterranean. But they could do nothing against God's judgment.

8:10-11 **Then the third angel blew his trumpet, and a great flaming star fell out of the sky, burning like a torch. It fell upon one-third of the rivers and on the springs of water. The name of the star was Bitterness. It made one-third of the water bitter, and many people died because the water was so bitter.**[NLT] One-third of the

living things in the sea died as a result of the second trumpet.
When *the third angel blew his trumpet,* the results affected all the
inland waters—*one-third of the rivers* and *the springs of water.* This
occurred when *a great flaming star* fell out of the sky. This may be
a comet.

The star is named *Bitterness*—other versions say "Wormwood,"
which is the name of a plant with a very bitter taste (see also Proverbs 5:3-4; Jeremiah 9:15; 23:15; Lamentations 3:15, 19; Amos
5:7). This pictures the bitterness of sorrow and death. This reversed
the miracle that God had performed for his people in the wilderness
at Marah—turning the bitter water sweet so that it would be drinkable (Exodus 15:22-25). Here, sweet water was turned bitter, making it undrinkable and causing many people to die.

This also compares to the first plague against Egypt when the
water was turned to blood and made undrinkable (Exodus 7:24).
This judgment affects one-third of all the fresh water on the
earth—horrible, but still not total and final judgment.

**8:12 The fourth angel sounded his trumpet, and a third of the sun
was struck, a third of the moon, and a third of the stars, so that
a third of them turned dark. A third of the day was without
light, and also a third of the night.**[NIV] The *fourth angel sounded
his trumpet* and the celestial bodies were affected. The picture is
of the sun and stars losing some of their light, but more than that,
there was a *third of the day* during which there was absolutely
no light at all. This compares to the ninth plague of darkness that
descended upon Egpyt (Exodus 10:21-29). In Egypt, the darkness
was so total that "during all that time [three days] the people
scarcely moved, for they could not see" (Exodus 10:23 NLT). During a portion of the day and a portion of the night, there was absolute darkness on the earth.

The prophet Isaiah spoke of the day of the Lord: "The heavens
will be black above them. No light will shine from stars or sun or
moon" (Isaiah 13:10 NLT; see also Mark 13:24). Joel wrote, "It is
a day of darkness and gloom, a day of thick clouds and deep
blackness" (Joel 2:2 NLT). Amos wrote, "That day will not bring
light and prosperity, but darkness and disaster" (Amos 5:18 NLT).

The darkness of the fourth trumpet judgment set the stage for
the last three trumpets that would bring demonic activity on the
earth.

**8:13 As I watched, I heard an eagle that was flying in midair call
out in a loud voice: "Woe! Woe! Woe to the inhabitants of the
earth, because of the trumpet blasts about to be sounded by
the other three angels!"**[NIV] This verse provides a transition from
the four trumpet blasts that caused havoc on nature to the three

coming blasts that would let loose demonic forces to attack people on the earth.

Habakkuk used the image of a vulture to symbolize swiftness and destruction (see Habakkuk 1:8). The picture is of a strong, powerful bird, here called an *eagle* (also a carrion bird), flying over all the earth, warning of the terrors yet to come. While the first four trumpet judgments were horrible, the eagle is saying that worse was yet to come: *Woe to the inhabitants of the earth, because of the trumpet blasts about to be sounded by the other three angels.* There is one "woe" for each remaining trumpet blast. The word "woe" is a Greek interjection *ouai,* meaning "alas for." The word is not an announcement of judgment but portrays the miserable condition of those who have rejected the gospel (see also Matthew 23:13-33; Luke 11:42-52). John uses three woes in 18:10-19 to refer to the various plagues and disasters of the final judgment. Many Jewish scholars of John's day referred to the "woes" of the Messiah. These were sufferings experienced by humanity in general before the kingdom could be established (see Daniel 12:1; also Revelation 12:1-6).

While both believers and unbelievers experience the terrors described in 8:7-12, the "inhabitants of the earth" refers to the unbelievers who will meet spiritual harm through the next three trumpet judgments. God has guaranteed believers protection from spiritual harm (7:2-3; 9:4).

The first two "woes" are the fifth and sixth trumpets, described in chapter 9. Then there is a vision recorded in 10:1–11:13, after which the seventh trumpet is blown, bringing in the bowl judgments.

HOW LONG?
In Revelation 6:10, the martyrs called out to God, "How long will it be before you judge the people who belong to this world for what they have done to us?" (NLT). In 8:3, incense mixed with the prayers of the saints ascends to God, and God responds with judgment in answer to the anguished prayers of the suffering and martyred believers.

As we see the world's wickedness, we too may cry out to God, "How long?" In the following chapters, the judgment comes at last. We may be distressed and impatient, but God has his plan and his timing, and we must learn to trust him to know what is best. Judgment is coming—be sure of that. Thank God for the time he has given you to turn from sin. Use the available time to warn others to turn to him.

Revelation 9

Revelation 9 records the fifth and sixth trumpet judgments—the first two "woes" (or "terrors") of the eagle (8:13). The first four trumpet judgments had brought disaster upon nature; with the fifth and sixth, demons were sent to attack the people of the earth and torment them. Ironically, the demonic forces destroyed their own worshipers. They were sent against those who did not have the seal of God and had, therefore, chosen to side with Satan (9:4).

9:1-2 The fifth angel sounded his trumpet, and I saw a star that had fallen from the sky to the earth. The star was given the key to the shaft of the Abyss. When he opened the Abyss, smoke rose from it like the smoke from a gigantic furnace. The sun and sky were darkened by the smoke from the Abyss.[NIV] The first "woe" or "terror" occurred when the *fifth angel sounded his trumpet*. When the trumpet was blown, John saw *a star that had fallen from the sky to the earth*. There is much debate as to the identity of this star, whether the "star" is Satan, a fallen angel, Christ, or a good angel. Most likely, the star is a good angel, but some scholars point to 9:11 and identify this angel with the "angel of the Abyss," thus, a demon (see also 12:4, 9; Isaiah 14:12; Luke 10:18). If the star is a demon, he loosed evil forces upon the inhabitants of the earth. The evil forces, however, were only allowed to harm those who belonged to them, not the sealed believers (9:4).

Most likely, this "star" is a good angel, because he *was given the key to the shaft of the Abyss,* and that key, normally, would be held by Christ (1:18), and because in 20:1 an angel came down from heaven with this key. If it is a good angel, then he (just as those blowing the trumpets) was simply obeying God's directions to let loose calamity upon the earth. Most importantly, this angel is under God's control and authority.

The Abyss, also called the Bottomless Pit, is the eternal destination of the wicked. It is full of smoke and fire, for when it was opened, *smoke rose from it like the smoke from a gigantic furnace.* The Abyss is the abode of the demonic forces (see Luke 8:31;

2 Peter 2:4; Jude 6; also referred to in 9:11; 11:7; 17:8; 20:1-3).
The original readers would have conceived the Abyss to be in the
depths of the sea. In those days, people did not have the knowledge
of the ocean floor. All they knew was that if a ship sank, it went
down, never to be seen again. The sea pictured evil, for the evil
beast himself would rise out of the sea (13:1). The image of smoke
and heat would portray a volcano rising from the sea. There is so
much smoke upon the opening of this Bottomless Pit that *the sun
and sky were darkened.*

DEMONS
God allowed demons to torment people (9:3-6). These demons
were not created by Satan, because God is the Creator of all.
Rather, they are probably fallen angels who joined Satan in his
rebellion. God limits what they can do; they can do nothing without his permission. Their main purpose on earth is to prevent,
distort, or destroy people's relationship with God. Whenever
Jesus encountered a demon-possessed person, that person
was being tortured (see, for example, Mark 9:14-29 and Luke
8:26-29). Because demons are corrupt and degenerate, their
appearance reflects the distortion of their spirits. While it is
important to recognize their evil activity so we can stay away
from them, we must avoid any curiosity about or involvement
with demonic forces or with the occult. Attempting to confront
demons should be done under the authority and protection of
the church leaders.

9:3-6 **Then locusts came from the smoke and descended on the
earth, and they were given power to sting like scorpions. They
were told not to hurt the grass or plants or trees but to attack
all the people who did not have the seal of God on their foreheads. They were told not to kill them but to torture them for
five months with agony like the pain of scorpion stings. In
those days people will seek death but will not find it. They
will long to die, but death will flee away!**[NLT] Out of the billow-
ing smoke that arose from the Abyss come *locusts.* God had also
sent a plague of locusts on Egypt (Exodus 10:1-20). This locust
plague, however, fulfilled the words of the prophet Joel, who
described a locust plague as a foreshadowing of the "day of the
LORD," meaning God's coming judgment (Joel 1:6–2:11). In the
Old Testament, locusts symbolized destruction because they
destroyed all vegetation (Deuteronomy 28:42; 1 Kings 8:37;
Psalm 78:46). In what is called a plague, millions of locusts
(grasshoppers) travel in a column many feet deep and miles in
length. So many destroy everything in an area—grass, trees, and
crops. This locust infestation spells destruction on agricultural

societies. In the 1950s, locusts devoured several hundred thousand square miles of vegetation in the Middle East.

Here, however, these locusts were *told not to hurt the grass or plants or trees.* This is a very different kind of "locust" plague, for they looked like horses (9:7; Joel 2:4) and they were *given power to sting like scorpions.* God controls even these evil forces. God told them what to do and limited the time in which they could do it. These "locusts" were terrifying. In fact, they were demons—evil spirits ruled by Satan who tempt people to sin. They did not attack vegetation but, instead, attacked *all the people who did not not have the seal of God on their foreheads* (7:3). This invasion of demons tortured people who did not believe in God. Believers, however, were protected from this (3:10; 7:3-4). The demons were not allowed to kill people but to cause *agony like the pain of scorpion stings.* These would be so painful that people *will long to die,* but would be unable to do so. God would not allow them to escape punishment by dying—instead, they would have to suffer. The

> Sinner, this is your present position. No hot drops have as yet fallen, but a shower of fire is coming. . . . As yet the water-floods are dammed up by mercy. . . . O that the hand of mercy may now lead you to Christ! He is freely set before you in the gospel . . . Thou knowest thy need of Him; believe in Him, cast thyself upon Him.
> *Charles Spurgeon*

demons could only torment people for *five months*—the lifespan of a locust, as well as the length of the harvesttime on earth during which locust plagues could come. The limitations placed on the demons show that they are under God's authority.

SAFE AND SEALED

The seal of Jesus on the foreheads of believers represents his ownership and protecting authority. The word "sealed" is significant elsewhere in the New Testament. In Matthew 27:65, Pilate applied his seal of authority to the tomb of Jesus so no one could steal the body. In Ephesians 1:13, Paul used this word to describe God's mark on a person who believes in Christ—he or she is "marked with the promised Holy Spirit" (NRSV). Obviously, God's seal is more than a mark; it is the Holy Spirit's presence in believers.

In Revelation 5, Christ alone demonstrated the power to break the seals that secure the account of the end of history. He also reminded the Asian churches (chapters 2–3) that his power to open or shut doors cannot be broken. The power to overcome and a sense of spiritual security cannot flow from our ability to believe or our success in obedience; our safety lies in the power of Jesus Christ. How much of your security have you entrusted to him?

9:7-10 The locusts looked like horses armed for battle. They had gold crowns on their heads, and they had human faces. Their hair was long like the hair of a woman, and their teeth were like the teeth of a lion. They wore armor made of iron, and their wings roared like an army of chariots rushing into battle. They had tails that stung like scorpions, with power to torture people. This power was given to them for five months.NLT This description is very similar to what locusts actually look like upon close observation (see Joel 2:4), but these locusts are exaggerated and much bigger than life—supernatural locusts. That they *had human faces* probably indicates that these were not mere insects but were intelligent beings. These locusts were not just out for food but were sent to make war against their own followers. *Their teeth were like the teeth of a lion* is also a description found in Joel's prophecy (Joel 1:6). These locusts had *armor made of iron,* making them invincible. No one would be able to fight against them. Their wings had the roaring sound of *an army of chariots rushing into battle.* This was the most fearsome sound of warfare in the ancient world. No one could stand against war chariots. Joel also described "the noise they make—like the rumbling of chariots . . . like a mighty army moving into battle" (Joel 2:5 NLT).

These armed locusts were only allowed to attack those who did not have the seal of God on their foreheads. God's people were protected from the stinging of these scorpions. They were *given* power (they did not have it themselves—it was "given" by God) *to torture people*—but only their own people. Even the length of time that they could torture people was limited by God—they were given only *five months* (noted in commentary on 9:5), the life span of a locust as well as the length of harvesttime.

WHAT TO LOOK FOR
John recorded his vision in the book of Revelation, writing what God had instructed him to write. John's description features many symbols drawn from the Old Testament. We do not know if we should regard these locusts as actual giant locusts, as mere representatives of evil, or as foreshadowing weaponry of advanced human technology. God has left this interpretation vague for a very creative reason. We can ponder and form opinions, but they should never divide us.

9:11 They had as king over them the angel of the Abyss, whose name in Hebrew is Abaddon, and in Greek, Apollyon.NIV This army of locusts had *a king over them.* He was *the angel of the Abyss.* Most likely, this was not the same angel who unlocked the

Abyss in 9:1 but a different angel, an emissary of Satan (see commentary on 9:1).

This angel's name is given in both *Hebrew (Abaddon)* and in *Greek (Apollyon),* both meaning "Exterminator" or "Destroyer." The Greek name may relate to the god Apollo, who was believed to be the leader of all the gods and was adopted as the patron god of the emperor. One of the symbols of Apollo was a locust. Roman emperors, such as Domitian, liked to portray themselves as the incarnate Apollo. Ironically, John may have linked this leader from hell (the locust king) with the emperor. Most likely, this is a powerful demon, similar to a commander in the hierarchy of demons, but not Satan himself.

9:12 **The first woe has passed. There are still two woes to come.**[NRSV] In the Old Testament, the word *woe* always refers to coming judgment (it is also translated "destruction"). It is the strongest exclamation of warning for coming judgment in the Bible (Isaiah 5; Jeremiah 4:13; 48:1, 46; Zechariah 11:17). Though carried out by demonic powers, these events are actually divine judgments. Satan is at the mercy of God's power. At this point, *the first woe has passed,* but *there are still two woes to come.*

This warning had a twofold purpose:

(1) To warn non-Christians that those who refuse to believe in God and Christ will certainly be punished;

(2) To renew hope in believers.

The warning will save people from agonizing punishment if they repent and turn to Christ. How strange it seems to us that some still refuse to believe.

9:13-16 **The sixth angel sounded his trumpet, and I heard a voice coming from the horns of the golden altar that is before God. It said to the sixth angel who had the trumpet, "Release the four angels who are bound at the great river Euphrates." And the four angels who had been kept ready for this very hour and day and month and year were released to kill a third of mankind. The number of the mounted troops was two hundred million. I heard their number.**[NIV] When *the sixth angel sounded his trumpet,* a voice came *from the horns of the golden altar that is before God.* It is unknown whether this was the voice of God or of another angel. The "horns of the golden altar" refer to the altar in the temple and its four projections, one at each corner (see Exodus 27:2). According to 6:9, this altar was where the souls of all who had been martyred were waiting for God's punishment to be executed on their enemies. Their prayers called for vengeance, and God was releasing it in these "woes" (8:13).

The voice told the angel *who had the trumpet* to set into motion the sixth trumpet judgment and the second "woe" that must be sent on the earth. The angel would *"release the four angels who are bound at the great river Euphrates."* The word "angels" here means fallen angels or demons, for in Scripture, God's angels are never bound. These four unidentified demons would be exceedingly evil and destructive. But note that they did not have the power to release themselves and do their evil work on earth. Instead, they were held back by God and would be released at a specific time, doing only what God allowed them to do. They had *been kept ready for this very hour and day and month and year.*

The "river Euphrates" was the eastern boundary of the land that God had promised to Abraham (Genesis 15:18). In John's day, it was the eastern boundary of the Roman Empire, the dividing line between the "civilized" peoples and the "barbarian" hordes (such as the Parthians whom the Romans had tried to conquer but could not—see commentary on 6:1-2). Throughout the Old Testament, the nations that had come to conquer Israel (Assyria, Babylonia) had crossed the Euphrates (see Isaiah 8:5-8; Jeremiah 2:18).

The four "angels" (demons) seem to be in command of a huge horde of demonic horsemen—*mounted troops* numbering *two hundred million.* These angels were unbound and *released to kill a third of mankind.* During the first "woe," the unbelievers were being tormented but could not die (9:6). In this woe, a third of all people on the earth were killed. How they are killed is described in 9:18. Again, this affects only those who did not have the seal of God on their foreheads (9:4, 20). As with the torture inflicted during the sixth trumpet, these demons were attacking their own followers.

This could correspond to the plague in Egypt of the death of the firstborn sons. In that final plague, the angel of death came and killed the firstborn sons of the Egyptian families but passed over the homes of the Israelites (Exodus 11). Many men died in Egypt that night, but that will not compare to the terror that will come upon the earth when these demonic mounted troops arrive. In 6:7-8, one-fourth of mankind had been killed; here, one-third more was killed. Thus, over one-half of the people in the world would have been killed by God's great judgments. Even more would have been killed if God had not set limits on the destruction.

In John's day, two hundred million mounted troops in an army was inconceivable. In the censuses taken in the Roman Empire, the number of people in the entire Empire totaled around two hundred million. So for the people of that day, that meant one demonic horseman for every person in the Empire. At the height of World War II, all soldiers on both sides numbered about seventy million.

This huge army, led by the four demons, killed one-third of the earth's population. But the judgment was still not complete.

The deathless torment of the locusts gives way to an unmatched slaughter of human lives. Throughout history, plagues have caused the death of millions, often striking high percentages of populations. But this disaster surpasses them all. The sixth trumpet announces the death of one-third of humanity. The math itself should have shocked the people into realizing that this is more than a natural disaster. But so hardened are the surviving two-thirds of earth's inhabitants that they remained unrepentant (9:21).

9:17-19 **The horses and riders I saw in my vision looked like this: Their breastplates were fiery red, dark blue, and yellow as sulfur. The heads of the horses resembled the heads of lions, and out of their mouths came fire, smoke and sulfur. A third of mankind was killed by the three plagues of fire, smoke and sulfur that came out of their mouths. The power of the horses was in their mouths and in their tails; for their tails were like snakes, having heads with which they inflict injury.** NIV John saw this army of two hundred million mounted troops as *horses and riders* with brightly colored *breastplates.* The *fiery red, dark blue, and yellow as sulfur* indicate their "colors"—to show that they are identified with the army of destruction. They were released to kill *a third of mankind* through *fire, smoke and sulfur* that comes *out of their mouths.* This sort of destruction had fallen on the evil cities of Sodom and Gomorrah (see Genesis 19:24). Sulfur, or brimstone, was found near regions with volcanic activity and, in the Bible, it represents the wrath of God (see 14:10; Isaiah 30:33; 34:9). Many interpreters see modern canons or tanks in this picture. John reminds us that these figures were *in my vision* and, most likely, are symbolic representations of demonic hordes, not descriptions of actual human armies. The figure of the horse is more like the description of the Leviathan in Job 41:19-21, "Fire and sparks leap from its mouth. Smoke streams from its nostrils like steam from a boiling pot on a fire of dry rushes. Yes, its breath would kindle coals, for flames shoot from its mouth" (NLT).

This destruction came from the *mouths* of the millions of horses with their *heads of lions.* This was demonic power, a

huge army sent out to destroy. But the destruction came not
from the riders but from the horses. They had power *in their
mouths and in their tails* with which they inflicted injury. Their
tails were *like snakes* and had *heads.* Throughout history,
snakes have often been closely associated with demons (12:9;
Genesis 3:1).

The entire picture in this *vision* is horrifying. There is much
symbolism in these descriptions. The main point to remember
is that God released these demonic hordes to kill their own followers. This should warn those who refuse to repent.

**9:20-21 But the people who did not die in these plagues still refused
to turn from their evil deeds. They continued to worship
demons and idols made of gold, silver, bronze, stone, and
wood—idols that neither see nor hear nor walk! And they
did not repent of their murders or their witchcraft or their
immorality or their thefts.**[NLT] This outpouring of judgment
upon the earth was a final attempt by God to bring people to
repentance. They had a chance to *turn from their evil deeds* but,
unfortunately, they did not. They saw what was occurring but
still refused to turn to God, desiring instead to continue to *worship demons and idols.* God proved to them his awesome power
and authority over their *idols that neither see nor hear nor
walk.* The uselessness of idols is a common theme in the Bible,
but idols were a constant problem and temptation for God's
people (see also Deuteronomy 4:28; Psalms 115:5-7; 135:17;
Jeremiah 10:1-16; Daniel 5:23).

Idolatry is demonic; it is worship of Satan (1 Corinthians
10:20). Demons hate the very people who worship them, tortur-
ing and killing them, yet people still prefer those demons over
God. They *did not repent* and turn to God. For example, in the
occult today, people worship demons. Their practices include
sacrifices of babies, murder, mutilation, and sacrifices of animals. These people are worshiping very destructive powers.
With the popularity of the occult in books and movies, the
church must strongly teach about the destructive and hateful
power of demons.

This is why there has to be eternal punishment. God does
everything he can do to draw people to himself, but these
people want to continue in their idol worship and live out what
that worship leads to—*murders, witchcraft, immorality,* and
thefts. They have chosen their side and so must remain there.
God does not want anyone to perish (2 Peter 3:9); however,
when God's call is consistently rejected, then judgment must
fall.

SLIPPERY SLOPE
These people were so hardhearted that even plagues did not drive them to God. People usually don't fall into immorality and evil suddenly—they slip into it a little bit at a time until, hardly realizing what has happened, they are irrevocably mired in their wicked ways. Any person who allows sin to take root in his or her life can find himself or herself in this predicament. Temptation entertained today becomes sin tomorrow, then a habit the next day, then death and separation from God forever (see James 1:14-15). To think you could never become this evil is the first step toward a hard heart. Acknowledge your need to confess your sin before God.

Revelation 10

Chapter 10 introduces an interlude between the sixth and seventh trumpets, much as chapter 7 was an interlude between the sixth and seventh seals. This interlude extends from 10:1 to 11:14. No corresponding interlude exists between the sixth and seventh bowl judgments, for at that time, the end will have come and there will be no time for further warning.

As noted earlier, the Scripture does not state whether these events follow in sequence, are cyclical, or are merely intensifying with each set of seven judgments. God has chosen not to explain these visions totally. This book reveals God's judgment upon evil and his bringing of his own to be with him forever. When and how that all happens is for us to discuss and study in order to be morally and spiritually prepared. Believers should not allow their different beliefs regarding the end times to distract them from the hope in Christ's return.

10:1 Then I saw another mighty angel coming down from heaven, surrounded by a cloud, with a rainbow over his head. His face shone like the sun, and his feet were like pillars of fire.[NLT] John then saw *another mighty angel coming down from heaven.* This may have been the same angel mentioned in 5:2, who also spoke with a loud voice and was involved with the opening of a scroll (10:2).

Some have suggested that this angel was actually Christ because of the divine imagery surrounding this angel's appearance—*surrounded by a cloud, rainbow over his head,* face *like the sun,* and feet *like pillars of fire.* While this description sounds much like the description of Christ in 1:13-16, most likely, it is not Christ, for he is never called an "angel" anywhere else in Revelation. Also, he would not speak with an oath, as described in 10:6. Others suggest that this is the same angel as described in Daniel 12:7. This angel is a very powerful, high-ranking angel who has come down from heaven to announce the final judgments on the earth. The "cloud" usually described the presence of God in the Old Testament (Exodus 13:21; 40:34; 2 Chronicles 5:13-14). The "rainbow" had been a promise to Noah that God would not destroy the earth again with a flood (Genesis 9:8-17). The angel's face "shone like the sun," much like the face of Christ at the Transfiguration (Matthew 17:2). The feet "like pillars of fire" could recall the pillar of fire in the wilderness (Exodus 14:20).

10:2 And in his hand was a small scroll, which he had unrolled. He stood with his right foot on the sea and his left foot on the land.^{NLT} This powerful archangel was carrying *a small scroll* that *he had unrolled.* Two scrolls appear in Revelation. The first contains a revelation of judgments against evil and was unrolled by the Lamb (chapters 5 and 6). The contents of the second little scroll are not indicated, but it also may contain a revelation of judgment. Ezekiel also saw a scroll in a vision: "Both sides were covered with funeral songs, other words of sorrow, and pronouncements of doom" (Ezekiel 2:9-10 NLT).

So large and powerful was the angel that he *stood with his right foot on the sea and his left foot on the land.* Many of John's readers may have immediately pictured the Colossus of Rhodes, a statue built in Rhodes, an island between Crete and Turkey. The magnificent statue of Apollo, the sun god, was one of the seven wonders of the ancient world. It stood about 105 feet high—one foot was on the island and the other foot was on the mainland. It was the greatest statue ever built in the ancient world. Ships would sail in the waterway between the statue's legs. It was destroyed by an earthquake in 227 B.C.

This angel standing on the sea and on the land indicates that his words would affect all creation, not just a limited part, as did the seal and trumpet judgments. The seventh trumpet (11:15) would usher in the seven bowl judgments, which would bring an end to the present world. When this universal judgment comes, God's truth would prevail.

POWER PERSPECTIVE
This powerful angel conveyed his high rank and his authority from God by straddling the land and the sea. His huge size contrasts with the smallness of God's enemies. When things are going bad in your life, remember that this angel represents the kind of power that is on your side. God's angelic forces are with you (Matthew 18:10; Hebrews 1:14). Keep your problems in their proper perspective by remembering that God's power is available to you to deal with your problems.

10:3-4 And he gave a great shout, like the roar of a lion. And when he shouted, the seven thunders answered. When the seven

thunders spoke, I was about to write. But a voice from heaven called to me: "Keep secret what the seven thunders said. Do not write it down."ᴺᴸᵀ The *shout* of this mighty angel sounded to John *like the roar of a lion.* When the angel spoke, *the seven thunders answered.* This is a picture of the awesome sight of God on Mount Sinai: "Moses spoke, and God thundered his reply for all to hear" (Exodus 19:19 NLT). This thunderous reply was spoken by God and must have been understandable, for John began to write down what was said. He was stopped from doing so, however, by another *voice from heaven: "Keep secret what the seven thunders said. Do not write it down."* The words "keep secret" are literally "seal up." The prophet Daniel was also told to seal up part of the vision he saw (Daniel 12:4).

The words of these "seven thunders" could refer to seven judgments that were not disclosed to those on the earth. They could also have been warnings that were not given to the people on earth because they had adamantly refused to repent of their sins (9:20-21). It is also possible that these thunders may have spoken of God's truths that would be too wonderful for God's people to take in, so God asked that they not be recorded. Job had proclaimed at the end of his trials, "I was talking about things I did not understand, things far too wonderful for me" (Job 42:3 NLT). Paul, after being caught up into paradise in a vision, wrote, "I was caught up into paradise and heard things so astounding that they cannot be told" (2 Corinthians 12:4 NLT). Some truths of God are so wonderful that the human mind would not be able to comprehend them. So God doesn't even tell about it but will wait until his people come to heaven for them to find out.

WE JUST DON'T KNOW
People have always wanted to know what will happen in the future, and God reveals some of it in this book. But John was stopped from revealing certain parts of his vision. An angel also told the prophet Daniel that some visions he had seen were not to be revealed yet to everyone (Daniel 12:9), and Jesus told his disciples that the time of the end was known by no one but God (Mark 13:32). God has revealed all we need to know to live for him now. In our desire to be ready for the end, we must not place more emphasis on speculation about the last days than on living for God while we wait.

10:5-7 Then the mighty angel standing on the sea and on the land lifted his right hand to heaven. And he swore an oath in the name of the one who lives forever and ever, who created heaven and everything in it, the earth and everything in it, and the sea

and everything in it. He said, "God will wait no longer. But
when the seventh angel blows his trumpet, God's mysterious
plan will be fulfilled. It will happen just as he announced it to
his servants the prophets."[NLT] The angel lifted *his right hand to
heaven* (see also Daniel 12:7) and *swore an oath in the name of the
one who lives forever and ever*—referring to God, "the one who is,
who always was, and who is still to come" (1:4 NLT). This description highlights the truth that God is eternal and controls all of
time—what a comfort for persecuted believers. It also implies that
he controls all of creation, for he created *heaven, earth,* and *the sea*
and everything in them.

The oath declares that *God will wait no longer.* With the
sounding of the seventh trumpet, God would bring about the
end of history—*God's mysterious plan will be fulfilled.* "Mystery" is a key word in the New Testament. The word is almost
synonymous with the word "revelation." In the Bible, the word
"mystery" refers to a divine secret. Paul wrote about two different mysteries. First: "This mystery is that through the gospel
the Gentiles are heirs together with Israel, members together of
one body, and sharers together in the promise in Christ Jesus"
(Ephesians 3:6 NIV, see also Romans 11:25; 16:25). The second
mystery about which Paul wrote: "God's secret plan has now
been revealed to us; it is a plan centered on Christ, designed
long ago according to his good pleasure. And this is his plan:
At the right time he will bring everything together under the
authority of Christ—everything in heaven and on earth" (Ephesians 1:9-10 NLT). This second mystery is about to be revealed
with the final trumpet. All of time has been pointing forward
to this moment. All prophecy will be fulfilled—everything will
occur just as God had announced *to his servants the prophets.*
From the very beginning, God had promised that, despite the
Fall and people's sin, he would one day defeat evil. From the
moment Adam sinned, all of history has been pointing toward
this blowing of the final trumpet.

In 6:10, the martyrs had asked, "How long will it be before you
judge the people who belong to this world for what they have done
to us?" (NLT). In this verse, the angel solemnly declared that God
would "wait no longer." The time of final judgment had come. God
would stop giving warnings and offers of repentance. All restraint
would be removed, and the Antichrist would be revealed (2 Thessalonians 2:3). The forces of God and Satan would meet in final confrontation, as foretold by Daniel (Daniel 12:1).

Although the seal and trumpet judgments were meant to bring
punishment to an evil world, there was also the opportunity for
repentance—unbelievers could still call out to God for salvation.

When the bowl judgments began, however, the spiritual battle between God and Satan intensified. There would be no more offer of repentance because when these judgments fell, they were final.

YOUR KINGDOM COME
By saying that God's mysterious plan would be fulfilled, John was pointing to God's removal of all evil and the final exaltation of Christ as Lord. This would be a pronouncement bringing fear to God's enemies. For God's chosen ones, however, it would bring hope and peace. Do you really long for Christ's return? Can you say, "Your kingdom come"? Do you long for God and his people to be vindicated? Believers ought to truly desire for God's justice to be carried out and his plan fulfilled. We should want Christ to come because of the triumph of his kingdom—not because things are bad or because we want out of our struggles but because of the sacredness of God's name. We should strive for this attitude. Pray expectantly for the fulfillment of God's plan.

10:8-9 **Then the voice from heaven called to me again: "Go and take the unrolled scroll from the angel who is standing on the sea and on the land. " So I approached him and asked him to give me the little scroll. "Yes, take it and eat it," he said. "At first it will taste like honey, but when you swallow it, it will make your stomach sour!"**[NLT] *The voice from heaven* had previously commanded John not to write down what the seven thunders had said (10:3-4). This time, the voice called to John *again* and told him to go to the magnificent angel, the awesome person *standing on the sea and on the land.* John was to approach the angel and ask for the *little scroll* that was in the angel's hand. So John obeyed. When he took the scroll, the angel told him to *take it and eat it.*

Some think that this scroll is the Word of God, but that is probably too general. More likely, the scroll represents the revelations of God as given to John in this book. Like the prophet Ezekiel, John would eat this scroll that would *taste like honey* (see also Psalm 119:103; Jeremiah 15:16) but would make his *stomach sour.* Ezekiel also had a vision in which he was told to eat a scroll. That scroll was filled with judgments against the nation of Israel (Ezekiel 2:9–3:3). Ezekiel said that the scroll "tasted as sweet as honey" (3:3 NLT) but that its contents brought destruction—just like the scroll that John was told to eat. This could mean that the scroll John ate was full of words of comfort as well as gloom. Through the command to eat this scroll, God was confirming John's prophetic role, as he did with Ezekiel. Receiving the Word of God can be a pleasant experience, but it often results in the unpleasant task of speaking judgment on evil. Believers know that victory is sure, but they are pained by the difficulties they must endure and by many people's stubborn refusal to repent.

This may also mean that the message on the scroll was for the church passing through difficult times. Those who think that Christians will go through these days of tribulation may consider that the scroll is a picture of John's message for the church. It was "sweet" because God will triumph in the end; but it would be "sour" because the church will face a terrible time of persecution. The little scroll would tell of those horrible days to come. It may be that as the scroll of chapter 5 described woes that would fall on all mankind, the little scroll would describe the difficulties that the church would face in the last days.

SOLD OUT
In 10:5-9, God is affirming that he will be with all those who follow him. Believers must be willing to accept that their faith will bring difficulty into their lives—it will be sweet to the taste but sour to the stomach. Those in ministry will find it difficult when they must share the truth of God's word. Many may have to die for their faith. Believers must be totally sold out to God, willing to eat this little scroll, no matter what.

10:10-11 So I took the little scroll from the hands of the angel, and I ate it! It was sweet in my mouth, but it made my stomach sour. Then he said to me, "You must prophesy again about many peoples, nations, languages, and kings."NLT John *took* and *ate* the little scroll, and it did just as the angel had said— tasted *sweet* but made his stomach *sour.* Then the angel gave John another command, *"You must prophesy again about many peoples, nations, languages, and kings"* (see also 7:9). John would prophesy about a world that had turned from God. There would be no distinctions among people—the message would be for all. The only distinction left would be those who had the mark of the Beast and those who had been sealed by God. The following chapters contain these prophecies.

Revelation 11

This section contains many elements that have stimulated much discussion among interpreters. There is no authoritative way to determine if the statements should be taken literally, or if they figuratively represent forces at work in the future. If they refer to literal events, we will not know until they happen. If they are figurative, we must have some idea to what the figures correspond. Two prophets, or witnesses, arrived and gave messages from God. The Beast entered the vision and began his evil attacks. Through it all, however, God is in control, offering people a final chance to repent of their sin and turn to him.

11:1 Then I was given a measuring stick, and I was told, "Go and measure the Temple of God and the altar, and count the number of worshipers."^{NLT} In 10:8-10, John had become a participant in his vision—taking the little scroll from the angel and eating it. In this chapter, John again was participating, for he was *given a measuring stick* and told to *go and measure the Temple of God and the altar, and count the number of worshipers.*

Prophets often were asked to perform symbolic actions in order to dramatize their message to the people. For example, Isaiah 20:2-4 records that Isaiah was told to go around "naked and barefoot" for three years as a sign of the judgment that would come upon Egypt and Ethiopia by the Assyrians. Ezekiel also publicly acted out God's messages—such as demonstrating the siege of Jerusalem by lying on his side for extended periods, cooking his food in an unusual way, and weighing the food carefully (see Ezekiel 4).

John's action recorded here is much like Ezekiel's in Ezekiel 40–42. Ezekiel had been told, in a vision, to watch a man who would carefully measure every part of the temple. God had told Ezekiel, "Watch and listen. Pay close attention to everything I show you. You have been brought here so I can show you many things. Then you will return to the people of Israel and tell them everything you have seen" (Ezekiel 40:4 NLT). In Ezekiel's day, the building of the temple envisioned a time of complete restoration to the exiles, a time when God would return to his people.

However, the temple built in 520-515 B.C. (see Ezra 5–6) did not match Ezekiel's vision (Haggai 2:3; Zechariah 4:9-10). Therefore, the vision of the temple in Ezekiel has been interpreted in four main ways: (1) It is the temple that Zerubbabel should have built in 520-515 B.C. and is the actual blueprint that should have been used, but due to disobedience (Ezekiel 43:2-10) it was never followed. (2) It is a literal temple to be rebuilt during the millennial reign of Christ. (3) It is a symbolic temple, representing the true worship of God by the Church right now. (4) It is a symbolic temple, representing the future and eternal reign of God, when his presence and blessing fill the earth.

Whether the temple in Ezekiel is literal or symbolic, it seems clear that it envisions God's final perfect kingdom. This gave hope to the people of Ezekiel's time who had just seen their nation and its temple destroyed, with no hope of rebuilding it in the near future. The details given in this vision in Revelation give believers even more hope than what Ezekiel saw.

There are two main interpretations of the temple that John was told to measure. (1) The temple, the altar, and the worshipers are literal and focus on the Jews and their place in these final days. (2) The temple, the altar, and the worshipers are symbolic and refer to the "true Israel," the church, consisting of all believers in Christ.

Those who believe that this is a reference to the Jews have two slightly different views. Some understand the temple to be a real, physical, rebuilt Jewish temple in Jerusalem. This view envisions the Antichrist permitting the rebuilding of the temple in Jerusalem and the restoration of Jewish worship. After three and a half years, however, the Antichrist will break his treaty with the Jews and destroy the city. Then Christ will return to deliver the Jewish people.

Others who also consider this section to refer to the Jews believe that the temple and the city of Jerusalem are not to be taken literally. Instead, they say, John was predicting the eventual salvation of the Jewish people (see also Romans 11:26). The temple, altar, and worshipers represent the believing Jews, while the outer courtyard represents the unbelieving Jews.

The second way of interpreting this passage is that it refers not just to the Jews but to all believers. In this view, the temple is a symbol of the church (all true believers—whether Jews or Gentiles).

Some who believe that the believers have already been raptured (taken to heaven) by this time will say that this action is primarily focused on the Jews, as a way to draw them to Christ before the end. Those who believe that the Christians are still on the earth understand this to refer to God's protection of his people, similar to his sealing them in 7:3 (see also 1 Corinthians 3:16-17; 2 Corinthians 6:16; Ephesians 2:19-22; 1 Peter 2:4-10).

John measured the temple and the altar and then counted the worshipers, showing that God was building walls of protection around his people to spare them from spiritual harm, although they could face physical harm (see 13:7). John was told not to measure "the outer courtyard" for that area had been "turned over to the nations" (11:2); however, the temple would be a place of safety reserved for all those who had remained faithful to God. Similarly, an angel would measure the new Jerusalem in 21:15-17. The measurements symbolically show the perfection of this new home for God's people. Its inhabitants are protected from all evil.

Ezekiel had been told to describe the temple in his vision to the people in Israel "so they will be ashamed of all their sins" (Ezekiel 43:10 NLT). The basic law of the temple is "holiness" (Ezekiel 43:12), and the description was meant to contrast God's holiness against idol worship. John's measuring of the temple differentiates God's people from those who worshiped the Beast.

We simply do not know if this scene is in heaven or on earth, so we must ask what God, through his Spirit, wishes us to grasp from John's actions. Most likely, this temple refers to all believers. As Peter wrote, "And now God is building you, as living stones, into his spiritual temple" (1 Peter 2:5 NLT). While there may be a special role for faithful Jews in the future, we simply do not know what it will be. The measuring most likely means that God will protect his people (see 11:19).

11:2 "But do not measure the outer courtyard, for it has been turned over to the nations. They will trample the holy city for 42 months."[NLT] The *outer courtyard* of the temple that had been standing in Jerusalem was also called the Court of the Gentiles. It was set aside as a place of worship for Gentiles who had converted to Judaism and the worship of the one true God. In Jesus' day, it had become a marketplace so that the Gentiles did not even have room to come and worship. This is why Jesus became angry at the religious leaders and cleared out the merchants (see Matthew 21:12-17; John 2:13-16). A low wall separated the Court of the Gentiles from the area where Jews could worship. A sign warned any Gentile from passing into the area set aside for "pure" Jews—Jews by birth. The penalty for disregarding the sign was death (see Acts 21:27-29).

In this case, as the area where John did no measurements, the outer courtyard represents those who would not be spiritually protected from the punishments to come. That these people were in the outer courtyard could mean that they were considered not to be a part of God's people. They decided either that they didn't want the persecutions promised if they were to remain faithful, or they were never believers in the first place and had been lured away. But they remained separated by God in the outer courtyard and were, therefore, excluded from the measuring and remained unprotected from the troubles to come.

This courtyard had been *turned over to the nations* who *will trample the holy city for 42 months.* This statement could refer to Jesus' words about a time of great apostasy (Mark 13) and the coming of the Antichrist, who will rule over the nations, trample the holy city, and set himself up as god (see also 2 Thessalonians 2:3-4). During this time, many will turn to the worship of evil. God's true and faithful people, however, will be protected from spiritual harm (see 3:10). The entire city, including the temple, will be trampled, so God's people will face persecution and death, but they will come safely to heaven.

The outer courtyard had been turned over "to the nations." The word "nations" has also been translated "Gentiles." The Greek word, *ethne,* is used several times in Revelation and never means "Gentiles" as opposed to Jews. Instead, it stands for peoples of the earth—groups of people such as believers (2:26; 21:24, 26) or those in rebellion against God (11:18; 14:8; 19:15). In this case, the "nations" are those in rebellion against God. They "trample the holy city," causing spiritual apostasy and physical suffering.

Some literally interpret the "holy city" as Jerusalem. (See Nehemiah 11:1; Isaiah 48:2; 52:1; Daniel 9:24; Matthew 27:53 where Jerusalem is referred to as "the holy city.") The city of Jerusalem has been oppressed throughout history by the forces of Assyria, Babylon, Medo-Persia, Greece, Rome, and the forces of Islam (see 2 Kings 25:8-10; Psalm 79:1; Isaiah 63:18; Lamentations 1:10). In A.D. 70, the Romans sacked Jerusalem and burned the temple. The city has since been rebuilt, but without a temple for the Jews. Instead, a mosque now stands in the location of Solomon's temple. Those who have interpreted this literally believe that one day the Jews' temple will be rebuilt in the "holy city," Jerusalem.

Others see the "holy city" as a symbolic reference to the Jews. If these references to the temple, courtyard, and holy city refer just to Jews, then this would be the only place in Revelation where it occurs. Thus, this has caused many to interpret this as another reference to believers, with the holy city as the church. The Antichrist's forces would attack and persecute the Christians. But God placed a time limit on this persecution; it would last only for forty-two months.

The expression "42 months" occurs only here and in 13:5, although its equivalent can be found in other places. In 11:3 and 12:6, it is "1,260 days" (42 months x 30 days for each month). In 12:14, it is simply stated as "three and a half years." Some versions translate 12:14 as "a time, times, and half a time," (a year, two years, and half a year), equaling three and a half years. This "three and a half years" is half of seven years, an important length of time in Daniel's prophecy.

In his vision, Daniel saw a king who "will speak against the Most High and oppress his saints and try to change the set times and the laws. The saints will be handed over to him for a time, times, and half a time" (Daniel 7:25 NIV). This king would make a seven-year treaty: "He will confirm a covenant with many for one 'seven.' In the middle of the 'seven' he will put an end to sacrifice and offering. And on a wing of the temple, he will set up an abomination that causes desolation" (Daniel 9:27*NIV). Finally, at the end of his prophecy, Daniel asked "the man clothed in linen" when the vision would be accomplished. The answer: "It will be for a time, times and half a time. When the power of the holy people has been finally broken, all these things will be completed" (Daniel 12:7 NIV). And the angel added, "From the time that the daily sacrifice is abolished and the abomination that causes desolation is set up, there will be 1,290 days" (Daniel 12:11 NIV).

In Daniel, the trampling and the setting up of an "abomination" in the temple has been interpreted as (1) the desecration of the temple by Antiochus IV Epiphanes in 168-167 B.C. (see Daniel 11:31); (2) the destruction of the temple by the Roman general Titus in A.D. 70 when one million Jews were killed; or (3) the future reign of the Antichrist (see Matthew 24:15; Revelation 13:5-7). As with so much of Bible prophecy, Daniel may have been seeing all those events rolled into one. Jesus, when speaking of the future, had said, "The time will come when you see what Daniel the prophet spoke about: the sacrilegious object that causes desecration standing in the holy place. . . . That will be a time of greater horror than anything the world has ever seen or will ever see again. In fact, unless that time of calamity is shortened, the entire human race will be destroyed. But it will be shortened for the sake of God's chosen ones. Jerusalem will be conquered and trampled down by the Gentiles until the age of the Gentiles comes to an end" (Matthew 24:15, 21-22; Luke 21:24 NLT).

Daniel's prediction had come true when Antiochus Epiphanes had sacrificed a pig to Zeus on the sacred temple altar. Jesus' words also were remembered when General Titus placed an idol on the site of the burned temple after destroying Jerusalem. Yet both Daniel and Jesus were describing more than current events; they were also foreseeing the end times. The Antichrist will also become like a god and will be worshiped by the peoples of the earth (Revelation 13). There will not be the danger of the "entire human race" being destroyed, as Jesus had said, until the events recorded here in Revelation occur.

In Revelation, the three and a half years are equivalent to the length of time the holy city will trampled (11:2), the two witnesses prophesy (11:3), the woman is protected from the Dragon (12:6, 14), and the Antichrist (the Beast) reigns (13:5-7). That these time periods are the same length may or may not mean that they will occur at the same time. They all may be simultaneous. Another explanation is that the first three and a half years of that seven-year period involve the preaching of the two witnesses and the protection of the woman in the desert (a symbol explained in chapter 12), while the second three and a half years is the time of the Antichrist's (the Beast's) reign and the trampling of the holy city.

Another question involves whether these are actual calendar years or symbolic lengths of time. The answer is unknown, although John used numbers as symbolic in other places in Revelation (see 2:10; 4:4; 7:4). The numbers here could be symbolic but still describe distinct periods of time. In Revelation, however, the number seven symbolizes perfection and completeness, so it is possible that the seven years simply refers to the completion of time, God's perfect timing. The main point is that God has set time limits and is in complete control of all of the events that will occur at the end of history. His plan will be completed; the plans of evil will be thwarted.

 MAKE SURE
The trampling of the city and the courtyard turned over to the Gentiles indicate that many nominal believers will join those who reject God. During this apostasy, many will leave the faith. The question for us should not be whether any of these people were ever saved, but "Where am I in my commitment to Christ?" Many *will* leave the faith—we do not want to be among them. We are protected, but the dangers are real. We want to stand with those in God's temple, not those in the outer courtyard. Don't play spiritual games; truly surrender yourself to Christ.

11:3 "And I will give power to my two witnesses, and they will be clothed in sackcloth and will prophesy during those 1,260 days."[NLT] The little word "and" (in Greek, *kai*) ties this verse to 11:2. Despite the fact that the holy city will be trampled and God's people will suffer under the Antichrist, God *will give power* to *two witnesses.* During this time of tribulation, the merciful God will still offer people a chance to hear and respond to the truth.

There has been much speculation about the identity of these two witnesses—are they people, or do they represent groups of people, or even sets of ideas? They are described further as "the two olive trees and the two lampstands that stand before the Lord of all the earth" (11:4) and as "two prophets" (11:4, 10), which still leaves their identity unknown. There are two views about the identity of the two witnesses.

The first view is that these witnesses are two men sent to prophesy to the Jews. In this regard, various names of Old Testament saints have been suggested:

(1) Enoch and Elijah, because both had been taken to heaven without dying (Genesis 5:24; 2 Kings 2:11).

(2) Moses and Elijah, because both bear much resemblance to Moses and Elijah. The two witnesses could consume their enemies with fire (11:5; as did Elijah in 2 Kings 1:10-14), shut the skies so that no rain would fall (11:6; as did Elijah in 1 Kings 17:1, 7), turn river and oceans into blood, and send plagues (as did Moses in Exodus 7–11). Moses and Elijah also appeared with Christ at his transfiguration (see Matthew 17:1-7). Jewish tradition anticipates that Moses and Elijah will return before the end (see Deuteronomy 18:15-18; Malachi 4:5-6).

The other view is that the two witnesses symbolize the witnessing church. In the Old Testament, God required two or more witnesses to confirm a testimony (Deuteronomy 19:15); therefore, these two witnesses have been sent to tell God's truth. It is possible that these two men will actually be Moses or Elijah, or they may be two men who speak in the spirit and power of Moses and Elijah. Some think that because Moses represents the law and Elijah represents the prophets, the "two witnesses" symbolize the spread of God's Word through the witness of believers during this time.

These two witnesses are described as *clothed in sackcloth,* the ancient garb of the prophets of God (Isaiah 20:2; Daniel 9:3; Zechariah 13:4). Wearing sackcloth was a sign of mourning (Isaiah 37:1-2; Jeremiah 4:8; 6:26; Jonah 3:5-8). These prophets were in mourning for what was happening to God's people and the evil that runs rampant in the world.

These witnesses *will prophesy during those 1,260 days,* that is, during the same time period of forty-two months (forty-two multiplied by thirty days per month) that the holy city is being trampled (11:2).

TO BE A WITNESS
As representatives of every believer who has witnessed for Jesus Christ, the two final, faithful witnesses are a picture of both invincibility and vulnerability. They win, they lose, they win again. Truth remains victorious, even though human channels fail. Their message—and God's plan—march on in spite of death, for even death proves to be a defeated foe.

Seldom do we face the possibility of death when we share our faith. Why should Satan threaten our lives when fear of embarrassment or rejection is enough to keep us silent? But if Jesus has truly changed our lives, we will find a way to let others know. Not to witness represents more than just fear; it also reveals selfishness. Have those near you heard what Jesus has done for you?

11:4 These two prophets are the two olive trees and the two lampstands that stand before the Lord of all the earth.^{NLT} John described these *two prophets* as *two olive trees*. This picture is in Zechariah 4:14. Zechariah saw a vision of a lampstand and two olive trees. He asked what the olive trees meant, and the angel replied, "They represent the two anointed ones who assist the Lord of all the earth" (NLT). In the context of Zechariah, these two anointed ones may have referred to Joshua and Zerubbabel who had the special task of completing the rebuilding of God's temple in Jerusalem after its destruction by the Babylonians (Zechariah 4:6-10; 8:11-14). Zechariah's vision had been given to encourage and strengthen Joshua and Zerubbabel in their difficult task, for the people who were rebuilding the temple had been facing much opposition. Surely it must have encouraged them to hear from God's prophet that God was on their side. As God worked through his chosen leaders, the temple would be completed, "'Not by might nor by power, but by my Spirit,' says the Lord Almighty" (Zechariah 4:6 NIV).

Zechariah's vision has also been considered as a further prophecy regarding these two witnesses who arise during the time of great tribulation on the earth. Like Joshua and Zechariah, the two witnesses stood before the Lord, doing his work despite great opposition.

John also described the two witnesses as *two lampstands*. There is much debate about what the "lampstands" symbolize. Many think they symbolize the church because the churches to whom John wrote are called "lampstands" (1:12-13, 20). The two witnesses may symbolize Jews and Christians joined in the church, or they could be the martyrs (two churches were especially being persecuted as reported in the letters in chapters 2 and 3—the churches at Smyrna and Philadelphia).

Oil and light often symbolize spiritual revival, and the two witnesses will speak God's message and spark a revival among the people on the earth. Some take this to mean that there will be a great harvest among the Jews who will become believers through the testimony of these two prophets. In any case, the power and authority of the prophets (or the church as a whole) to witness comes from God alone—not by might or by power, but by his Spirit (Zechariah 4:6).

11:5 If anyone tries to harm them, fire flashes from the mouths of the prophets and consumes their enemies. This is how anyone who tries to harm them must die.NLT These two witnesses, here called *prophets,* were divinely protected so that they could give the testimony that God had called them to give. *If anyone tries to harm them, fire flashes* from their mouths *and consumes their enemies.* Their ability to do this was a judgment from God against those who would stop them from delivering their message. Note, Elijah had called down fire from heaven (1 Kings 18:36-38; 2 Kings 1:10-14). It is unknown what aspects of this description are literal and which are symbolic. But the point is that no one will be able to stop these two prophets until God's appointed time (see 11:7). This parallels Jesus' experience, since he could not be killed before his time had come (John 7:30; 8:20). Fire probably refers to judgment from God.

11:6 They have power to shut the skies so that no rain will fall for as long as they prophesy. And they have the power to turn the rivers and oceans into blood, and to send every kind of plague upon the earth as often as they wish.NLT Like Elijah, these prophets *have power to shut the skies so that no rain will fall.* Elijah had done the same, as recorded in 1 Kings 17:1, 7. These prophets would stop the rain from falling *for as long as they prophesy*—meaning 1,260 days (11:3) or three and a half years, the same amount of time that Elijah had kept the rain from falling. "Elijah . . . prayed earnestly that no rain would fall [and] none fell for the next three and a half years" (James 5:17 NLT; see also Luke 4:25).

Like Moses, these prophets also *have the power to turn the rivers and oceans into blood, and to send every kind of plague upon the earth as often as they wish* (Exodus 7–11). With the devastation already caused by the seals and the trumpets, the additional horror of a drought and no drinkable water would bring great suffering to those left on the earth. Through these difficulties, God would call people to turn to him. This would be their last and only hope. They must believe the message of these prophets from God.

These prophets were given power to do miracles to authenticate their message. The same God who worked through Moses and Elijah would work through these two witnesses.

11:7 **Now when they have finished their testimony, the beast that comes up from the Abyss will attack them, and overpower and kill them.**^{NIV} At the end of the 1,260 days (three and a half years), the two witnesses would have *finished their testimony.* God had given them that amount of time to preach the message of salvation, but then God would remove their supernatural protection and powers and would allow *the beast that comes up from the Abyss* to *attack, overpower, and kill them.*

Who is this "beast"? In Revelation, the word "beast" refers to the Antichrist. This is the first of thirty-six references to this person in this book. He is also mentioned in other places in the Bible. Daniel described the Beast as a "little horn," who would speak arrogantly (Daniel 7:8-27). The Antichrist would blasphemously set himself against God by persecuting believers and defiling the Lord's holy place (Daniel 9:27; 11:20-39). Jesus also predicted a sacrilegious figure who would terrorize God's people (Mark 13:14, 20). Paul wrote of a man of lawlessness who would seek to dethrone God and use Satan's power to deceive people (2 Thessalonians 2:3-4, 9-10). John is the only biblical writer to use the term "Antichrist," described as an opponent of Christ (1 John 2:18, 22; 4:3; 2 John 7).

This vision presents a figure who fulfills these earlier prophecies. Abruptly introduced here, more details are given in coming chapters. This man of evil, known as the Beast, would be dedicated to opposing God. Using Satan's power (12:9), the Beast would gain control over the world, force people to worship him, establish the wicked kingdom of Babylon, and persecute those who refuse to worship him (13:16-17).

Some individuals in history stand out as so evil that people of their time have considered them to be the Antichrist of Scripture—people like Caligula, Nero, Stalin, and Hitler. The Bible teaches, however, that *many* antichrists will appear, but one will stand out. John also wrote, "Dear children, this is the last hour; and as you have heard that the antichrist is coming, even now many antichrists have come. This is how we know it is the last hour" (1 John 2:18 NIV). People who have been completely "against Christ" have done their evil in this world, but one will come who will be even more wicked and powerful. He will be *the* Antichrist, the Beast, as first mentioned here in 11:7. This Beast will come out of a great rebellion against God and then will be revealed (2 Thessalonians 2:3, 7). While postmillennial-

ists typically interpret these passages as having already been fulfilled, most other Christians believe that these prophecies refer to
a figure in the future, *the* Antichrist, who will arise at the very
end of history to oppose God.

This Beast *comes up from the Abyss,* which represents the
satanic underworld (see also 17:8). The Abyss, or bottomless
pit, was the place from which the demonic locusts had come
to attack the people on the earth (9:1-12). The Antichrist is
the epitome of the satanic perversions and wickedness that are
present in every age. This is actually a foreshadowing—later,
the Beast will be called up out of the Abyss (the sea, 13:1).

The Beast would attack and kill the two witnesses. Up to this
point, the witnesses had been supernaturally protected from harm
for 1,260 days. But then God would allow them to be killed by
the Antichrist. Just as the "little horn" was "waging war against
the holy people and was defeating them" (Daniel 7:21 NLT), so
the Antichrist would kill God's representatives. Whether these
two witnesses are two literal individuals or represent groups of
people, the Antichrist would be allowed to attack, overpower,
and kill them.

STAND FIRM
When the seven angels sound the trumpets one at a time,
God's terrible judgment begins. In the midst of judgment, however, two witnesses arise, standing against evil and for righteousness. When they are killed, the evil world rejoices. The
truth is, mankind loves sin and hates God. When we speak out
for God's power and love, the world hates us. Eventually, however, God will come as judge, eradicating sin and punishing evildoers. Until that day, we must stand firm against evil, despite
opposition and persecution, knowing that God's justice will
prevail and we will be saved.

**11:8 Their bodies will lie in the street of the great city, which is
figuratively called Sodom and Egypt, where also their Lord
was crucified.**^{NIV} The witnesses would complete the task, and
God would allow Satan, through the Antichrist (the Beast), to
kill them. They would become martyrs for God—added to the
number of martyrs already awaiting God's justice (6:11).

After the Beast would kill them, he would refuse even to give
them a burial, preferring to desecrate their bodies by allowing
them to *lie in the street of the great city.* In the eastern world, to
be deprived of burial is an act of great indignity.

John wrote that the city is *figuratively called Sodom and
Egypt,* but more exactly, it would be the place where *their Lord*

was crucified. Some commentators believe that the city where the witnesses will be killed is Jerusalem, figuratively called Sodom and Egypt because of the sin and idolatry there. Sodom represents the epitome of sexual sin and idolatry; Egypt represents the height of persecution and hatred of God's people. Both Sodom and Egypt had been destroyed by God's power (Genesis 19:24-25; Exodus 12:31-33; 14:27-28). If this is literally the city of Jerusalem, this once great city and capital of Israel would become enemy territory, a place of immorality and persecution of God's people. Jerusalem had been destroyed by the Romans in A.D. 70. Nearly a million Jews had been slaughtered, and the Temple treasures had been carried off to Rome. The original readers of Revelation would have been able to understand the low point to which Jerusalem would be brought in the last days.

Others, however, believe that the "great city" refers to Rome, but probably not the actual city because later an earthquake would destroy one-tenth of this city, killing seven thousand people (11:13). If one-tenth of Rome were to be destroyed by an earthquake, the death toll would be much higher, for in those days, Rome's population was half a million to a million. The "great city" could symbolically refer to the universal power of Rome (the word "city" is often used in a symbolic sense in Revelation). The Antichrist would have world dominion, even more universal than the Roman Empire. When the Antichrist kills the witnesses (whether they are two men, symbolic of the Jews, or symbolic of the church, see 11:3), he would be acting with Satan's power against God's own people.

11:9-10 **For three and a half days members of the peoples and tribes and languages and nations will gaze at their dead bodies and refuse to let them be placed in a tomb; and the inhabitants of the earth will gloat over them and celebrate and exchange presents, because these two prophets had been a torment to the inhabitants of the earth.**NRSV The bodies of the two witnesses would not be buried but left in the street (11:8) *for three and a half days.* That time period corresponds to the three and a half years of their ministry (1,260 days; 11:3). For the mid-Tribulation position, these three and a half days are the Great Tribulation.

Refusing to let the bodies *be placed in a tomb* was the greatest dishonor that could be given. In ancient religions, this meant consigning them to wander in nothingness in the afterlife. That people from all over the world would *gaze at their dead bodies* and agree with the refusal to bury them shows the utter hatred that all the inhabitants of the world would have for these two witnesses. All cultures have respect for the dead and a desire to bury them, but no one would care to bury these two witnesses. (Surely the latest form of satellite technology will make it possible for the entire world to see these dead bodies.)

In fact, *the inhabitants of the earth* are said to be so happy about the deaths of these men that they *gloat, celebrate,* and *exchange presents* with one another. The "inhabitants" are the pagans, not the believers. The deaths of the two witnesses become a time of worldwide celebration. It is interesting to note that this could be in direct contrast to the Jewish Feast of Purim when Jews gave gifts to one another. Esther 9:19-22 describes the beginning of this Feast—it was a time of celebration after Haman's plot to destroy all the Jews had been defeated and he was killed. In Revelation, these people are glad that the two prophets are dead, so they also celebrate with a kind of national holiday *because these two prophets had been a torment* to them. The words of these prophets had pricked people's consciences, and they did not want to hear the message. The ability of the prophets to inflict physical affliction in the form of drought, plagues, and spoiled water supply (11:6) had also been a torment to the people who had blamed the prophets for those troubles. The world today rejoices when God's spokesmen for truth and morality are silenced or suffer setbacks.

> Christ . . . is the root of the martyr line; his Spirit is the life-breath of his witnesses. All through the centuries . . . there has been an unbroken succession of pure and noble souls who have stood for Jesus Christ even unto death. Let us dare to stand with them and our Lord, that he may not be ashamed of us at his coming.   *F. B. Meyer*

The Antichrist silenced the two witnesses—whether they were actual men or the witness of the church at large—to the great glee of his own followers. But God saw to it that their glee would be short-lived.

BE PREPARED
The whole world rejoices at the deaths of these two witnesses who have caused trouble by saying what the people didn't want to hear—words about their sin, their need for repentance, and the coming punishment. Sinful people hate those who call attention to their sin and who urge them to repent. They hated Christ, and they hate his followers (1 John 3:13). When you obey Christ and take a stand against sin, be prepared to experience the world's hatred. But remember that the great reward awaiting you in heaven far outweighs any suffering that you face now.

11:11-12 But after the three and a half days a breath of life from God entered them, and they stood on their feet, and terror struck those who saw them. Then they heard a loud voice from heaven saying to them, "Come up here." And they went up to heaven in a cloud, while their enemies looked on.ᴺᴵⱽ Because God always controls events and timing, these two witnesses remained dead for only *three and a half days* (see 11:9). Their bodies had been left out for all to see, but suddenly, *a breath of life from God entered them,* and *they stood on their feet.* Just as Christ had died and had been buried for three days before being resurrected, so these witnesses were dead for three and a half days and then were resurrected. Later, the Antichrist would copy this resurrection (13:3).

Obviously, the merriment surrounding their death stopped, and *terror struck those who saw them.* Next, a voice from heaven said, *"Come up here."* Then the two witnesses *went up to heaven in a cloud.*

Midtribulationists base much of their view on these verses. They believe that the church will be raptured after three and a half years of the Tribulation, at the sounding of the seventh trumpet (which occurs in 11:15; see also 1 Corinthians 15:52). According to this view, the church will face persecution for the first three and a half years of the seven-year Tribulation period (Daniel 7:25; 9:27). In the second half of the Tribulation, the Antichrist and those who chose to follow him will be the target of God's wrath. Midtribulationists also believe that the book of Revelation is chronological, so that this rapture will occur halfway through the years of tribulation. The pretribulationists take the voice from heaven in 4:1 telling John to "come up here" to be a reference to the rapture of the believers. Midtribulationists see the two witnesses as representing the believers being raptured at the midpoint of the Tribulation, calling the two witnesses to "come up." That they go up to heaven "in a cloud" compares to 1 Thessalonians 4:16-17, "All the Christians who have died will rise from their graves. Then, together with them, we who are still alive and remain on the earth will be caught up in the clouds to meet the Lord in the air" (ɴʟᴛ). In a sense, Malachi 4:5 will be fulfilled again: "Look, I am sending you the prophet Elijah before the great and dreadful day of the Lord arrives" (ɴʟᴛ). The first time, John the Baptist fulfilled Malachi's prophecy as the forerunner of the first coming of the Messiah; in this case, it is fulfilled again as another like Elijah is a forerunner of the second coming of the Messiah.

Those who believe that the book of Revelation is cyclical

(that is, the visions are repetitions of one another, intensifying as they go) may see this as the rapture of the church. They would say, however, that the Rapture will occur at the end of the Tribulation rather than in the middle, for this event occurs just before the last trumpet.

Some suggest that this is comparable to Ezekiel's vision of the valley of dry bones (Ezekiel 37:1-14), a vision of the spiritual regeneration of Israel. If these two witnesses represent the Jews, then this event pictures the salvation of the Jews.

The two witnesses ascend to heaven in full view of their enemies who had been gleeful over their deaths. The main point is that God alone possesses authority over life and death and that only those who believe in him will be taken to be with him forever.

11:13 And in the same hour there was a terrible earthquake that destroyed a tenth of the city. Seven thousand people died in that earthquake. And everyone who did not die was terrified and gave glory to the God of heaven.[NLT] As part of the vindication of his two witnesses, God sent *a terrible earthquake* immediately after the ascension of the two witnesses—an earthquake that *destroyed a tenth of the city.* Ezekiel had prophesied of an earthquake that would precede the end of history (Ezekiel 38:19-20). Zechariah also had seen the Mount of Olives split in two (Zechariah 14:3-5).

In this earthquake, *seven thousand people* were killed. This seems to indicate that the "city" is not Rome (see commentary on 11:8) because Rome's population was between a half million and a million, and an earthquake destroying a tenth of the city of Rome would have a much higher death toll. The population of the city of Jerusalem was between fifty and seventy thousand people.

The survivors were *terrified,* but they gave *glory to the God of heaven* (see 14:6-7). It is possible that these survivors were converted by the miraculous acts they had just seen, or that this glory they gave to God was no more than forced homage. That is, they may have recognized that God is all-powerful but may not have repented of their sins. In the end, every knee will bow, whether they want to or not (Philippians 2:10). Everyone will one day be forced to submit—demons and unrepentant people.

11:14 The second woe has passed. The third woe is coming very soon.[NRSV] The flying eagle had warned of three "terrors" or "woes" to come upon the earth (8:13). The first woe was recorded in 9:1-12; the second woe in 9:13-21 and 11:1-13. The *third woe is coming very soon.* Most likely, 11:18 hints at the

third woe which will include the battle of Armageddon—the final
battle between God and Satan. This will begin when the angel
sounds the seventh trumpet.

 GLORIFY HIM!
The ultimate goal of God's saving plan, and indeed of creation
itself, is that everything will glorify God. "Glory" refers to the
splendor, radiance, and magnificence of God. It refers not only
to God in his essential nature but to the praiseworthy effects of
what God has accomplished.

We glorify God because his glory is true and real, and we
acknowledge his greatness. In so doing, we see our rightful
position as his servants. When we glorify him in our singing, our
speaking, and our living, we experience some of his transcendence and thus edify and uplift our own spirits. Glorifying God
prompts us to moral action and loving service.

THE SEVENTH TRUMPET / 11:15-19

The first six trumpets had been blown in 8:6–9:21, then there
was an interlude, just as there had been an interlude between the
sixth and seventh seals (see 6:1–8:5). In addition, the fifth trumpet had brought in what was considered the first of three "woes"
(see 8:13), the sixth trumpet ushered in the second woe, and the
seventh trumpet would bring the third woe.

**11:15 Then the seventh angel blew his trumpet, and there were loud
voices shouting in heaven: "The whole world has now become
the kingdom of our Lord and of his Christ, and he will reign
forever and ever."**[NLT] *The seventh angel blew his trumpet,* in
essence announcing the arrival of the King. There was now no
turning back. The coming judgments were no longer partial but
complete in their destruction. God unleashed his full wrath on the
evil world that refused to turn to him (9:20-21). When his wrath
would begin, there would be no escape.

Those who think the book of Revelation is cyclical contend
that this seventh trumpet heralds the end of the world and the
return of Christ, which occurs after the bowl judgments (chapter
19). These *voices* in heaven were most likely angels singing, as
they had in 5:11. This event is so certain that the angels sang of
it as though it had already occurred. They were *shouting* that the
whole world *has now* become Christ's kingdom. These voices
were declaring the triumph of Christ and his establishment on the
throne, reigning *forever and ever.*

Daniel had predicted a time when God's kingdom would

destroy the kingdoms of this world, "During the reign of those kings, the God of heaven will set up a kingdom that will never be destroyed; no one will ever conquer it. It will shatter all these kingdoms into nothingness, but it will stand forever" (Daniel 2:44 NLT).

Zechariah had prophesied, "And the Lord will be king over all the earth. On that day there will be one Lord—his name alone will be worshiped" (Zechariah 14:9 NLT). The announcement of the reign of the king occurs here, but Christ's final triumph over the world does not occur until the return of Christ (19:11). The song of triumph by the heavenly hosts introduces the great themes of the following chapters. The end times had begun. When Christ first came, he brought in the kingdom, yet his fulfilled kingdom was still to come. The kingdom is with God's people spiritually but has not been fulfilled historically. This verse refers to that final consummation. This is a worship pageant, portraying in heaven what will be unfolded on earth.

11:16-17 And the twenty-four elders, who were seated on their thrones before God, fell on their faces and worshiped God, saying: "We give thanks to you, Lord God Almighty, the One who is and who was, because you have taken your great power and have begun to reign.NIV The *twenty-four elders* are mentioned again as *seated on their thrones before God* and then falling on their faces in worship. For more information on these elders, see commentary at 4:4 and 7:11. They fell prostrate before God in worship.

First, these elders *give thanks* to God, calling him *Almighty,* and *the One who is and who was.* This is much like the song they had sung in 4:8 and 4:11. There, however, they had referred to God as "the one who always was, who is, and who is still to come" (NLT). Here, God "is" and "was," but no longer "is to come" because he had come and fulfilled history. He had taken his *great power,* meaning he had unleashed his power against evil, and had *begun to reign.*

11:18 "The nations were angry; and your wrath has come. The time has come for judging the dead, and for rewarding your servants the prophets and your saints and those who reverence your name, both small and great—and for destroying those who destroy the earth."NIV The *nations* of the world *were angry,* but Christ's *wrath* would subdue them; he would destroy *those who destroy the earth.* This is much like Psalm 2: "Why do the nations rage? Why do the people waste their time with futile plans? The kings of the earth prepare for battle; the rulers plot together against the Lord and against his anointed one. But the one who rules in heaven laughs. The Lord scoffs at them. Then in anger he rebukes them, terrifying them with his fierce fury" (Psalm 2:1-2, 4-5 NLT). This anger of the nations will be described in chapters 12–19. But the outcome was already determined. The nations would no longer be afraid (as in 6:15-17); instead, they would be filled with defiant rage that would manifest itself in an attempt to fight against Christ, as described in coming chapters.

Not only did Christ bring wrath, he also brought judgment and rewards. The judgment is described in chapter 20. No one will escape judgment, for Christ will even judge *the dead.* All believers (God's *servants*—the *prophets* and the *saints, those who reverence* his *name*) will be rewarded according to their deeds. Throughout Revelation, the prophets are held in high esteem, separate from the rest of the believers, although joined with them as those who reverence God (see also 16:6; 18:20, 24; 22:6, 9). Unbelievers will be brought from the grave to face judgment and punishment for their sins. For more on judgment and rewards, see commentary in chapter 20.

WOE OR JOY
Although the seventh trumpet announces the third "woe," what actually occurs is a great victory shout. The triumph of "the kingdom of our Lord and of his Christ" is irreversible. The elders respond with joyful thanksgiving.

But while some rejoice over Christ's accomplishment, others turn away. The rebels greet the victory chant with anger. To them it sounds like a curse. Judgment time has come. Their own hopes of victory have been crushed.

Whether we have received or rejected Christ, now will determine our future response to his day of coronation. Will you be filled with rejoicing or regretting? At the sound of the seventh trumpet, there will be no more deciding. The time to decide is now. Have you chosen joy with Christ or woe without him?

11:19 Then God's temple in heaven was opened, and within his temple was seen the ark of his covenant. And there came flashes of lightning, rumblings, peals of thunder, an earthquake and a great hailstorm.[NIV] John saw *God's temple in heaven.* Most likely this was not a physical temple sitting in the clouds, for the point is made later that there would be no temple in the new Jerusalem because "the Lord God Almighty and the Lamb are its temple" (21:22 NLT). John had already seen God's throne and the altar in heaven (4:2; 6:9; 8:3). What John was seeing is the place where God dwells and the ark of the covenant, which had always symbolized God's presence and faithfulness among his people. God's promises would be fulfilled and his purposes completed.

THE GREATEST REWARD
In the Bible, God gives rewards to his people according to what they deserve. Throughout the Old Testament, obedience often brought reward in this life (Deuteronomy 28), but obedience and immediate reward are not always linked. If they were, good people would always be rich, and suffering would always be a sign of sin. If we were quickly rewarded for every faithful deed, we would soon think that we were pretty good. Before long, we would be doing many good deeds for purely selfish reasons. While it is true that God will reward us for our earthly deeds (see Revelation 20:12), our greatest reward will be eternal life in his presence.

The phrase "within his temple" refers to the Most Holy Place (also called the Holy of Holies), the place in the temple where the *ark of his covenant* resides. In Old Testament days, the ark of the covenant was the most sacred treasure of the Israelite nation. The high priest could enter the Most Holy Place (Hebrews 9:3; or the "inner room," Hebrews 9:7 NIV), the innermost room of the temple, one day each year to atone for the nation's sins. The Most Holy Place was a small room that contained the ark of the covenant (a gold-covered chest containing the original stone tablets on which the Ten Commandments were written, a jar of manna, and Aaron's staff). The top of the chest served as the "atonement cover" (the altar) on which the blood would be sprinkled by the high priest on the Day of Atonement. The Most Holy Place was the most sacred spot on earth for the Jews. Only the high priest could enter; the other priests and the common people were forbidden to come into the room. Their only access to God was through the high priest, who would enter the Most Holy Place once each year with animal's blood to atone first for his own sins and then for the people's sins (see also Leviticus 16; Hebrews 10:19).

A curtain separated the Most Holy Place from the rest of the temple. When Jesus died on the cross, "the curtain in the Temple was torn in two, from top to bottom" (Matthew 27:51 NLT). The tearing of this curtain that separated the Most Holy Place from view symbolized that the barrier between God and humanity was removed. Then all people were free to approach God because of Christ's sacrifice for sin.

So Christ has now become the High Priest over all the good
things that have come. He has entered that great, perfect
sanctuary in heaven, not made by human hands and not part

of this created world. Once for all time he took blood into that
Most Holy Place, but not the blood of goats and calves. He
took his own blood, and with it he secured our salvation
forever. We can boldly enter heaven's Most Holy Place because
of the blood of Jesus. This is the new, life-giving way that
Christ has opened up for us through the sacred curtain, by
means of his death for us." (Hebrews 9:11-12; 10:19-20 NLT*)*

In this vision of God's open temple, John saw heavenly worship before God himself. There would be no sin to act as a barrier between God and his people. In addition, the ark of the covenant symbolized God's presence with his people. That John saw the ark also assured the readers of God's presence and protection in their coming trials.

The *flashes of lightning, rumblings, peals of thunder, an earthquake and a great hailstorm* all indicate God's signature on these events. These events occur here, at the sounding of the seventh trumpet, and they also occurred at the opening of the seventh seal (8:5). This will occur again at the pouring out of the seventh bowl (16:18-21).

Revelation 12

The seventh trumpet (11:15) ushers in the bowl judgments (15:1–16:21), but in the intervening chapters (12–14), an interlude, John saw several signs regarding the cosmic warfare in Revelation—the conflict between God and Satan. He saw the source of all sin, evil, persecution, and suffering on the earth, and he understood why the great battle between the forces of God and Satan must soon take place. In these chapters the nature of evil is exposed, and Satan is revealed in all his wickedness.

In 12:1-6, the reader is given a description of the scene; the rest of the chapter (12:7-17) amplifies various parts of that basic scene. The picture of warfare between good and evil—between God and Satan—is found in 12:1-6. The next three sections—12:7-12; 12:13-17; and chapter 13—expand the story of 12:1-6. Much like a symphony where the first movement sets the theme and the rest of the movements supply variations on the theme, so the first six verses set the theme and the next three "movements" supply the variations. The scenes focus on three characters—the dragon, the woman, and the child. The first scene records the birth of the child (12:1-6), the second highlights the expulsion of the dragon from heaven (12:7-12), and the third shows the dragon attacking the woman and her children (12:13-17). Not many of these details can be traced to specific people or events but are used to depict God's victory over evil and our need to trust in him.

Interestingly, God chose as his pattern for telling this story a common theme in the mythology of other religions—a prince is born, a usurper wants to kill the prince, the prince is protected, the usurper is killed. Such a story occurs in the Greek myth of Apollo and the Egyptian myth of Isis and Horus. This use is called "redemptive analogy."

12:1 A great and wondrous sign appeared in heaven: a woman clothed with the sun, with the moon under her feet and a crown of twelve stars on her head.NIV A clue to understanding this chapter is in the first phrase—what John would describe as a *sign*—a picture of something with deeper significance. The *woman* here represents much more than a woman. Pictured as a superhuman figure, she was *clothed with the sun* and had *the moon under her feet.* She was also wearing a victor's crown, *a crown of twelve stars.*

In the Old Testament, the nation of Israel is pictured as the wife of God (Isaiah 54:5-6; Jeremiah 3:6-8; 31:32; Ezekiel 16:32; Hosea 2:16). This woman represents the faithful people in Israel who had been waiting for the Messiah who would be born from among them (Isaiah 9:6-7; Micah 5:2). They had recognized and had accepted the Messiah when he had come. Later in the chapter, this woman will represent all believers—Jews and Gentiles.

Three other symbolic women appear in Revelation: (1) a woman named Jezebel, symbolizing paganism (2:20); (2) the scarlet woman, symbolizing the apostate church (17:3-6); (3) the bride of the Lamb, symbolizing God's people, the true church (19:7). The woman's crown of twelve stars symbolizes the twelve tribes of Israel.

THE FRONT LINES
The great and wondrous sign of the woman and the dragon that John saw reveals the mighty force of the conflict between good and evil. This may seem far removed until we realize that much of the daily conflict we experience reflects the much larger conflict of Christ against Satan. Those for Christ stand against the evil system of this world. Those who fight with Christ against evil are on the front lines of battle in this war.

12:2 She was pregnant and cried out in pain as she was about to give birth.[NIV] God had set apart the Jews for himself (Romans 9:4-5), and that nation had given birth to the Messiah, who would "rule all nations with an iron rod" (12:5; see also Psalm 2:9). In this part of the vision, John saw that this woman, Israel, *was pregnant and . . . about to give birth* to the Messiah (see also Isaiah 26:17-18; 54:1; 66:7-12; Hosea 13:13; Micah 4:9-10; 5:2-3; Matthew 24:8). When Mary gave birth to a tiny baby in Bethlehem, the entire universe took notice, for this event held cosmic significance.

This picture also symbolizes the nation of Israel agonizing for centuries as it awaited the coming Messiah, the deliverer, who would destroy evil and usher in God's eternal kingdom.

12:3 Then another sign appeared in heaven: an enormous red dragon with seven heads and ten horns and seven crowns on his heads.[NIV] In these verses *another sign* appears *in heaven.* This time, it is not a "great and wondrous sign" as in 12:1, but merely a sign—for the wonder of the dragon pales in comparison to the glory of the woman.

In this sign, John saw *an enormous red dragon,* who was Satan
(12:9). He had power over the kingdoms of the world, signified by
his heads, horns, and crowns. The color red is probably not that
important to the vision; however, it may symbolize blood, for the
red dragon had killed the saints. Satan is described as "a murderer
from the beginning" (John 8:44 NLT). John's original readers would
have immediately identified this dragon as the enemy of God's
people because such creatures are mentioned
by the prophets (see Psalm 74:14; Isaiah
27:1; Ezekiel 29:3). A dragon, or leviathan, in
the Old Testament, often stood for a king who
opposed God and his people.

> The Bible teaches that the devil is a real person and that he controls the affairs of this evil world. His great objective is to defeat the will and program of God in the world, in the church, and in the Christian.
>
> *Billy Graham*

Satan was originally created for God's
glory. But Satan arrogantly rebelled against
God because he desired to be like God
instead of giving glory to God (1 Timothy
3:6; Jude 6).

Satan first appears in the third chapter
of the first book of the Bible. God created
humans for his glory, and he placed Adam and Eve in a paradise
called the Garden of Eden (Genesis 1–2). Satan, disguised as a serpent, led Adam and Eve into sin (Genesis 3). That first sin enslaved
all future people—"When Adam sinned, sin entered the entire
human race. Adam's sin brought death, so death spread to everyone, for everyone sinned" (Romans 5:12 NLT). People are enslaved
to Satan, the prince of evil (Matthew 12:22-32; 1 John 5:19).

Scripture describes Satan as the "ruler" or "god of this world"
(John 14:30; 2 Corinthians 4:4; 1 John 5:19). His rule pervades
every area of this world. Oppressive and unjust political struc-
tures reflect Satan's reign (Revelation 12:13; 13:4-8; 18:1-20).
Even the curse of death and sickness that God pronounced in
Eden is the result of Satan's work (John 8:44).

THE RED DRAGON
Satan, the prince of this world, is an angel who rebelled against
God. Satan is real, not symbolic, and is constantly working
against God and those who obey him. Satan tempted Eve in the
garden and persuaded her to sin; he tempted Jesus in the desert
but was not able to persuade him to fall (Matthew 4:1-11). Satan
has great power, but people can be delivered from his reign of
spiritual darkness because of Christ's victory on the cross. Jesus
is much more powerful than Satan. Jesus' resurrection shattered
Satan's deathly power (Colossians 1:13-14). To overcome Satan
we need faithful allegiance to God's Word, determination to stay
away from sin, and the support of other believers.

After Adam and Eve's sin in the Garden of Eden, God had promised to destroy Satan and his demons and reestablish his own kingdom. Speaking to the serpent, God had said, "You and the woman will be enemies, and your offspring and her offspring will be enemies. He will crush your head, and you will strike his heel" (Genesis 3:15 NLT). The offspring who ultimately crushes Satan's head is God's promised Savior, Jesus Christ. Jesus demonstrated his power over Satan through his miracles and exorcisms (Matthew 12:28-29). Hearing of his disciples' success on their first mission to spread his word, Jesus had said, "I saw Satan falling from heaven as a flash of lightning. And I have given you authority over all the power of the enemy" (Luke 10:18-19 NLT). Jesus' sacrificial death on the cross and his resurrection sealed his victory over Satan. Christ "disarmed the evil rulers and authorities" (Colossians 2:15 NLT; see also John 12:31; 16:11).

Although a great battle had been won, the war was not over. Since Eden, Satan has been the avowed enemy of God and his people, as pictured in John's vision. In the end, Satan will fight against God's people and will wage a final war against God. At that time, Satan will be decisively defeated.

This dragon is pictured as having *seven heads and ten horns and seven crowns on his heads.* These are not supernatural, heavenly crowns, as the crown of twelve stars on the woman's head (12:1); instead, these heads and crowns symbolize nations over which Satan has control. Throughout Revelation, the number seven signifies completeness, so the seven heads and seven crowns could picture the totality of Satan's control over the earth. The dragon has authority only in this world. The "ten horns" allude to Daniel 7:7 and 24, "Then in my vision that night, I saw a fourth beast. . . . It was different from any of the other beasts, and it had ten horns. Its ten horns are ten kings that will rule that empire" (NLT). The ten horns, or ten kings, are also mentioned in Revelation 17:12. The huge statue in Nebuchadnezzar's vision also had ten toes (Daniel 2:41-42). It is unclear whether these ten kings will be actual kings and nations or even the exact number ten, but Revelation 17:12-14 says they will make war against Christ. As the King of kings, Christ will conquer them.

12:4 His tail swept a third of the stars out of the sky and flung them to the earth. The dragon stood in front of the woman who was about to give birth, so that he might devour her child the moment it was born.[NIV] This verse describes the fall of Satan. Next, John saw a vision of the dragon standing *in front of the woman who was about to give birth, so that he might devour her child the moment it was born.* This reminds us of the slaugh-

ter of the young boys in Bethlehem by Herod (Matthew 2:16).
Herod was Satan's emissary, used by Satan to attempt to kill the
child Jesus.

**12:5 She gave birth to a boy who was to rule all nations with an
iron rod. And the child was snatched away from the dragon
and was caught up to God and to his throne.**^{NLT} The woman
gave birth to a boy. This boy child is Jesus, born to a devout Jew
named Mary (Luke 1:26-33), born to the entire nation of Israel.
But this boy would not be killed by Satan, for he would be born
to rule all nations with an iron rod (see Psalm 2:6-9). As a shepherd defends his flock, so Christ will defend his church against
those who attempt to destroy it. The iron rod pictures Jesus as the
ultimate warrior. His life on earth is not pictured in this story, for
John immediately saw the child *snatched away from the dragon*
and *caught up to God and to his throne.* Jesus came to earth,
accomplished his work, and then returned to heaven. This is the
Ascension (Acts 1:9). Satan may have fought Jesus, but nothing
stopped him from doing what he had been sent to earth to do.

**12:6 And the woman fled into the wilderness, where God had pre-
pared a place to give her care for 1,260 days.**^{NLT} The *wilderness* represents a place of spiritual refuge and protection from
Satan, probably not meant to be literal because this chapter is
mostly symbolic. John the Baptist had lived in the wilderness
before beginning his public ministry (Luke 1:80; 3:2). After he
had been tempted by Satan in the wilderness, Jesus had been ministered to by the angels (Mark 1:13). Jesus had withdrawn to the
wilderness with his disciples before returning to Jerusalem the
last time (John 11:54). After the apostle Paul had been converted,
he had gone away "into Arabia" (most likely, into the wilderness,
Galatians 1:17) before returning to begin his ministry. Thus, in
this verse, *the woman fleeing into the wilderness* is a picture of
her escaping to a place of protection.

In this place *prepared* by God, he cared for her *for 1,260
days*—the same number noted for the trampling of the holy city
(11:2), the ministry of the two witnesses (11:3), and the rule of
the Beast (13:5). God would care for his people during the entire
time when evil would be in control in the world. In the wilderness, God's people would be hounded by the people on the earth
(those who would follow the Beast), but God would watch over
them. Many would be martyred, but God would care for them.
The word translated "care for" is literally "nourish." The woman
will be provided with food miraculously, just as Elijah was cared
for in the wilderness by God (1 Kings 17:2-4). God also provided
manna in the wilderness for his people (Exodus 16:4).

Some think that this woman pictures the Jewish believers only. Others suggest that she symbolizes all believers, the true Israel. Depending on one's view of when the believers will be taken to heaven (before, in the middle of, or after this time of Great Tribulation), these symbols may be identified in different ways. Because God has chosen not to make it clear, it is best to simply understand that God is promising spiritual protection for his people who are still on the earth during this difficult time.

TRUE SECURITY
Because God aided the woman's escape into the desert, we can be sure that he offers security to all true believers. Satan always attacks God's people, but God keeps them spiritually secure. Some will experience physical harm, but all will be protected from spiritual harm. God will not let Satan take the souls of God's true followers. When Satan's attacks seem overpowering, remember that God is ruler over all. Trust him.

12:7-9 **Then there was war in heaven. Michael and the angels under his command fought the dragon and his angels. And the dragon lost the battle and was forced out of heaven. This great dragon—the ancient serpent called the Devil, or Satan, the one deceiving the whole world—was thrown down to the earth with all his angels.**NLT This is the first expansion on the pictures described in 12:1-6. What John saw next fills in for the readers more detail of what was described in 12:4 regarding Satan's expulsion from heaven: "His tail swept a third of the stars out of the sky and flung them to the earth" (NIV).

Satan's expulsion from heaven began as a *war in heaven* between *Michael and the angels* of God and *the dragon* (Satan) *and his angels.* These events most likely describe the time of the second binding of Satan associated with the death and resurrection of Christ (see 12:4). Some believe it relates to the eviction of Satan before the creation of humans in Genesis, but that view is based more on conjecture. Others see it as something that will occur just before the return of Christ. If the passage refers to the Resurrection, Christ's victory over death caused Satan to try to reestablish himself in heaven. According to Scripture, Satan had some sort of access (Job 1:6-7; Zechariah 3:1). In either case, this event fulfills a portion of Daniel's vision (Daniel 12:1-2).

Michael is a high-ranking angel (called an archangel). Throughout Jewish literature, Michael is named as the one who comes to the aid of God's people. He was seen as one of their protectors (see also Daniel 10:13, 21; 12:1; Jude 9). Notice that the battle here was not between God and Satan or between Christ and Satan but between

Michael and Satan. Warfare raged, and *the dragon lost the battle.* As a result, Satan and his minions were *forced out of heaven.* Having lost their place, they are already vanquished foes. Satan was *thrown down to the earth,* and he went about his work of *deceiving the whole world*—his final revolt before his destruction (20:10).

Here, the great dragon is identified as *the ancient serpent called the Devil, or Satan.* The devil is not a symbol or legend; he is very real. The devil, God's enemy, constantly tries to hinder God's work, but he is limited by God's power and can do only what he is permitted to do (Job 1:6–2:6). The name Satan means "accuser" (12:10). He actively looks for people to accuse and attack (1 Peter 5:8-9). Satan likes to pursue believers who are vulnerable in their faith, who are spiritually weak, or who are isolated from other believers. He "prowls around like a roaring lion, looking for some victim to devour" (1 Peter 5:8 NLT). Members of the first-century church understood Satan's intentions. They warned one another to resist evil (James 4:7) and even expected "to enter into the Kingdom of God through many tribulations" caused by their enemy (Acts 14:22 NLT; see also John 16:33). Although Satan's final destruction is certain, believers are presently waiting for Christ to crush Satan and to end all evil (Romans 16:20).

Some consider this verse to describe warfare in the ancient past, but others think that Satan's fall to earth took place at Jesus' resurrection or ascension and that the 1,260 days (12:6) are a symbolic way of referring to the time between Christ's first and second comings. Still others say that Satan's defeat will occur in the middle of a literal seven-year Tribulation period, following the rapture of the church and preceding the second coming of Christ and the beginning of Christ's one-thousand-year reign. Regardless of the interpretation, God's clear teaching is that Christ is victorious—Satan has already been defeated because of Christ's death on the cross (12:10-12). Even though God permits the devil to do his work in this world, God is still in control. And Jesus has complete power over Satan; he defeated Satan when he died and rose again. One day Satan will be bound forever, never again to do his evil work (20:10).

Satan fell to the earth with "all his angels"—referring to demons. This world is their prison, where, as the enemies of God, they work against God's people. Satan is not omnipresent—he cannot be everywhere at once, so his demons work for him. Demons are fallen angels, sinful spiritual beings who have Satan as their leader (Matthew 25:41; Luke 11:15). Revelation highlights three evil powers who will oppose God's people during the end times: Satan, pictured as a dragon (Revelation 12:9); the Beast, better known as the Antichrist (13:1-10); and the false prophet (13:11; 16:13).

Demons serve as agents of this evil trinity. They seduce people, will establish the notorious kingdom of Babylon, and will lead a worldwide offensive against God's people (16:1-14).

REAL ENEMIES
These are demons over whom Satan has control. They are not fantasies—they are very real. Believers face a powerful army whose goal is to defeat Christ's church. When a person trusts in Christ, these beings become that person's enemies, trying every trick to turn him or her away from Christ and back to sin. Although assured of victory, believers must engage in the struggle until Christ returns because Satan is constantly battling against all who are on the Lord's side. Believers need supernatural power to defeat Satan, and God has provided this by giving his Holy Spirit and his armor. If you feel discouraged, remember Jesus' words to Peter: "On this rock I will build my church, and the gates of Hades will not overcome it" (Matthew 16:18 NIV).

12:10-11 Then I heard a loud voice shouting across the heavens, "It has happened at last—the salvation and power and kingdom of our God, and the authority of his Christ! For the Accuser has been thrown down to earth—the one who accused our brothers and sisters before our God day and night. And they have defeated him because of the blood of the Lamb and because of their testimony. And they were not afraid to die."NLT Verses 10-12 comprise a hymn of praise to God for the defeat of Satan when he was thrown out of heaven. Despite Satan's power on this earth, he is and always will be a vanquished foe. This hymn has three stanzas, shouted by *a loud voice* that was heard *across the heavens*—possibly an angel. Some have suggested that this could not be an angel because the words "our brothers and sisters" usually refer to humans. In 19:10, however, an angel says, "I am a servant of God, just like you and other believers who testify of their faith in Jesus" (NLT), thus, in a sense, equating the angels and humans in their being servants of God.

First, the voice proclaims the victory of God's kingdom and Christ's authority: *"It has happened at last—the salvation and power and kingdom of our God, and the authority of his Christ!"* Salvation means deliverance—not just spiritual salvation from sin, but freedom from the clutches of Satan. This had occurred because of God's power (strength exerted for believers) and kingdom (his rule in believers' lives), and because of the authority of his Son. Both the Father and the Son have given this deliverance.

Second, the message describes the victory and its appropriation by believers through their faith in Christ: *"For the Accuser has been thrown down to earth."* This has already been described in 12:4, 8-9 (see commentary above).

Third, there is a promise that Satan is ultimately and forever defeated *because of the blood of the Lamb and because of their testimony.* The critical blow to Satan had come when the Lamb, Jesus Christ, had shed his blood for sinful humanity. The victory had been won by sacrifice—Christ's death to pay the penalty for sin. Those who accept this sacrifice become victors along with the Lamb. They confirm their loyalty to the Lamb through their testimony—some even to the point of death. The martyrs who were *not afraid to die* revealed their ultimate victory in that final act of faith. When a believer dies, Satan may think he has gained a victory. In reality, however, he has lost. In fact, he loses every time a believer dies. The victory of the saints is the heart of Revelation. In each of the letters to the seven churches (chapters 2–3), Christ had promised that those who are victorious will receive great reward.

> The same serpent who accuses the saints in heaven also deceives . . . the nations into thinking that the people of God are dangerous, deluded, even destructive. . . . God's people in every age must expect the world's opposition, but the church can always defeat the enemy by being faithful to Jesus Christ.
>
> *Warren Wiersbe*

TRUE LOYALTY
These martyrs were not afraid to die. Satan's power over death had been broken and their loyalty to Christ was deep. Another translation of 12:11 reads, "They did not love their lives so much as to shrink from death" (NIV). We must ask, "How deep is my loyalty to Christ? Do I love him that much? Do I love my life so much as not to shrink from being ridiculed for my faith?" If we can't say that, we are probably not ready to step up to martyrdom. Take heart from the martyrs' testimony and strive to love Christ more each day, to set priorities that focus on him, and to break away from attractions and loyalties that might weaken your faith. By so doing, you can move toward the goal of loyal devotion to Christ even to the point of death.

12:12 "Rejoice, O heavens! And you who live in the heavens, rejoice! But terror will come on the earth and the sea. For the Devil has come down to you in great anger, and he knows that he has little time."NLT This third stanza of the hymn calls those in heaven to *rejoice.* But those left on earth will face *terror.* The reason? *The Devil has come down to you in great anger, and he knows that he has little time.* Knowing that his doom is sealed and that he will ultimately be defeated, Satan, in great anger, lashes out, attempting to take as many people with him as he can, as well as causing suffering and pain to those who are on God's side.

The Devil began to step up his persecution knowing that *he has little time.* Some believe that all of church history has been the "last days," so Satan has been constantly battling against God's people. Others interpret this as happening right before the end of history, when Satan will increase his persecution of God's people. Although the devil is very powerful, as can be seen by the condition of our world, he is always under God's control. That is, he can only do what God permits him to do. One of the reasons God allows Satan to work evil and bring temptation is so that the false believers will be weeded out from Christ's true believers. Knowing that the last great confrontation with Jesus was near, Satan was desperately trying to recruit as great an enemy force as possible for this final battle.

THE WAR IS WON
The angel shouted the victory cry, "Rejoice, O heavens!" because Satan would be defeated. The war will be won by God. In the process, we need to make sure we don't lose our individual battles. Too many Christians sing "Victory in Jesus" but then sit idly by, assuming that the work is all God's to do and they will be carried along in the victory. Not only must we be spiritually fit and morally strong, but we also must not be a hindrance to the cause of Christ by hurting others or dividing the church. The war is real, and we must be on guard to serve in the battle well.

12:13 And when the dragon realized that he had been thrown down to the earth, he pursued the woman who had given birth to the child.^{NLT} Verses 7-12 describe the war in heaven and expand on verse 4; verses 13-17 describe the war on earth, expanding on verse 6. *The dragon realized that he had been thrown down to the earth* and was angry. He had lost the war in heaven (12:8), lost access to God, and, thus, no longer was allowed to accuse the believers (12:10-11). He could not attack the child because the child had been taken up to heaven (12:5), and knew that his time was short (12:12). In his attempt to bring as many people with him, and in his anger at God's people, the dragon *pursued the woman who had given birth to the child.* The word "pursued" is the same word translated "persecute." Satan is stalking and killing God's people, hoping to do as much damage as possible.

The woman had "fled into the wilderness" (12:6 NLT) because of the pursuit of the dragon, but God would care for her there (see 12:14). The woman symbolizes God's people. It is unclear if this refers to the Jews or to all believers. But those on earth at this time who believe in Jesus will be hounded by Satan. His anger at Christ will be redirected at Christ's people.

12:14 But she was given two wings like those of a great eagle. This allowed her to fly to a place prepared for her in the wilderness, where she would be cared for and protected from the dragon for a time, times, and half a time.^{NLT} This verse repeats 12:6, "And the woman fled into the wilderness, where God had prepared a place to give her care for 1,260 days" (NLT). The text says that the woman *was given two wings like those of a great eagle,* picturing divine protection and deliverance (see also Exodus 19:4; Deuteronomy 32:10-11; Psalm 91:4; Isaiah 40:31). Eagles were the largest birds known in Palestine. These great wings *allowed her to fly to a place prepared for her in the wilderness,* a place of safety, *where she would be cared for and protected.* God had prepared this safe place, as noted in 12:6.

> The antagonism directed against the church has its origin in the hatred of Satan for Christ.
> *Robert H. Mounce*

The 1,260 days mentioned in 12:6 correspond to the *time, times, and half a time* mentioned here. "Time" means one year; "times" means two years; and "half a time" means half a year. This equals three and a half years, or forty-two months (see 11:2), or 1,260 days (forty-two months multiplied by thirty days per month). Thus, the woman would be protected during the time of persecution. This could refer to the time period of the trampling of the holy city (11:2) or to the time when the Antichrist reigns (13:5) or to both, depending on how these time periods fall. The point is that God has prepared a place of spiritual protection for his people during the time when Satan will rampage across the earth. Many will die, but that will be their greatest victory over Satan. The time of that rampage has an end because God will bring an end to Satan and all evil.

12:15-16 Then the dragon tried to drown the woman with a flood of water that flowed from its mouth. But the earth helped her by opening its mouth and swallowing the river that gushed out from the mouth of the dragon.^{NLT} The dragon spewed water *from its mouth,* hoping to *drown the woman.* A flood is a common Old Testament picture of overwhelming evil (see Psalms 18:4; 32:6; 69:1-2; 124:2-5; Nahum 1:8). This is a flood of lies and deceit in an attempt to drown the woman in sin. This could refer to the river of lies that will threaten Christians in the last days (see 13:14; Matthew 24:24; 2 Thessalonians 2:9-11). This provides an interesting contrast to the river of life flowing from God's throne (22:1).

Next, John saw that *the earth helped her by opening its mouth and swallowing the river* so that the flood could not hurt the woman. God used the earth to protect his people. God delivered Israel from Pharaoh by parting the Red Sea; once again, God supernaturally intervenes on behalf of his people (see Exodus 14:21-22; see also Isaiah 26:20; 42:15; 43:2; 50:2).

12:17 **Then the dragon became angry at the woman, and he declared war against the rest of her children—all who keep God's commandments and confess that they belong to Jesus.**NLT If the woman represents faithful Jews, then the phrase "the rest of her children" could refer to all believers—the entire church. If the woman represents all believers (both Jew and Gentile), then "the rest of her children" could refer to all who come to Christ through the testimony of God's people or to those specifically chosen for martyrdom. Because Satan could not bring down the group (the Jewish believers or the church at large), he waged war against individuals. "The rest of her children" could also refer to all of God's people after the first child, Jesus. All believers are considered to be Jesus' family (Romans 8:29; Hebrews 2:11).

The *dragon* was very *angry.* The reasons are noted in the commentary on 12:13. The woman had escaped to the wilderness, and the dragon had not been able to kill her, even with a great flood. So Satan *declared war against the rest of her children—all who keep God's commandments and confess that they belong to Jesus.* This stresses the obedience that is a central part of endurance.

NO TIME FOR INDECISION
The apostle Paul wrote that believers are in a spiritual battle (Ephesians 6:10-12). John wrote that the outcome has already been determined. Satan and his followers have been defeated and will be destroyed. Nevertheless, Satan battles daily to bring more into his ranks and to keep his own from defecting to God's side. Those who belong to Christ have gone into battle on God's side, and he has guaranteed them victory. God will not lose the war, but we must make certain not to lose the battle for our own souls. Don't waver in your commitment to Christ. A great spiritual battle is being fought, and there is no time for indecision.

12:18 **Then he stood waiting on the shore of the sea.**NLT Some versions place this verse at the beginning of 13:1 to accomodate a textual variation, "I stood upon the sand of the sea," (KJV), referring to John. But better textual evidence affirms the reading, "he [i.e., the dragon] stood."

The Beast was foreshadowed in 11:7 as the one who would

attack the two witnesses. He was described there as "the beast that comes up from the Abyss" (NIV). At this point, John would see the Beast arrive. The dragon stood on the edge of the sea (the Abyss), ready to call out one who would help him pursue God's people.

In 9:1-2, John had seen the abyss opened and an army of locusts ascending from it. As noted in the commentary there, the people of John's day would have pictured the "Abyss" as the depths of the sea. The sea usually represented evil in the ancient world. Later, John would describe the new heaven and new earth as a place where the "sea" no longer exists (21:1).

The dragon (Satan) had tried to kill the woman's child (Jesus) but could not. Then he had chased the woman (at first picturing God's people, Israel, then seeming to picture all believers), but she had been protected by God. So he had turned his attention to the rest of the woman's offspring and had "declared war against the rest of her children—all who keep God's commandments and confess that they belong to Jesus" (12:17 NLT). As noted in 12:17, having realized he could not bring down the church as a whole, the dragon had begun an assault against individual believers.

Revelation 13

Chapter 13 introduces Satan's (the dragon's) two evil accomplices: (1) the beast out of the sea (the Antichrist, 13:1-10) and (2) the beast out of the earth (the false prophet, 13:11-18). Together, the three evil beings form an unholy trinity in direct opposition to the Holy Trinity of God the Father, God the Son, and God the Holy Spirit.

Chapter 13 continues the expansion of John's vision of 12:1-6. This chapter provides more detail about the dragon's wrath and pursuit of the woman and her offspring (the church).

During the temptation in the desert, Satan wanted Jesus to demonstrate his power by turning stones into bread, to perform miracles by jumping from a high place, and to gain political power by worshiping him (see Matthew 4:1-11). Satan's plan was to rule the world through Jesus, but Jesus refused to do Satan's bidding. Thus, in the vision, Satan turned to the fearsome beasts described in Revelation 13. To the beast that came out of of the sea, he gave political power. To the beast that came out of the earth, he gave power to do miracles. Both beasts worked together to gain control of the whole world. This unholy trinity—the dragon, the Beast out of the sea, and the false prophet (16:13)—united in a desperate attempt to overthrow God, but their efforts were doomed to failure. See what became of them later in the book (19:19-21; 20:10).

13:1 And now in my vision I saw a beast rising up out of the sea. It had seven heads and ten horns, with ten crowns on its horns. And written on each head were names that blasphemed God.^{NLT} The Beast came from the Abyss (or bottomless pit, see 11:7) to do Satan's bidding. John described the Beast as horrible to look at, for it *had ten horns and seven heads, with ten crowns on his horns.* In 12:3, the dragon was described as having "seven heads and ten horns and seven crowns on his heads" (NIV). The dragon has the seven crowns on his seven heads; the Beast has the ten crowns on his ten horns. This could simply be a picture of the dragon's authority

THE ANTICHRIST

There are many theories regarding the person of the Antichrist, and each has its advocates who have Scripture to back up their views. The actual truth will probably not be clear until the events actually occur. Until then, believers are to remain watchful (Matthew 24:4–5), looking expectantly to Christ's return.

Early Christian Interpreters
Early Christian writings identify the Antichrist as the one who will exalt himself as God. These writers noted that the tribe of Dan is not on the list of the 144,000 "sealed" Jews (see Revelation 7:4-8) and that Dan is the perpetrator in Jeremiah's prophecy of "terror" (Jeremiah 8:15-16). They concluded, therefore, that the Antichrist would be a descendant of the tribe of Dan. This interpretation is not widely held today.

Postmillennialists and Amillennialists
Some in these two groups believe that the Antichrist will not be a person but, rather, an evil system. Scripture speaks of "many antichrists" (1 John 2:18), and anti-Christian forces have persecuted the church throughout history.

Most postmillennialists, however, believe that the prophecies regarding the Antichrist have already been fulfilled. Some think this was Nero, who committed suicide and, then, was expected to come back to life and reclaim his throne. In this theory, the seven-headed beast symbolizes the Roman Empire because the city of Rome was built on seven hills (see Revelation 17:9). There are parallels between the beast and Roman emperors, who took on blasphemous names, such as "lord" or "god" (see Revelation 13:1). Today, many doubt that the Antichrist is Nero or any other Roman emperor.

Dispensationalists
Dispensationalists believe that the Antichrist will emerge as the leader of the restored Roman Empire. He will make commitments to Israel (Daniel 7:8, 21-27; 9:24-27; Revelation 17:9-14), then will be assassinated and restored to life. According to this view, the Antichrist will exalt himself in the rebuilt Temple at Jerusalem and begin to persecute the Jews. This will cause Israel to turn to the Messiah. The time of great tribulation will end with military forces converging on Israel to defeat the Antichrist.

Historic premillennialists believe in an Antichrist who will be a powerful individual, but they do not believe that the Temple in Jerusalem will be restored.

---

over the Beast. It may also be that the ten horns represent national leaders who followed the Beast; their crowns symbolized their authority, but they actually belonged to the Beast—who belonged to Satan. Initially, this Beast was identified with Rome because the Roman Empire, in its early days, encouraged an evil lifestyle, persecuted believers, and opposed God and his followers. But the Beast also symbolizes the Antichrist—not Satan, but someone under Satan's power and control who would be able to draw the whole world to himself.

The heads and horns are further described in 17:9-14. See commentary there. John clearly described the evils of the Roman Empire. But even more, he described the hideous, satanic system that will manifest itself as the end draws near. The Beast, therefore, must be more than the Roman Empire. Revelation also seems to imply that this blasphemous creature will have a devastating effect on the believers.

On each head the Beast had *a blasphemous name.* Some have suggested that these refer to the divine names that had been given to various Roman emperors. Whether referring to the Roman emperors or not, these blasphemous names signified the Beast's challenge of God's sovereignty and his setting himself up as god.

Believers must not be too concerned about attempting to identify any person as the Antichrist. This has been done with many world leaders since the first century. However, God's timing is perfect, and when it happens, God will still be in control, even of the Antichrist.

13:2 This beast looked like a leopard, but it had bear's feet and a lion's mouth! And the dragon gave him his own power and throne and great authority.[NLT] This Antichrist seems like a combination of the four beasts that Daniel had seen centuries earlier in a vision (Daniel 7:4-8), combining the characteristics of a leopard, a bear, and a lion. In Daniel's vision, the lion with eagle's wings represented Babylon with her swift conquests (statues of winged lions have been recovered from Babylon's ruins). The bear that ravaged the lion was Medo-Persia. The three ribs in its mouth represented the conquests of three major enemies. The leopard was Greece, its wings picturing the swiftness of Alexander the Great's campaign as he conquered much of the civilized world in four years (334-330 B.C.). The leopard's four heads were the four divisions of the Greek Empire after Alexander's death. The fourth beast pointed to both Rome and the end times. Many Bible scholars believe that the ten horns on the fourth beast correspond to the ten kings who will reign shortly before God sets up his everlasting kingdom (see also Revelation 13:1). These ten kings had still not come to power at the time of John's vision recorded in the book of Revelation (17:12). The little horn is a future human ruler or the antichrist (see also 2 Thessalonians 2:3-4). God was illustrating the final end of all worldly kingdoms in contrast to his eternal kingdom.

In combining these four beasts, John's vision reveals the epitome of evil power. The *dragon* (Satan) gave the Beast (the Antichrist) *his own power and throne and great authority.* Those same words are used in the hymns in Revelation sung to God. So

SATAN'S WORK IN THE WORLD

Satan's . . .	Reference in Revelation
Hatred for Christ	12:13
Hatred for God's people	12:17
Power and authority	13:2
Popularity among unbelievers	13:4
Blasphemy against God	13:6
War against believers	13:7
Ability to deceive	13:14

Satan attempted to again make a false copy, by giving his Beast his power, throne, and authority. As the dragon (12:17) was in opposition to God, so the Beast from the sea was against Christ and may be seen as Satan's false messiah.

The early Roman Empire was strong and also anti-Christ (or against Christ's standards); many other individual powers throughout history have been anti-Christ. The original readers would have immediately identified Antichrist with one of the Caesars. Certainly the emperors were against Christ ("antichrists," 1 John 2:18). Many Christians believe that Satan's evil will culminate in a final Antichrist, who will run an evil world system. He will focus all the powers of evil against Christ's followers.

The Antichrist will appropriate the powers of government and religion in himself. As a political figure, the Antichrist will become so powerful that opposing him will be futile. All nations on earth will serve him. Opposition against the Antichrist's rule will be brutally suppressed. Only those who are branded with the Beast's mark, showing their loyalty to him, will be able to participate in the world's economy.

Throughout history, many enemies of God and the church have arisen. The people who faced the persecutions of Nero, Hitler, or Stalin couldn't imagine that anything worse was yet to come. Believers may have to face many antichrists. Christians will only know the identity of this Antichrist in retrospect.

13:3 One of the heads of the beast seemed to have had a fatal wound, but the fatal wound had been healed. The whole world was astonished and followed the beast.[NIV] Using spectacular miracles, the Antichrist persuaded the world to accept his false teachings. The Beast seduced the world by imitating Christ's resurrection when he recovered from *a fatal wound* (from a sword, see

13:14). Because the Beast, the Antichrist, is a false messiah, he will be a counterfeit of Christ and will even parody Christ's resurrection (13:14). People across *the whole world* will be *astonished* and will follow him because they will be awed by his power and miracles. Paul had written, "This evil man will come to do the work of Satan with counterfeit power and signs and miracles. He will use every kind of wicked deception to fool those who are on their way to destruction because they refuse to believe the truth that would save them" (2 Thessalonians 2:9-10 NLT).

The Antichrist will unite the world under his leadership (13:7-8), and he will control the world economy (13:16-17). People are impressed by power and will follow those who display it forcefully or offer it to their followers. But those who will follow the Beast will only be fooling themselves: he will use his power to manipulate others, to point to himself, and to promote evil plans. God, by contrast, uses his infinitely greater power to love and to build up.

BE NOT DECEIVED
Satan uses counterfeit miracles to draw people to him. John 8:44 says, "[Satan] was a murderer from the beginning and has always hated the truth. There is no truth in him. When he lies, it is consistent with his character; for he is a liar and the father of lies" (NLT). Revelation shows Satan copying the work of God and thus deceiving people. But he would not be able to deceive if people were not so easily astonished by his displays of power and intelligence and so prone to follow. Pray each day for discernment to tell the difference between good and evil, so you will be immune to counterfeits. Saturate your life with God's love and serve him. Then, you will be able to withstand Satan's temptations.

13:4 They worshiped the dragon, for he had given his authority to the beast, and they worshiped the beast, saying, "Who is like the beast, and who can fight against it?"NRSV The ultimate goal of the dragon was, of course, to draw people away from Christ and to himself. He wanted people's worship. Thus, the people who were astounded by the Beast followed him and even worshiped him (ultimately worshiping the dragon, Satan). Worshiping anything other than Christ *is* worshiping Satan. At this point, the Beast gained complete governmental and religious power. The question "Who is like the beast?" is a parody of God's Word, when God's people asked, "Who is like the Lord?" (see, for example, Exodus 15:11; Micah 7:18). Here, the peoples of the earth asked, *"Who can fight against the beast?"* Some scholars think the Beast will actually bring world peace so that no one can fight against him. But that peace will be based on domination and without real substance; thus, it will be shallow and short-lived.

13:5-6 **The beast was given a mouth uttering haughty and blasphemous words, and it was allowed to exercise authority for forty-two months. It opened its mouth to utter blasphemies against God, blaspheming his name and his dwelling, that is, those who dwell in heaven.**NRSV Verses 5-7 record a series of passive verbs regarding the Antichrist—he "was given" a mouth and time to exercise his authority (13:5); he "was allowed to wage war," and he "was given authority to rule" (13:7). The passive voice indicates either that these had been given by the dragon, Satan (13:2), or by God. Either way, God has control over Satan's activities.

The Antichrist *was given a mouth to utter* proud words and *blasphemies,* exalting himself as God. This compares to the "little horn" that Daniel had seen, "The little horn had . . . a mouth that was boasting arrogantly" (Daniel 7:8 NLT; see also 7:20; 11:20-39). He blasphemed God by placing himself in God's position. "He will exalt himself and defy every god there is and tear down every object of adoration and worship. He will position himself in the temple of God, claiming that he himself is God" (2 Thessalonians 2:4 NLT). Setting himself up in the temple is what Jesus spoke of as "the abomination that causes desolation" (Mark 13:14 NIV).

The Antichrist slandered God's *name and his dwelling,* that is, those *who dwell in heaven.* (This shows that God's dwelling place is his people.) Such pride and blasphemy are the heart of this world. The Antichrist will be the archenemy of all who side with Christ. "Those who dwell in heaven" could refer to angelic beings or to the believers who will one day be safe there, for in Revelation, people are divided into two groups—those who belong to the earth, and those who belong to heaven. The Antichrist blasphemed anything that had to do with God and his Son. As a result, confessing faith in Christ as Lord may result in death (13:7). The Antichrist and his followers (the people who belong to this world) would slander the Christians, calling them evildoers (1 Peter 2:12).

Whether one subscribes to the pre-Tribulation or post-Tribulation theory, the text is clear that there will be believers on earth during the Tribulation. Those who believe that the Christians will have been taken before this time think that the believers on earth will be those who will become Christians during this time of tribulation. Those who believe the church will not be taken until after the Tribulation would assert that all believers on the earth at this time will face this persecution.

The Antichrist will unite all nations and all religions under his authority. Even so, the power given to the Beast will be limited by God. He will allow the Beast to exercise authority only for a short time—*forty-two months.* This is the same time period as noted in 11:2 for the trampling of the holy city, in 11:3 for the ministry of the two witnesses (stated as 1,260 days), and in 12:6 and 12:14 for the protection of the woman (God's people). (For more information on that time period, see commentary on 11:2.) Even while the Beast is in power, God is still in control (11:15; 12:10-12).

13:7 And the beast was allowed to wage war against God's holy people and to overcome them. And he was given authority to rule over every tribe and people and language and nation.NLT The Antichrist was responsible for unleashing the Tribulation, the most intense period of persecution God's people would ever experience (Mark 13:14, 20). The Beast would be *allowed* (by God) to *wage war against God's holy people and to overcome them* (see also 12:17; Daniel 7:21). The phrase "wage war" does not refer to a military campaign (at least not yet), but to harassing God's people. The Antichrist would "overcome" believers, but he could only do so physically, as part of this world. In reality, those who died for the faith are the ultimate overcomers, for they have participated in Christ's death (12:11). The Antichrist could not harm God's holy people spiritually.

The Antichrist would establish worldwide dominance—given by God—*to rule over every tribe and people and language and nation.* He would demand to be worshiped as God (13:8). And many *will* worship him—everyone except true believers. Refusal to worship the Beast would result in suffering for God's people, but they would be rewarded with eternal life. The ultimate irony is that although the Beast was given power to overcome, the believers were the final "overcomers." Every believer's death brings the end nearer (6:10-11).

13:8 All inhabitants of the earth will worship the beast—all whose names have not been written in the book of life belonging to the Lamb that was slain from the creation of the world.NIV The Beast had been given control over "every tribe and people and language and nation" (13:7) for the express purpose of gaining their worship. The coming battle had only two sides—those who worshiped Satan and those who worshiped God. *All inhabitants of the earth* (referring to those who refuse to accept Christ) *will worship the beast.* Awed by his miracles and awesome power, they will look to him as a god (13:3-4).

These people are *all whose names have not been written in the book of life.* As noted in 3:5, the Book of Life is a register in heaven of those who have trusted in Christ for their salvation (see also 17:8; 20:12, 15; 21:27). Only the people whose names are written in this register will be accepted into heaven. Despite the horrors of this time of tribulation, not one believer will be lost, for their names are in the book. Two types of people exist—those whose names are in the book and those whose names are not in the book. Clearly, the people who will worship the Beast will be those whose names are *not* in the book of life. They will have made the choice to reject Christ and worship the Beast. Such people were described in 9:20-21 as those who "still refused to turn from their evil deeds. They continued to worship demons and idols . . . and they did not repent" (NLT).

The Book of Life belongs *to the Lamb that was slain from the creation of the world.* There has been debate as to whether the phrase "from the creation of the world" refers to the names written in the book of life or the slaying of the Lamb. Some suggest that the names have been written "from the creation of the world" based on 17:8 (NIV), which refers to "the inhabitants of the earth whose names have not been written in the book of life from the creation of the world. . . ." If the phrase refers to the Lamb having been slain from the creation of the world, it would refer to God's plan from eternity past to have his Son redeem mankind from sin. In either case, the verse shows the distinction between those who belong to God and those who belong to Satan.

THE BOOK OF LIFE
The Book of Life is a record of heavenly citizenship. Registered there are the names of those who put their trust in Christ (3:5). This should comfort those facing severe trials. It guarantees that death will not erase Jesus' promise of eternal life in him. Jesus said, "I assure you, those who listen to my message and believe in God who sent me have eternal life. They will never be condemned for their sins, but they have already passed from death into life. Indeed, the time is coming when all the dead in their graves will hear the voice of God's Son, and they will rise again. Those who have done good will rise to eternal life, and those who have continued in evil will rise to judgment" (John 5:24, 28-29 NLT). Do you ever doubt what happens after death? Those who believe in Christ can take him at his word. Their destiny is certain.

13:9-10 Anyone who is willing to hear should listen and understand. The people who are destined for prison will be arrested and taken away. Those who are destined for death will be killed. But do not be dismayed, for here is your opportunity to have endurance and faith.ᴺᴸᵀ This phrase, "anyone who is willing to hear should listen and understand," also appears at the end of all the letters to the seven churches. It warns readers that they had better listen.

These verses come from Jeremiah 15:2: "Those who are destined for death, to death; those who are destined for war, to war; those who are destined for famine, to famine; those who are destined for captivity, to captivity" (ᴺᴸᵀ)—the basic point is that the captivity would be divine judgment upon the rebellious nation of Israel, and there was nothing anyone could do to stop it.

> This is a wise, sane Christian faith: that a man commit himself, his life, and his hopes to God; that God undertakes the special protection of that man; that therefore that man ought not to be afraid of anything!
>
> *George MacDonald*

These verses describe how believers should act during this time of tribulation by the Beast (see 14:12). They understand that God is in control. He already has it all in his plan—some *who are destined for prison will be arrested and taken away*. Some *who are destined for death will be killed*. John wrote that believers must stand up for their faith, but they must not take up arms in an attempt to fight. Their job, at this point, would be to show *endurance and faith*. God has the battle under control; this time of persecution would only draw closer the time of Christ's glorious return. See 1 Peter 2:19-24 for more on suffering patiently.

AS A TESTIMONY
The times of great persecution that John saw will provide an opportunity for believers to exercise patient endurance and faithfulness. The tough times we face right now are also opportunities for spiritual growth. If God wills for us to be put to death for our faith, then our death will serve as a testimony to the goodness of God. Paul wrote, "Don't be intimidated by your enemies. This will be a sign to them that they are going to be destroyed, but that you are going to be saved, even by God himself. For you have been given not only the privilege of trusting in Christ but also the privilege of suffering for him" (Philippians 1:28-29 ɴʟᴛ). Don't fall into Satan's trap and turn away from God when hard times come. Instead, use those tough times as opportunities for testifying for God.

13:11 Then I saw another beast that rose out of the earth; it had two horns like a lamb and it spoke like a dragon.ᴺᴿˢⱽ The first Beast had come out of the sea (13:1), but this second beast *rose out of the earth.* Later identified as the false prophet (16:13; 19:20; 20:10), he was a counterfeit of the Holy Spirit. This beast completed the unholy trinity with the dragon (Satan) and the Beast from the sea (the Antichrist). The false prophet would be in charge of the world-wide worship of the first Beast.

There is a further imitation of Christ, the Lamb of God, in that the false prophet has *two horns like a lamb* (5:6). Perhaps his very similarity to Christ will be part of his deceptiveness. He may appear good, helpful, and caring—an "angel of light" (2 Corinthians 11:14). Jesus had warned of false teachers, "Beware of false prophets who come disguised as harmless sheep, but are really wolves that will tear you apart" (Matthew 7:15 NLT). The beast looked like a lamb but spoke *like a dragon.* The source of his words was Satan himself—the dragon.

As with their interpretation of the first Beast, scholars are divided about the beast from the earth. The different thoughts are that the second beast represents either (1) a movement or power, or (2) an individual who, at the end times, will arise along with the Antichrist to take control of the world. Those who believe that this beast represents a movement or power point to the first Beast as representing the worldwide anti-God system, with the second beast representing false teachers who cause people to stray. These false teachers will be the opposite of the two godly witnesses in chapter 11.

13:12 **He exercised all the authority of the first beast on his behalf, and made the earth and its inhabitants worship the first beast, whose fatal wound had been healed.**NIV The first Beast's authority came from Satan; the second beast *exercised all the authority of the first beast on his behalf.* This second beast's job was to make *the earth and its inhabitants worship the first beast.* The false prophet was in position when the Antichrist was killed and came back to life. Then the false prophet made everyone worship the Antichrist.

13:13-15 **He did astounding miracles, such as making fire flash down to earth from heaven while everyone was watching. And with all the miracles he was allowed to perform on behalf of the first beast, he deceived all the people who belong to this world.**NLT The second beast was also empowered to do *astounding miracles, such as making fire flash down from heaven.* Again, in copycat style, this was the same miracle that the two witnesses for God could perform (11:5), which is a reference to a miracle of Elijah recorded in 1 Kings 18:36-38. Ironically, Elijah had performed that miracle so that God could show who was a true prophet and who was not. Christ had warned, "False messiahs and false prophets will rise up and perform miraculous signs and wonders so as to deceive, if possible, even God's chosen ones" (Mark 13:22 NLT).

This miracle and others *deceived all the people who belong to this world.* The phrase "people who belong to this world" refers to those who were deceived and worshiped the Beast, not to the believers on the earth at this time (see also 13:8). True believers must not be swayed or deceived by these great miracles that the false prophet will perform.

CONVINCED?
The Bible repeats many miracles performed as proofs of God's power, love, and authority. But here counterfeit miracles are performed to deceive. This is similar to Pharaoh's magicians, who duplicated Moses' signs in Egypt. True signs and miracles point to Jesus Christ, but miracles alone can be deceptive. That is why we must ask with respect to each miracle we see: Is this consistent with what God says in the Bible? The second beast gained influence through the signs and wonders that he performed on behalf of the first Beast. The second beast ordered the people to worship an image in honor of the first Beast—a direct flouting of the second commandment (Exodus 20:4-6). Allowing the Bible to guide our faith and practice will keep us from being deceived by false signs, however convincing they appear to be. Any teaching that contradicts God's Word is false.

He ordered them to set up an image in honor of the beast who was wounded by the sword and yet lived. He was given power to give breath to the image of the first beast, so that it could speak and cause all who refused to worship the image to be killed.[NIV] As with all worship that is not of the one true God, this worship of the Beast is idolatry. The false prophet ordered *them* (the people of the world) *to set up an image in honor of the beast who was wounded by the sword and yet lived.* Actually the Beast had been fatally wounded and then brought back to life (13:3, 12). This brings to mind the great statue that Nebuchadnezzar, king of Babylon, had built to himself and then had required everyone to worship (Daniel 3:1-11).

The false prophet *was given power to give breath to the image of the first beast, so that it could speak.* The statue seemed to live and supposedly spoke to its worshipers. This, again, convinced many on this earth. The God of the Christians seemed to be mysteriously silent and invisible, but this god could be seen and he spoke audibly. No wonder many followed. And no wonder the believers needed to be warned so that they would not be swayed from the truth.

The heart of the false prophet's power is in the next words, "all who refused to worship the image" would be "killed." Christianity had become a capital offense—for only those who followed Christ were unwilling to worship the Beast's image. This was universal persecution.

Note that the false prophet is "allowed to perform" miracles to deceive people (13:14) and "was given power to give breath" (13:15). Both verses use the Greek passive, *edothe,* which means that God permitted these events to occur (see also 13:5-6).

13:16-17 **He required everyone—great and small, rich and poor, slave and free—to be given a mark on the right hand or on the forehead. And no one could buy or sell anything without that mark, which was either the name of the beast or the number representing his name.**[NLT] The false prophet went further in the worship of the Beast by requiring *everyone,* no matter their age or social status, *to be given a mark on the right hand or on the forehead.* The mark is described as *the name of the beast or the number representing his name* (13:18). This mark of the Beast was designed to mock the seal that God had already placed on his followers (7:2-3). Just as God had marked his people to save them, so Satan's Beast marked his people to save them from the persecution that he would inflict upon God's followers. Identifying this particular mark is not as important as identifying the purpose of the mark. Those who accepted it showed their allegiance to Satan, their willingness to operate within the economic system he promoted, and their rebellion against God. To refuse the mark meant to commit oneself entirely to God, preferring death to compromising one's faith in Christ.

People will have to worship the Beast in order to receive the mark and to be able to *buy or sell anything.* Clearly those who refuse the mark (the Christians) will be set up for economic ruin, homelessness, and hunger. In the end times, no one will be able to buy or sell anything without the mark of the Beast. Those who receive the brand of the Beast will be readily identifiable. The mark will be stamped prominently on their right hands or foreheads. The mark will be the number 666 (13:18).

Those who receive the mark of the Beast will benefit economically for a brief time. Their short gain, however, will be quickly offset by the eternal consequences that await them. Revelation warns that those who accept the mark of the Beast will have to endure God's cup of anger (see 14:9-12; 20:7-15).

BE A SKEPTIC
In every generation, Christians need to maintain a healthy skepticism about society's pleasures and rewards. In our educational, economic, and civic structures, there are incentives and rewards. Cooperating Christians must always support what is good and healthy about our society, but we must stand against sin. In some cases, such as Satan's system described here, the system or structure becomes so evil that there is no way to cooperate with it.

13:18 Wisdom is needed to understand this. Let the one who has understanding solve the number of the beast, for it is the number of a man. His number is 666.[NLT] The meaning of this number has been discussed more than that of any other part of the book of Revelation. The three sixes have been said to represent many things including the unholy trinity of Satan, the first Beast, and the false prophet (16:13).

Wisdom is needed to understand this. Let the one who has understanding solve the number of the beast, for it is the number of a man. Throughout church history, people have assigned numerical values to the letters of names to try to identify the Beast. The first readers of this book probably applied the number to the Emperor Nero, a man symbolizing all the evils of the Roman empire. (The Greek letters of Nero's name represent numbers that total 666.) Some proposed figures include *Lateinos,* which alludes to the entire Roman Empire; *Neron Kaisar* (referring to Caesar Nero), under whose direction the church suffered intense persecution; and *Teitan,* for Titus, the Roman emperor who destroyed Jerusalem in A.D. 70. The number continues to be linked with various world leaders, institutions, and types of economic transactions.

Because the book of Revelation is filled with symbolism, this number probably is also symbolic. The number seven is used in the book as a symbol of God's perfection. Conversely, the number six symbolizes human imperfection. So 666, then, symbolizes *the number of a man*—all human beings and their continued imperfection. Three sixes together—666—implies a trinity of imperfection—a parody of the number seven. The number symbolizes the worldwide dominion and complete evil of this unholy trinity designed to undo Christ's work and overthrow him.

Revelation 14

Chapter 13 describes the onslaught of evil that will occur when Satan and his helpers control the world. Chapter 14 gives a glimpse into eternity to show believers what awaits them if they endure. Their suffering will not be meaningless; it will only be a prelude into eternity with God. This chapter explains what will happen to those who refuse to receive the mark of the beast, and what will happen eventually to the beast and his servants.

14:1 Then I saw the Lamb standing on Mount Zion, and with him were 144,000 who had his name and his Father's name written on their foreheads.^{NLT} The battle was still occurring on the earth—believers were being persecuted and killed for their faith, unable to buy or sell anything because they had refused to worship the beast (13:15-17). To encourage John, God revealed what would await believers in heaven, reminding him that believers have been sealed by God.

The *Lamb* is Jesus the Messiah, and *Mount Zion* is probably the heavenly Jerusalem. This scene contrasts with the dragon standing on the edge of the sea and the evil world empire (13:1). "Mount Zion," here, may refer to the earthly location where Christ will begin his millennial reign, or it may refer to the church, the heavenly Mount Zion—"You have come to Mount Zion, to the city of the living God, the heavenly Jerusalem, and to thousands of angels in joyful assembly" (Hebrews 12:22 NLT). Chapter 21 will describe that new city—the New Jerusalem. This scene pictures the ultimate victory of Christ and his followers. The battle may be raging on earth, but the war has already been won.

Standing with the Lamb are *144,000 who had his name and his Father's name written on their foreheads.* This contrasts with the reference in 13:16 to the unbelievers on earth who had received the mark of the beast on their foreheads.

This group of 144,000 represents the same spiritual reality as the group of 144,000 in 7:4, the number symbolizing completeness (see commentary on 7:4). The 144,000 mentioned in 7:4 had been sealed against the difficulties to come on earth. That is, all those who have been or will be saved are protected spiritually and sealed for heaven. In this passage, all those who had been sealed and promised heaven were standing with Christ. In other words, no believers will be lost, forgotten, or misplaced. Everyone who has been sealed with God's seal will one day be with Christ. All believers throughout history will be with Christ. The promise is certain. The number will be complete.

14:2 And I heard a sound from heaven like the roaring of a great waterfall or the rolling of mighty thunder. It was like the sound of many harpists playing together.^{NLT} John heard *a sound from heaven.* He described it as *the roaring of a great waterfall or the rolling of mighty thunder.* The voices he had heard previously had been from Christ (1:10-15; 4:1; 10:7-8; 11:12), the living creatures (6:1-7), an angel (5:2; 7:2), many angels (5:11-12), all of creation (5:13), the souls under the altar (6:10), and the eagle (8:13). Many different voices had spoken to John in his vision. Thus far, he has described them as sounding like "thunder" or a "waterfall." Here he also described the sound as *many harpists playing together.* This scene of great rejoicing in heaven includes victorious singing and instrumental music. This was not an angelic choir singing, but the 144,000 who had been redeemed (14:3).

HEAVENLY HARPS
The harps of heaven have received more than their share of abuse in people's imaginations. How often has eternal life been described as cherubs floating on clouds while plucking on odd-shaped stringed instruments?
   The Greek word used here (and in 5:8; 15:2; 18:22) is the source of our word "guitar" *(kithara).* This may improve your anticipation about the sounds of heaven. The presence of harps in heaven points to some exciting possibilities for us: (1) God may well include countless new learning opportunities in heaven; (2) our understanding of God will be so heightened that any opportunity to increase our praise will simply expand our own joy; and perhaps (3) some of us will finally learn to play a musical instrument.

14:3 And they sang a new song before the throne and before the four living creatures and the elders. No one could learn the song except the 144,000 who had been redeemed from the earth.^{NIV} The 144,000 who had been sealed by God and brought to their reward in heaven *sang a new song before the* *throne and before the four living creatures and the elders* (see commentary on 4:4 and 4:6). The angel choir had sung a "new song" in 5:9, but the new song mentioned here could only be sung by the people who had been *redeemed from the earth—* purchased by the blood of the Lamb (see also 7:14; 12:11; 19:13). The angels, creatures, and elders could not sing it, for they had not experienced redemption from sin so they could not *learn the song.* The redeemed sang a glorious song of praise to the Lamb, who was standing with them, and the hosts of heaven were the audience. Only because of his sacrifice were they able to be in heaven.

14:4-5 For they are spiritually undefiled, pure as virgins, following the Lamb wherever he goes. They have been purchased from among the people on the earth as a special offering to God and to the Lamb. No falsehood can be charged against them; they are blameless.^{NLT} *They* refers to the 144,000, the true believers whose robes had been washed and made white in Christ's blood (7:14) through his death. They are described as:

- spiritually undefiled but remaining pure,
- following the Lamb,
- purchased from among the people on the earth,
- offered as a special offering,
- not lying, and
- blameless.

The phrase "spiritually undefiled, pure as virgins" means that these had not been involved with the pagan world system. In the Old Testament, idolatry was often portrayed as spiritual adultery (Jeremiah 3:6; Hosea 2:5). Paul wrote of the church, "I promised you as a pure bride to one husband, Christ" (2 Corinthians 11:2 NLT). These believers were spiritually pure; they had remained faithful to Christ. They are pictured as the pure bride of Christ (see also 21:9).

They were *following the Lamb wherever he goes,* indicating that they had followed him exclusively—referring to following Christ's instructions and his example. Jesus had told his followers, "If any of you wants to be my follower . . . you must put aside your selfish ambition, shoulder your cross, and follow me. If you try to keep your life for yourself, you will lose it. But if you give up your life for my sake and for the sake of the Good News, you will find true life" (Mark 8:34-35 NLT). Some may also have followed Christ to martyrdom for their faith— dying, as he also had died.

That they *have been purchased from among people* means that
Christ had bought them with his blood (5:9; 7:14; 12:11; 19:13).
The price of people's sin was paid on the cross—a free gift.
But only those who accept that gift are saved. Paul had told the
leaders of the church in Ephesus, "Be shepherds of the church of
God, which he bought with his own blood" (Acts 20:28 NIV), and
he had reminded the believers in Corinth, "You are not your own;
you were bought at a price" (1 Corinthians 6:19-20 NIV).

The phrase "a special offering to God and the Lamb" (also translated "firstfruits" NIV) refers to the act of dedicating the first part of
the harvest as holy to God (Exodus 23:19; see also James 1:18).
These believers had been dedicated solely and completely to God.
They belonged to no one else—and never would.

No falsehood was found in these believers' mouths—*they
are blameless.* These believers, bought by Christ's blood and
redeemed, had also been made perfect in the presence of the Lamb.
In contrast to the evil world that loves "to live a lie" (22:15 NLT),
these people were blameless because of their faith in Christ.

UNDEFILED
Two qualities of the 144,000 redeemed believers stand out:
"They are spiritually undefiled, pure as virgins" and they are
"following the Lamb wherever he goes."

(1) Spiritual purity is not popular today, but God requires it
of his followers. To remain spiritually pure means resisting the
seductions and idolatries of the present world—power, wealth,
and sexual immorality. To do so requires daily application of God's
Word, for it has a purifying effect on the mind and heart. It
requires great resolution not to give in to these temptations.
Stand strong and don't give in.

(2) Following Christ, the Lamb, requires heroic effort to carry
out Christ's commission to face oppression and even death if
required. Too many shrink back when the work is difficult or the
future looks bleak. Join those who take their stand with Christ and
against sin.

THE THREE ANGELS / 14:6-12

In this section, three angels contrast the destiny of believers with
that of unbelievers. This is a transition between the picture of the
coming triumph of God's people and the pouring out of the seven
bowl judgments upon the earth. God will judge evil.

14:6-7 **Then I saw another angel flying in midair, and he had the eternal gospel to proclaim to those who live on the earth—to every
nation, tribe, language and people. He said in a loud voice,**

"Fear God and give him glory, because the hour of his judgment has come. Worship him who made the heavens, the earth, the sea and the springs of water."[NIV] *Another angel* flew and announced a message to the people of the earth (as did the eagle in 8:13). This angel had *the eternal gospel to proclaim to those who live on the earth,* described as *every nation, tribe, language and people* (for the same phrase, see also 7:9; 11:9; 13:7). The angel's message called people to *fear God* and *worship* him *because the hour of his judgment has come.* The "eternal gospel" was still the Good News. Even in these final moments of judgment, God gave the people the opportunity to repent. This may be the final fulfillment of Jesus' prophecy, "Unless the Lord shortens that time of calamity, the entire human race will be destroyed. But for the sake of his chosen ones he has shortened those days" (Mark 13:20 NLT).

The phrase "fear God and give him glory" is the essence of the believers' duty to God. The word "fear" refers to respect and reverential awe. The word "glory" means to recognize God's power and give him the honor he is due.

Some commentators see this as an announcement of judgment rather than as an appeal. The people of the world have had their chance to proclaim their allegiance to God, and now God's great judgment is about to begin. Most likely, however, this is a final, worldwide appeal to all people to recognize the one true God. No one would have the excuse of never hearing God's truth. Because this is the vision of a scene in the future, it is unknown if God will, at that point, give the world one more chance. What is known, however, is that he offers that chance to those who read and study John's vision now.

The message is proclaimed to everyone; therefore, no one can have the excuse that they did not know the gospel message. As Paul said in Romans, "They have no excuse whatsoever for not knowing God" (Romans 1:20 NLT). This is a key theme of Revelation—whenever there has been a time of judgment, there has been a preceding time of warning, when people are given the opportunity to repent. However, those who refuse want nothing to do with God; their punishment is justified.

NOTHING TO FEAR
If you are reading this, you have already heard God's truth. You know that God's final judgment will not be put off forever. Have you joyfully received the everlasting Good News? Have you confessed your sins and trusted in Christ to save you? If so, you have nothing to fear from God's judgment. The Judge of all the earth is your Savior!

CITIZENS OF HELL

Who will be in hell? Sadly, hell will be populated by people who have willingly rebelled against God and stubbornly refused any offer of repentance. (Verses are quoted from NLT.)

Reference	Verse
Matthew 25:41-46	". . . Away with you, you cursed ones, into the eternal fire prepared for the Devil and his demons! For I was hungry, and you didn't feed me . . . when you refused to help the least of these my brothers and sisters, you were refusing to help me."
Romans 6:23	"For the wages of sin is death . . ."
1 Corinthians 6:9-11	". . . Those who do wrong will have no share in the Kingdom of God . . . Those who indulge in sexual sin, who are idol worshipers, adulterers, male prostitutes, homosexuals, thieves, greedy people, drunkards, abusers, and swindlers—none of these will have a share in the Kingdom of God."
2 Peter 2:4	"For God did not spare even the angels when they sinned; he threw them into hell . . ."
Revelation 20:10	"Then the Devil, who betrayed them, was thrown into the lake of fire that burns with sulfur, joining the beast and the false prophet. There they will be tormented day and night forever and ever."
Revelation 20:15	"Anyone whose name was not found recorded in the Book of Life was thrown into the lake of fire."
Revelation 21:8	"But cowards who turn away from me, and unbelievers, and the corrupt, and murderers, and the immoral, and those who practice witchcraft, and idol worshipers, and all liars—their doom is in the lake that burns with fire and sulfur. This is the second death."
Revelation 21:27	"Nothing evil will be allowed to enter [heaven]—no one who practices shameful idolatry and dishonesty—but only those whose names are written in the Lamb's Book of Life."

14:8 Then another angel followed him through the skies, shouting, "Babylon is fallen—that great city is fallen—because she seduced the nations of the world and made them drink the wine of her passionate immorality."[NLT] A second *angel followed* the first angel *through the skies.* The angel shouted that *Babylon—that great city is fallen* (see also Isaiah 21:9; Jeremiah 51:8). In the Old Testament, Babylon was the name of both an evil city and an immoral empire—a world center for idol worship. Outside that city, Nebuchadnezzar had built a great statue to himself and had required everyone to worship it (Daniel 3:1-6; compare Revelation 13:14-15). King Nebuchadnezzar had reached the apex of power and pride, only to find himself judged by God (Daniel 4:28-33). The Babylonians had ransacked Jerusalem and had taken many of the people of Judah into captivity (see 2 Kings 24 and 2 Chronicles 36). Just as Babylon had been Judah's worst enemy, the Roman Empire was the worst enemy of the early Christians. John, who probably did not dare speak openly against Rome, was applying the name "Babylon" to this enemy of God's people (Rome)—and, by extension, to all of God's enemies of all times.

> God will never send anybody to hell. If man goes to hell, he goes by his own free choice. . . . God has done everything within His power to keep you out. He even gave His Son to die on that cross to keep you out. . . . You can go to heaven or to hell. The choice is yours.   *Billy Graham*

"Babylon" is the name given to the civilization that was seduced by the beast (see also 17:1-9). This world system is filled with idolatry, corruption, and sexual sin (18:2-3, 7), a wellspring of ungodly religion, government, and economics.

The angel's words here are a prediction: the actual fall of the city would not occur until the judgment of the last bowl (16:19). God would judge this evil power *because she seduced the nations of the world and made them drink the wine of her passionate immorality.* Later, Babylon is described as the "great prostitute" with whom the rulers of the world have had "immoral relations" and the people who belong to this world have "been made drunk by the wine of her immorality" (17:2 NLT). This draws from the prophecy of Jeremiah, "Babylon has been like a golden cup in the Lord's hands, a cup from which he made the whole earth drink and go mad" (Jeremiah 51:7 NLT). This pictures the godlessness and sinfulness of those who have been lured away from God into a world system that fulfills their lusts and passions but ultimately destroys them. Ultimately, God will destroy this evil and judge the people.

14:9-11 **Then a third angel followed them, shouting, "Anyone who worships the beast and his statue or who accepts his mark on the forehead or the hand must drink the wine of God's wrath. It is poured out undiluted into God's cup of wrath. And they will be tormented with fire and burning sulfur in the presence of the holy angels and the Lamb. The smoke of their torment rises forever and ever, and they will have**

**no relief day or night, for they have worshiped the beast
and his statue and have accepted the mark of his name.**"ᴺᴸᵀ
A *third* angel *followed* the first two, *shouting* a warning to *anyone who worships the beast and his statue* (13:14), or *accepts
his mark on the forehead or the hand,* so that they can continue
to function in the world (13:16-18).

In chapter 13, the believers were told how difficult it would be
for them if they refused the mark of the beast. In these verses, an
angel explained to the nonbelievers what would happen to them
if they *do* receive the mark of the beast. Their eventual judgment
would be much worse and the consequences eternal. While those
who belong to God would suffer and be killed, they would have a
glorious eternity awaiting them (14:1-5). Those who worship the
beast and accept his mark, however, would be choosing to operate according to the Antichrist's world economic system and
would ultimately face God's judgment. To get what the world values, these people would have turned away from God and violated
Christian principles.

Thus, they must *drink the wine of God's wrath.* The Old
Testament often pictures God's anger as being in a cup, ready
to be poured out (see Job 21:20; Psalm 75:8; Isaiah 51:17;
Jeremiah 25:15-38). This cup of wrath is "undiluted." This
refers (in antithetical form) to the normal Roman practice of
diluting wine with water. God's wrath will be in its strongest
form. The full extent of his anger, undiluted by mercy and
grace, would soon be poured out on those who had adamantly
refused to turn from sin and receive his salvation.

Their future torment will be *with fire and burning sulfur*—
a picture taken from the destruction of Sodom and Gomorrah,
sinful cities that the Lord had destroyed with "fire and burning
sulfur" rained down from heaven (Genesis 19:24). Fire and
sulfur are used as instruments of torture in 19:20; 20:10; and
21:8. The actual picture may be symbolic, but there is no doubt
as to the horror and finality of this judgment, for *the smoke of
their torment rises forever and ever.* In contrast to the redeemed
who could "rest from all their toils and trials" (14:13 NLT), the
unbelievers would have *no relief day or night* from their torment. Having chosen the side of the *beast,* they would suffer
for it. Jesus described eternal punishment as "unquenchable
fires" (Mark 9:44 NLT). For more on eternal punishment, see
commentary at 20:10.

God has promised that he will punish sin (Romans 2:6-11;
12:19). The wicked will be paid back for how they have
rejected God and mistreated their fellow human beings
(Matthew 13:41-42; 16:27). Jesus promised that Satan, his

demons, and the wicked would be thrown into hell at the final
judgment (Matthew 25:41). Although Scripture uses images
of fiery sulfur, destruction, and darkness for hell (Matthew
7:13; 18:8; Jude 13; Revelation 14:10), few details are given.
Jesus used the Greek word *gehenna* to describe hell. The
word alludes to the valley of Ben Hinnom, where, at times,
Old Testament Israelites would sacrifice their children to false
gods (2 Chronicles 28:3), and later where they burned their
garbage and refuse (Jeremiah 7:31). Jesus repeatedly warned
that hell would be a fate far worse than physical death. Scripture consistently describes hell as a place where one is utterly
alone, rejected by one's Creator, and excluded from his presence (Matthew 25:12, 41; Luke 13:24-28; 2 Thessalonians
1:8-9).

ETERNAL SEPARATION
The ultimate result of sin is unending separation from God.
Because human beings are created in God's image with an
inborn thirst for fellowship with him, separation from God will
be the ultimate torment and misery. Sin always brings misery,
but in this life we can choose to repent and restore our relationship with God. In eternity, there will no longer be opportunity
for repentance. If in this life we choose to be independent of
God, in the next life we will be separated from him forever.
Nobody is forced to choose eternal separation from God, and
nobody suffers this fate by accident. What neighbor, coworker,
friend, or relative needs to hear the Good News of God's
grace? Consider how you can tell him or her soon, before it's
too late.

**14:12 Let this encourage God's holy people to endure persecution
patiently and remain firm to the end, obeying his commands and trusting in Jesus.**[NLT] A similar statement is in
13:10 regarding the difficulties that believers will face under
the Antichrist: "But do not be dismayed, for here is your opportunity to have endurance and faith" (NLT). This verse follows
the promise of God's punishment for the wicked as an encouragement *to God's holy people to endure persecution patiently
and remain firm to the end.* The phrase "endure persecution
patiently" does not refer to a way to be saved. Instead, such
endurance is evidence that a person is really committed to
Jesus. Persistence is not a means to earn salvation but the
by-product of a truly devoted life (see Matthew 10:22; 2 Thessalonians 1:4). To "remain firm" will take perseverance
because believers' faith will be challenged and opposed. The
assurance of salvation will keep believers strong in times of

PERSEVERE TO THE END

Scripture Verse	Lesson
Luke 21:19—"By standing firm, you will gain life." (NIV)	Perseverance grows out of commitment to Jesus Christ. Standing firm is not the way to be saved but the evidence that a person is really committed to Jesus. Endurance is not a means to earn salvation; it is the by-product of a truly devoted life.
2 Timothy 4:5—"But you should keep a clear mind in every situation. Don't be afraid of suffering for the Lord. Work at bringing others to Christ. Complete the ministry God has given you." (NLT).	God will make believers' perseverance worthwhile. He will help his people complete whatever work he has called them to do; he will help them draw others into the kingdom.
Hebrews 3:6—"But Christ, the faithful Son, was in charge of the entire household. And we are God's household, if we keep up our courage and remain confident in our hope in Christ." (NLT)	Perseverance keeps believers courageous and hopeful because they can trust Christ. Because Christ lives in Christians and because he is completely trustworthy to fulfill all his promises, believers can remain courageous and hopeful.
Revelation 14:12—"This calls for patient endurance on the part of the saints who obey God's command-ments and remain faithful to Jesus." (NIV).	Believers' ability to persevere is related to the quality of our relationship with God. The secret to perseverance is trust and obedience. Trust God to give you the patience to endure even the small trials you face daily. The fact of God's ultimate triumph can encourage believers to remain steadfast in their faith through every trial and persecution.

persecution (see Mark 13:13; 2 Timothy 4:5; Hebrews 3:6, 14). This news about God's ultimate triumph should encourage God's people to remain faithful through every trial and persecu-tion, even death. The result of refusing to worship the Anti-christ will be temporal; but the result of turning from Christ will be eternal.

THE HARVEST OF THE EARTH / 14:13-20

The final verses of this chapter give two visions of final judg-ment. Verses 14-16 describe the harvest of the earth compared to a grain harvest. Verses 17-20 picture the horror of this final judg-ment of God upon sin.

PATIENT AND FIRM
Jesus said to rejoice when we're persecuted. Persecution can be good because (1) it takes our eyes off earthly rewards, (2) it strips away superficial belief, (3) it strengthens the faith of those who endure, and (4) our attitude through it serves as an example to others who follow. We can be comforted to know that many of God's prophets were persecuted (Elijah, Jeremiah, Daniel). The fact that we are being persecuted proves that we have been faithful. Eventually, God will reward the faithful by receiving them into his eternal kingdom, where there will be no more persecution.

In the midst of terrible persecution, we can have hope, knowing that salvation is ours. Times of trial serve to sift true Christians from false or fair-weather Christians. When you are pressured to give up and turn your back on Christ, don't do it. Remember the benefits of standing firm, and continue to live for Christ.

14:13 And I heard a voice from heaven saying, "Write this down: Blessed are those who die in the Lord from now on. Yes, says the Spirit, they are blessed indeed, for they will rest from all their toils and trials; for their good deeds follow them!"[NLT] The angels had spoken, and John heard another *voice from heaven.* This time John was commanded to *write this down,* emphasizing its importance to the readers. The voice pronounced the second of seven beatitudes in Revelation: *Blessed are those who die in the Lord from now on.* (The first beatitude is in

> The blood of the martyrs is seed. *Tertullian*

1:3.) Believers would face persecution and death at the hands of the Antichrist and his worldwide power and influence. The phrase "from now on" doesn't mean that some martyrs for the faith would not be blessed; in fact, those already dead are waiting for the final vindication (6:9-11). The phrase probably means that they are blessed from the moment of their death because they immediately go to be with Christ. As persecution increases, such blessing is just as certain for those who remain faithful. To "die in the Lord" does not necessarily refer to martyrdom; all believers die "in the Lord" and go to heaven to be with Christ.

Those who die in the Lord *are blessed indeed, for they will rest from all their toils and trials.* The torment of unbelievers will leave them with "no rest day or night" (14:11 NRSV), but the believers who go to be with Christ will have "rest." This "rest" does not mean that heaven will be one big easy chair. The "toils" and "trials" refer to the difficulties of remaining steadfast in the faith in the evil world. Their "rest" is the cessation of persecution. In addition, *their good deeds follow them.* The unbelievers may have done

BEATITUDES IN REVELATION

Seven times in Revelation, God promises blessings upon the believers. (Verses are quoted from NLT.)

Reference	Verse
1:3	"God blesses the one who reads this prophecy to the church, and he blesses all who listen to it and obey what it says."
14:13	"Blessed are those who die in the Lord from now on. Yes, says the Spirit, they are blessed indeed, for they will rest from all their toils and trials; for their good deeds follow them!"
16:15	"Blessed are all who are watching for me, who keep their robes ready so they will not need to walk naked and ashamed."
19:9	"Blessed are those who are invited to the wedding feast of the Lamb."
20:6	"Blessed and holy are those who share in the first resurrection. For them the second death holds no power, but they will be priests of God and of Christ and will reign with him a thousand years."
22:7	"Blessed are those who obey the prophecy written in this scroll."
22:14	"Blessed are those who wash their robes so they can enter through the gates of the city and eat the fruit from the tree of life."

some "good deeds" during their time on earth, but those deeds will not save them. In the end, those good deeds will be destroyed. But God remembers believers' good deeds; indeed, they are the basis for the rewards he will give (1 Corinthians 3:13-15; Ephesians 6:8).

PRODUCING ETERNAL PRODUCE
While it is true that money, fame, and belongings can't be taken with us from this life, God's people *can* produce fruit that survives even death. God will remember our love, kindness, and faithfulness. Furthermore, those who accept Christ through our witness will join us in the new earth. Be sure that your values are in line with God's values, and decide today to produce fruit that lasts forever.

14:14 Then I looked, and there was a white cloud, and seated on the cloud was one like the Son of Man, with a golden crown on his head, and a sharp sickle in his hand![NRSV] This is an image of judgment: *one like the Son of Man* is *seated on the cloud* separating the faithful from the unfaithful like a farmer harvesting his crops. This will be a time of joy for Christians who have been persecuted and martyred because they will receive their long-awaited reward. Christians should not fear the Last Judgment. Jesus said, "I assure you, those who listen to my message and believe in God who sent me have eternal life. They will never be condemned for their sins, but they have already passed from death into life" (John 5:24 NLT).

The identity of the "one like the Son of Man" has been debated. Some suggest that it is Christ (see also Daniel 7:13-14). Others believe that it is not Christ, but another angel, because in 14:15 "another angel" gives this one a command (to begin harvesting), and they don't think that Christ would be commanded by an angel. Most likely, however, this is Christ, for nowhere else in Scripture is an angel designated as "like the Son of Man." In the vision, Christ may be waiting for the angelic messenger to announce the time of the harvest, just as other angels have announced the judgments. He wore *a golden crown on his head, and he had a sharp sickle in his hand*—waiting for the announcement that the harvest of the earth was to begin.

14:15-16 **Then another angel came out of the temple and called in a loud voice to him who was sitting on the cloud, "Take your sickle and reap, because the time to reap has come, for the harvest of the earth is ripe." So he who was seated on the cloud swung his sickle over the earth, and the earth was harvested.**[NIV] *Another angel came out of the temple*—referring to the presence of God—bringing with him the command to *begin reaping*.

The phrase "the harvest of the earth is ripe" takes the Old Testament picture of divine judgment as a "harvest" (see Jeremiah 51:33; Hosea 6:11; Joel 3:13). One of Jesus' parables also describes the end times as a harvest: "Let both grow together until the harvest. Then I will tell the harvesters to sort out the weeds and burn them and to put the wheat in the barn" (Matthew 13:30 NLT).

Without any further detail, the one *seated on the cloud swung his sickle over the earth, and the earth was harvested.* There is some debate about who was being harvested—God's people, or the sinners. Some scholars have suggested that 14:14-16 pictures the harvesting of God's people, while 14:17-18 pictures the harvest of sinners. Most likely, however, as Jesus' parable seems to indicate, 14:14-16 indicates the harvest of all people. This is a general picture of the final judgment, with the elect being taken to heaven and the unbelievers being sent to eternal punishment, as recorded in the following verses.

14:17-18 **After that, another angel came from the Temple in heaven,
and he also had a sharp sickle. Then another angel, who has
power to destroy the world with fire, shouted to the angel
with the sickle, "Use your sickle now to gather the clusters of
grapes from the vines of the earth, for they are fully ripe for
judgment."**NLT *Another angel* arrived *from the Temple in heaven,*
also from the presence of God (14:15). This angel *also had a
sharp sickle.* This is probably a third picture of the same reality
of coming judgment. First was the cup of unmixed wine to be
poured out (14:10), second was the grain harvest (14:15-16), and
third was the grape harvest (14:17-20). This third image stresses
the violent nature of this final judgment. The Old Testament also
pictures divine judgment as a grape harvest (see Isaiah 63:1-6;
Lamentations 1:15; Joel 3:13). Revelation 19:15 describes the
return of the victorious Christ: "He trod the winepress of the
fierce wrath of almighty God" (NLT).

The angel *who has power to destroy the world with fire* could
refer to the angel who had authority over the fire on the altar
(8:3-5). The altar is connected both with the souls of the martyrs
(6:9) and the prayers of the saints (8:3), both of which play a part
in bringing about this final drama of ultimate judgment.

The angel with the sickle is told to *gather the clusters of
grapes from the vines of the earth, for they are fully ripe for judgment.* While the previous picture of the harvest in 14:14-16 may
have pictured both the bringing of the righteous to heaven and
the destruction of the wicked, this picture is only of the judgment
of the wicked. The clusters of grapes probably have no special
symbolism other than indicating that the time for harvest had
come. They were "ripe for judgment," which means there would
be no more waiting.

14:19-20 **The angel swung his sickle on the earth, gathered its grapes
and threw them into the great winepress of God's wrath.
They were trampled in the winepress outside the city, and
blood flowed out of the press, rising as high as the horses'
bridles for a distance of 1,600 stadia.**NIV Obeying the command (14:18), the angel with the sickle *swung* it across the
earth and *gathered its grapes* (picturing the unbelievers who
will receive punishment) *into the great winepress of God's
wrath.* A "winepress" was a large vat or trough where grapes
would be collected and then smashed. The juice would flow out
of a duct that led into a large holding vat. The unbelievers are
collected and *trampled in the winepress outside the city,* possibly referring to Jerusalem. Since Jesus was crucified outside
the walls of Jerusalem, this great scene of judgment is pictured

there (see also Joel 3:12-14; Zechariah 14:1-4; John 19:20; Hebrews 13:12).

The grisly detail of the blood flowing out pictures the ultimate horror of this judgment. The distance of *1,600 stadia* equals about 180 miles, approximately the north-south length of Palestine. Others suggest that 1,600 squares the number 4 (for the four corners of the earth) and multiplies by 1,000 or the square of 10 (signifying both the entire world and completeness). The hyperbole is meant to show the total and complete destruction of the wicked.

GRAPES OF WRATH
To those unaccustomed to vivid descriptions of God's anger in judgment, these are disturbing images. People dislike the idea of other people, even evil ones, being trampled like grapes. The depth and length of the blood flow provides a sickening scene of the immensity of God's judgment. But unless we face the necessity of God's judgment, we will never see our desperate need for his mercy. A god with only grandfatherly kindness would not inspire our repentance, obedience, or worship. God has promised a harsh harvest for those who reject him. Those who know God well enough to fear his wrath know God well enough to desire his grace. The crushing wrath of God is coming. Blessed are those who have had their sins forgiven, and blessed are those who lead others to God's mercy.

Revelation 15

Seven angels were given seven bowls from which they would pour out the seven "bowl judgments," the last plagues to be visited upon the earth. These plagues would bring the final and complete punishment upon wickedness. These would bring about the end of the Antichrist's reign.

Some believe that all of this will occur at the end of the seven-year period of tribulation, with the seven bowls following in rapid succession after the seal and trumpet judgments. Others who see the book of Revelation as presenting a series of cyclical events say that this is the most severe of the series of seven judgments, also heralding the end.

15:1 I saw in heaven another great and marvelous sign: seven angels with the seven last plagues—last, because with them God's wrath is completed.[NIV] This next event that John *saw in heaven* is also called *another great and marvelous sign.* The vision of the woman in 12:1 was "a great and wondrous sign" (NIV), and the vision of the dragon in 12:3 was a "sign" (NIV). Clearly, these symbols point to significant events.

John described *seven angels* who had *the seven last plagues.* These plagues were in golden bowls, given to these angels by one of the four living creatures (15:6-7). The seven last plagues are also called the seven bowl judgments. They actually begin in the next chapter. Unlike the previous plagues from the seals, which had destroyed one-fourth of the earth (chapters 6–8), and the trumpets, which had destroyed another third of the earth (chapters 8–11), these plagues were directed only against the Antichrist's followers but affected the entire earth. These judgments were complete and final, culminating in the abolition of all evil and the end of the world.

The seven bowls were directed to every part of the world: the land, the sea, rivers and lakes, the sky, and the beast's (Antichrist's) kingdom. These plagues would be filled with horrors, but the sign itself was "great and marvelous" because through these plagues God would end the reign of terror by the Antichrist, the reign of Satan, and evil itself.

15:2 And I saw what looked like a sea of glass mixed with fire and, standing beside the sea, those who had been victorious over the beast and his image and over the number of his name. They held harps given them by God.^{NIV} John *saw what looked like a sea of glass mixed with fire.* This is similar to the "sea of glass" described in 4:6, located before the throne of God. Here it was mixed with fire to represent wrath and judgment. Those who stood beside it had been *victorious over the beast* (the Antichrist, 13:1ff), *and his image* (13:14), *and over the number of his name* (13:18). Those who had "been victorious" were those who had refused to receive the mark of the beast, had refused to worship his image, and thus had faced persecution, difficulty, and perhaps even martyrdom. This is the complete group of all believers (see also 14:1-5). Clearly they were preparing for a song of worship and praise (see also 5:8).

15:3-4 And sang the song of Moses the servant of God and the song of the Lamb: "Great and marvelous are your deeds, Lord God Almighty. Just and true are your ways, King of the ages. Who will not fear you, O Lord, and bring glory to your name? For you alone are holy. All nations will come and worship before you, for your righteous acts have been revealed."^{NIV} The *song of Moses* had celebrated Israel's deliverance from Egypt and the defeat of the Egyptian army at the Red Sea (Exodus 15). The song would be sung in the afternoon service each Sabbath as a reminder to the Jews of God's deliverance and sovereignty.

The *song of the Lamb* here celebrated the ultimate deliverance of God's people from the power of Satan. John was describing not two separate songs but one song celebrating deliverance and victory. They had been delivered from the power of the Antichrist, but they were in heaven because they had been delivered from sin through the death of the Lamb.

Each line comes from a phrase in the Old Testament psalms or prophets.

Great and marvelous are your deeds (Exodus 15:11; Psalms 86:10; 139:14)
Lord God Almighty (Amos 4:13)
Just and true are your ways (Deuteronomy 32:4)
Who will not fear you, and bring glory to your name (Jeremiah 10:7; Psalm 86:9)
You alone are holy (Psalm 99:9)
All nations will come and worship before you (Psalm 86:9; Malachi 1:11; Revelation 14:6-7)
Your righteous acts have been revealed (Psalm 98:2)

The song glorifies God and his ultimate victory over all the world. That "all nations will come and worship" him does not mean that eventually everyone will be saved. The thought is very much like that recorded in Philippians 2, "at the name of Jesus every knee will bow"; it means that whether in grateful worship or defeated submission, eventually all nations will give the honor to Christ that is his due (see commentary at 14:6-7).

JUST AND TRUE
John quotes the song of Moses and the Lamb, "Just and true are your ways, King of the ages." Can we sing that song whole-heartedly? Some believers falter quickly in their commitment to God and the justice of his ways when they are confronted with personal trials and difficulties.
Beware of the following pitfalls to trusting God's control:

- *Questioning God's timing*—we may say that God is just but challenge his timetable. Trusting God means resting in his choice of methods and sequence, even when they don't coincide with our preferences.
- *Resenting the outcome*—we may say that we trust God and then rebel at his decision to take a loved one or to end a cherished relationship. We do not know the future, so resenting his decisions is premature. Trusting God means letting him determine the outcome.
- *Quarreling over a pet issue*—we may say that God is good and then question his decisions, getting bogged down defending God and his treatment of a sincere pagan or an unreached but innocent child. This intellectualism may cause us to doubt God's goodness. Taken to the extreme, these doubts may cause indecision and weaken our trust in God.

Have patience and trust God to be as just and wise in the future as he has been in the past.

15:5-6 **After this I looked and in heaven the temple, that is, the tabernacle of the Testimony, was opened. Out of the temple came the seven angels with the seven plagues. They were dressed in clean, shining linen and wore golden sashes around their chests.**[NIV] The *tabernacle of the Testimony* is a Greek translation for the Hebrew "Tent of Meeting" (see Numbers 17:7; 18:2). The imagery recalls the Exodus in the wilderness when the ark of the covenant (the symbol of God's presence among his people) resided in the tabernacle. The tabernacle was a portable place of worship that the Israelites would carry with them as they journeyed through the wilderness. Later, when they settled in the Promised Land, a permanent structure was built—the temple. Both words, tabernacle and temple, refer to the place of God's residence among his people.

John again saw this "tabernacle" *opened* (see also 11:19). The *seven angels* who come out of the temple *were dressed in clean, shining linen and wore golden sashes around their chests* (see also Daniel 10:5). Their garments, reminiscent of the high priest's clothing (and of Christ's—1:13), show that they were free from corruption, immorality, and injustice. They had come out from God's presence to do God's bidding. These angels would be in charge of the *seven plagues*—that is, the bowls with the plagues—just as seven angels had blown the seven trumpets (8:6).

15:7-8 **Then one of the four living creatures gave to the seven angels seven golden bowls filled with the wrath of God, who lives for ever and ever. And the temple was filled with smoke from the glory of God and from his power, and no one could enter the temple until the seven plagues of the seven angels were completed.**NIV In what appears to be a solemn ceremony, *one of the four living creatures* (see commentary at 4:6) *gave seven golden bowls to the seven angels.* These four living creatures, identified as powerful angels, are mentioned several times in Revelation (4:6; 5:6; 6:1; 7:11; 14:3; 15:7; 19:4). One of these four creatures gave each angel a golden bowl.

Bowls (also called basins) would be used in the temple for various purposes, such as collecting the blood of the sacrifices (Exodus 27:3; 1 Kings 7:50; 2 Kings 25:15). In this case, these bowls were *filled with the wrath of God* which would be poured out on the earth. When these bowls would be poured out, there would be no escape, and the judgment would be complete. This destruction is described in the bowl judgments. The *smoke* that filled the temple is the manifestation of God's *glory* and power (see also Exodus 19:18; 40:34-35; 1 Kings 8:10-11; Isaiah 6:4).

God's glory filled the temple, appearing like smoke, and God set in motion the final phase of judgment. The fact that *no one* would be able to *enter the temple until the seven plagues of the seven angels were completed* indicates that the time for intercession had passed. No one could come before God to stay his hand. It seems that even the time of worship and praise was suspended as God brought about this final act of history. It is as if heaven was waiting.

THE ONLY RESPONSE
John saw the Temple filled with the glory and power of God. The key to God's eternal glory and power is his holiness (4:8). God's glory is not only his strength but also his perfect moral character. God will never do anything that is not morally perfect. This reassures us that we can trust him, yet it places a demand on us. Our desire to be holy (dedicated to God and morally pure) is our only suitable response.

Revelation 16

This is the third of the three sets of judgments. First came the seal judgments (6:1–8:5), then the trumpet judgments (8:6–11:19), and finally the bowl judgments (16:1-21). Some view these three sets of judgments as one set of events with three different descriptions; some see them as occurring consecutively; others see repetition with increasing intensity. For more on these views, see the introductory comments on chapter 6. How these events will unfold is not revealed, but regardless of what happens, God will be completely in control. He will judge an evil and rebellious world.

These bowl judgments are very similar to the trumpet judgments, affecting every part of the world. The first four bowls, like the first four trumpets, affect the earth, sea, inland waters, and the sky; the last three affect humanity. The trumpet and the bowl judgments differ in three main ways: (1) the bowl judgments are complete, whereas the trumpet judgments are partial; (2) the trumpet judgments give unbelievers the opportunity to repent, but the bowl judgments do not; and (3) mankind is indirectly affected by several of the trumpet judgments but is directly attacked by all the bowl judgments.

Just as the trumpet judgments, the bowl judgments reenact the plagues of Egypt as recorded in Exodus 7–12 (see also the introductory comments at 8:6). The Egyptian plagues have the same purpose as the bowls of wrath—to prove to the world that God is all-powerful.

16:1 **Then I heard a mighty voice shouting from the Temple to the seven angels, "Now go your ways and empty out the seven bowls of God's wrath on the earth."**^{NLT} The scene in chapter 15 had been at the *Temple* of God in heaven, from which *seven angels* had come (15:5-8). Each of these seven angels had been given "a gold bowl filled with the terrible wrath of God" (15:7 NLT). *A mighty voice* shouted *from the Temple.* Isaiah had heard a similar voice, "What is that terrible noise from the Temple? It is the voice of the Lord taking vengeance against his enemies"

THE SEVEN BOWLS

Bowl Judgment	Results	Reference
1. Horrible malignant sores break out on everyone who has the mark of the beast.	Physical pain comes to those who have not repented.	16:2
2. The sea becomes blood and everything in it dies.	With the death of the sea, all ecosystems are affected.	16:3
3. Inland waters turn to blood.	With the death of the inland waters, there is no water to drink.	16:4
4. The sun scorches people.	People burned by the heat curse God for it.	16:8
5. Darkness covers the earth.	People are in anguish because of the darkness, but they curse God and refuse to repent. They still have the sores from the first plague and the burns from the fourth plague.	16:10
6. The great Euphrates River dries up.	The drying up of the river provides a way for the armies of the east to march westward without hindrance and gather at the battlefield of Armageddon.	16:12
7. An earthquake greater than any that has ever occurred changes the face of the earth. Then comes a terrible hailstorm.	The great city of Babylon is destroyed, islands are engulfed, mountains are flattened. People continue to curse God.	16:17-21

(Isaiah 66:6 NLT). This was probably the voice of God, for 15:8 had said that "no one could enter the Temple until the seven angels had completed pouring out the seven plagues" (15:8 NLT). The voice commanded the angels, *"Go your ways and empty out the seven bowls of God's wrath on the earth."*

16:2 So the first angel left the Temple and poured out his bowl over the earth, and horrible, malignant sores broke out on everyone who had the mark of the beast and who worshiped his statue.NLT The outpouring of these bowls occurred in rapid succession, one right after the other, but the effects of each seem to have lingered. For example, the *malignant sores* that people get here still affect them during the fifth plague (16:10-11), along with the sunburns they received during the fourth plague.

When the *first angel* poured out his bowl *over the earth,* everyone *broke out* in horrible sores. This does not compare directly with the first trumpet (during which grass and trees were destroyed), but it does compare with another of the plagues on Egypt—the plague of boils (Exodus 9:10-11). These sores affected *everyone who had the mark of the beast* (13:16) *and who worshiped his statue* (13:14-15). God's wrath was only upon the unbelievers.

Those who subscribe to the pre-Tribulation theory assert that because the believers have already been raptured, those who become believers after the Rapture will still be on the earth but will be protected from these plagues. Those who subscribe to the mid-Tribulation theory say that just before these universal plagues hit, the believers are raptured so that the only people left on the earth at this point will be unbelievers. Those who subscribe to the post-Tribulation theory say that the believers are still on the earth going through this difficulty. But even as these plagues hit, the believers will be protected by the seal of Christ they have received (7:3) and the promise of protection (3:10).

16:3 Then the second angel poured out his bowl on the sea, and it became like the blood of a corpse. And everything in the sea died.NLT The *second angel poured out his bowl of wrath.* This time the sea *became like the blood of a corpse,* killing everything in it. During the second trumpet, a third of the water of the sea had become blood, killing a third of the sea creatures (8:8-9). This time, the entire sea turned to blood, killing *everything* in it (see also Exodus 7:20-21).

At the time of John's writing, the Roman Empire lived by sea trade and much of their food came from the sea. This type of judgment would devastate civilization (for more on the importance of the sea to the Roman Empire, see commentary at 8:9).

16:4 Then the third angel poured out his bowl on the rivers and springs, and they became blood.NLT The *third angel poured out his bowl* of God's wrath, and this time *the rivers and springs—* the inland waters—also turned to *blood.* During the third trumpet judgment, one-third of the rivers and springs were turned bitter so that they were undrinkable (8:10-11). In this bowl judgment, *all* the inland waters were affected, leaving people with nothing to drink. Water, a basic necessity for human life, was gone.

16:5-6 And I heard the angel who had authority over all water saying, "You are just in sending this judgment, O Holy One, who is and who always was. For your holy people and your prophets have been killed, and their blood was poured out on the

earth. So you have given their murderers blood to drink. It is their just reward."^{NLT} The horror of the plague of blood upon all water led to a pause in heaven, during which time *the angel who had authority over all water* explained the logic and justice of the plague. Ironically, those who had shed believers' blood were left with blood to drink. They are punished with the methods of their own crimes. The *holy people* and the *prophets* had been killed, their blood *poured out on the earth.* So the *just reward* for the murderers was to give them *blood to drink.* God's judgment reflects his righteous and just nature.

God is referred to as the *Holy One, who is and who always was.* The phrase "and who is still to come" (1:8 NLT) is here excluded because at this point there would be no more future. This is similar to the song of the victorious in 15:2-4. The end of time had arrived.

TRUTH AND JUSTICE
The angel acclaimed God for his justice in dealing with those who had killed the martyrs. God's wrath may be hard for us to accept. In a moral universe, however, God must ultimately oppose and destroy ultimate evil. Those who join the revolt against God suffer with their leaders.

We must avoid the common misconception that God must be fair and kind in his dealings with humanity. This view of justice is merely a projection of a human idea. People who believe this notion appeal to tolerance and forgiveness and assume that God must play by our rules. In reality, God sets his own standard of justice. He uses his power according to his own moral perfection. Thus, whatever he chooses or decrees is fair, even if we don't understand it or like it. Those who rebel and reject God are not rejecting a "lifestyle option," but they are rejecting truth and justice itself.

16:7 And I heard the altar respond: "Yes, Lord God Almighty, true and just are your judgments."^{NIV} The *altar* in the Temple responded to the song with, *"Yes, Lord God Almighty, true and just are your judgments."* This second voice confirmed what the angel had said (16:5). The personification of the altar acclaiming God shows that everyone and everything will praise God, acknowledging his righteousness and perfect justice. The "altar" could refer to the souls under the altar—the martyrs—who had been waiting for this day to arrive (6:9-11).

16:8-9 The fourth angel poured out his bowl on the sun, and the sun was given power to scorch people with fire. They were seared by the intense heat and they cursed the name of God, who had control over these plagues, but they refused to repent and glorify him.^{NIV} After a brief interlude, *the fourth* *angel poured out his bowl on the sun.* This intensified the sun's heat so that it scorched *people with fire.* The fourth trumpet had caused the sun and the moon to stop giving light for portions of the day (8:12). This fourth bowl was much more serious. This is a picture of a solar explosion that reaches out and scorches the earth with fire. Fire is a common theme for judgment in the Bible (see, for example, Deuteronomy 28:22; Luke 16:24; 1 Corinthians 3:13; 2 Peter 3:7).

The people on earth *were seared by the intense heat.* They knew that these judgments had come from God, and they cursed him for sending them. But still they refused to recognize God's authority and repent of their sins. The contrast with those protected is unmistakable: "These are the ones coming out of the great tribulation. . . . they will be fully protected from the scorching noontime heat" (7:14, 16 NLT).

> If men and women will not yield to the love of God, and be changed by the grace of God, then there is no way for them to escape the wrath of God.   *Warren Wiersbe*

The reason for the phrase "they refused to repent" is to show the complete depravity of the people left on the earth. They had totally and irrevocably rejected God. They cursed (literally, blasphemed) his name. They had taken on the character of the Beast (13:6) and had committed the unforgivable sin by rejecting God with absolute finality. (See the commentary on 9:20-21 for more on hard hearts.)

DO IT NOW
Christians should not be surprised at unbelievers' hostility and hardness of heart. Even when the power of God is fully and completely revealed, many will still refuse to repent. If you find yourself ignoring God more and more, turn back to him now before your heart becomes too hard to repent. Don't wait until "just the right time" before turning to God. Do it now while you still have the chance. If you continually ignore God's warnings, you will eventually be unable to hear him at all.

16:10-11 **Then the fifth angel poured out his bowl on the throne of the beast, and his kingdom was plunged into darkness. And his subjects ground their teeth in anguish, and they cursed the God of heaven for their pains and sores. But they refused to repent of all their evil deeds.**[NLT] The fifth, sixth, and seventh bowls deal with Armageddon. The *fifth angel* poured out his bowl *on the throne of the beast.* This bowl was directed on the controller of the inhabitants of the earth—the Beast, the Antichrist, who had been placed into power by Satan (see chapter 13). His "throne" was merely an imitation of God's great throne in heaven (4:2-11).

When the fifth bowl was poured out, the Antichrist's *kingdom was plunged into darkness.* This was not like the partial darkness that had occurred during the fourth trumpet (8:12). This was total and complete darkness—like the plague visited upon Egypt, which is described as so dark that "during that time people scarcely moved, for they could not see" (Exodus 10:23 NLT).

Some take this "darkness" to refer to the total depravity and evil that comes from the leadership of the Antichrist. Others see it as a scientific phenomenon that after the flaring up of the sun (as described in the fourth bowl), the sun virtually burns itself out and it is dark. Whether physical or merely spiritual, this "darkness" caused great *anguish* among the people of the earth; they were in abject fear of this total physical and/or spiritual darkness. They were also still suffering *pains and sores*—probably from the boils in the first bowl (16:2) and the burns of the fourth bowl (16:8).

But the same phrase is repeated from 16:9: "they cursed the God of heaven" and "refused to repent." These people knew that God exists (none of them were atheists), but they decided that they hated him.

ANGER AT GOD
Tragically, the first time some people acknowledge that God is real occurs when they get angry at him. Until then, they may deny God's existence or admit to his existence but ignore any possibility that God could have any designs on their lives. The fifth bowl of judgment creates a loud darkness filled with angry outcries against God. Rebellious people blame God (thereby admitting his existence), but they still refuse to acknowledge that God should be worshiped.

Anger at God can provide a moment of awakening. It can help people realize the difference between themselves as creatures and God as Creator. It can draw them closer to God as they deal with their anger and questions.

Sustained anger, however, fed by self-pity and self-centeredness, will only cause people to reject God and his offer of grace. When you find yourself perplexed or angry with God, you can begin by consulting the book of Psalms (see especially Psalms 10, 13, 38, 64). The psalmist took his anger to God and found that God transformed it into trust. You can make the same discovery.

16:12 Then the sixth angel poured out his bowl on the great Euphrates River, and it dried up so that the kings from the east could

march their armies westward without hindrance.NLT When *the sixth angel poured out his bowl, the great Euphrates River* was *dried up.* In comparison, the sixth trumpet also mentions the Euphrates River and describes an invading army of demons (9:14-21).

The Euphrates River was a natural protective boundary between the Roman Empire and the empires to the east. As noted in the commentary on the first seal (6:1-2), the Parthians, from east of the Euphrates, had defeated the Roman army twice and so were much feared by the Romans. If the Euphrates River dried up, nothing could hold back invading armies—those hordes who had already defeated the Romans. The *kings from the east* have been identified in many ways. In 16:14, the kings from the east are joined by "the kings of the whole world," drawn together to the battlefield, a coalition that would bring its armies to the final battle against God Almighty and his hosts.

16:13-14 Then I saw three evil spirits that looked like frogs; they came out of the mouth of the dragon, out of the mouth of the beast and out of the mouth of the false prophet. They are spirits of demons performing miraculous signs, and they go out to the kings of the whole world, to gather them for the battle on the great day of God Almighty.NIV These *three evil spirits* confirm that these kings were the combined forces of evil coming to the final battle. One evil spirit came from *the mouth of the dragon* (12:3-9), a second *out of the mouth of the beast* (13:1-10), and the third *out of the mouth of the false prophet* (13:11-18). The evil trinity spawned three evil spirits *that looked like frogs.* Frogs were unclean animals in Jewish kosher law (Leviticus 11:10-11, 41). These were the *spirits of demons.*

Demons are fallen angels who had joined Satan in his rebellion against God and now are evil spirits under Satan's control (possibly described in 12:7-9). They are not mere fantasies—they are very real. Demons comprise a powerful army whose goal has always been to keep people from Christ, to tempt believers into sin, and to destroy Christ's church in any way possible. During these last days, the demons will be set loose to perform their destruction, ironically, on those who have rejected Christ and are on the side of Satan (see also commentary on 9:3). The demonic forces will come together to this final battle. These evil spirits will perform *miraculous signs,* convincing *the kings of the whole world to gather* for battle—uniting the rulers of the world against God. The imagery of the demons coming out of the mouths of the three evil rulers signifies the verbal enticements and propaganda that will draw many people to their evil cause.

In this vision, the battle is now set for *the great day of God Almighty*—God already knows that the demons are coming, and this is part of the plan. The final outcome has already been decided. "The great day of God Almighty" is also called "the day of the Lord." Throughout the Bible, the phrase "day of the Lord" is used in two different ways: (1) it can mean the end times (beginning with Christ's birth and continuing into the present); (2) it can mean the final judgment day at the end of time. In Scripture, the phrase is always used in connection with an extraordinary happening, whether a present event (such as a locust plague in Joel 1:15), a near future event, or the final period of history when God will defeat all the forces of evil. The final day of the Lord is pictured as a time when God will intervene directly and dramatically in world affairs. Predicted and discussed often in the Old Testament (Isaiah 13:6-12; Ezekiel 38–39; Joel 2:11, 28-32; 3:2; Zephaniah 1:14-18; 14:1-21), the day of the Lord will include both punishment and blessing. God will triumph completely. Christ will judge sin and set up his eternal kingdom.

The day of the final battle pictured in this text will be the time when the entire system of human opposition to God will be destroyed.

16:15 "Take note: I will come as unexpectedly as a thief! Blessed are all who are watching for me, who keep their robes ready so they will not need to walk naked and ashamed."[NLT] This is the third of seven beatitudes in Revelation—*blessed are all who are watching for me*. The first two are located at 1:3 and 14:13 (see the chart at 14:13). This is a warning to the Christian, spoken by the Lord. Jesus *will come as unexpectedly as a thief* (see also 3:3; Matthew 24:42-44; Luke 12:39-40; see also 1 Thessalonians 5:2, 4; 2 Peter 3:10). The teaching of the unexpectedness of Christ's return occurs throughout the New Testament. Believers who are still on the earth must be on their guard, watching, morally and spiritually prepared, with *their robes ready.* The word "robes" refers to purification attained by the cleansing of Christ's blood (7:9-14). Christ had also given this warning to the churches at Sardis (3:2-4) and Laodicea (3:18). The warning is that believers should not be swayed by the miraculous signs performed by the demons of the evil trinity. They must persevere, remain true to the faith, and wait with readiness. That way they *will not need to walk naked and ashamed.* Just as the robes refer to purity through Christ's blood, to be "naked" means having one's sinfulness exposed for all to see. This, of course, would lead to shame. For more on being rightfully clothed, see Colossians 3:12-17.

HOW TO BE READY
Christ will return unexpectedly (16:15), so believers must be ready when he returns. We can prepare ourselves by resisting temptation and by being committed to God's moral standards. It requires discernment to the deception of idolatry, which can be disguised as wealth, pleasure, or security. We must avoid spiritual apathy and laziness. In what ways does your life show either your readiness or your lack of preparation for Christ's return? Focus on living for God and serving him, not yourself and fulfilling your own desires.

16:16 And they gathered all the rulers and their armies to a place called *Armageddon* in Hebrew.[NLT] The evil spirits (16:13) *gathered all the rulers and their armies* (the kings of the east in 16:12, and the kings of the whole world in 16:14) *to a place called Armageddon in Hebrew.* Some archaeologists have located this battlefield near the city of Megiddo (southeast of the modern port of Haifa), which guarded a large plain in northern Israel. This is a strategic location near a prominent international highway leading north from Egypt through Israel, along the coast, and on to Babylon. Megiddo overlooks the entire plain southward toward Galilee and westward toward the mountains of Gilboa.

> Christ designed that the day of his coming should be hid from us, that being in suspense, we might be as it were upon the watch. *Martin Luther*

Over two hundred battles have been fought in this area (see, for example, Judges 5:19; 2 Kings 9:27). While this may be the location of the battle, the actual meaning of Armageddon is unknown. The word *har* in Hebrew means "mountain," but there is no mountain in the area of Megiddo. "Mountain" may have been used to describe God's presence—for he often would meet with people on mountains (Exodus 19:3, 11-23; 24:12; 1 Kings 19:11; Ezekiel 40:2; Matthew 17:1). The Aramaic meaning of the word "Armageddon" is "mount of the assembly"; thus, this may refer to the assembly of the kings who come to fight. John's unusual use of the explanation "in Hebrew" to a group of readers who for the most part probably did not know Hebrew probably alerts them to the symbolic nature of what he was writing (see also 9:11). Although the actual location is uncertain, we *are* told what will happen. This will truly be a "world war," except that the entire world will be on the same side. They will assemble to fight together against God. Some suggest that the entire world will come against Israel, God's people (see the descriptions of the views, below). Revelation describes this battle:

- *Revelation 14:14-20*—described as a harvest by an angel with a sickle, the battle will result in terrible bloodshed.

- *Revelation 16:16*—the name of the battlefield is "Armageddon."
- *Revelation 19:11-21*—the battle will be won by the rider on the white horse, Christ.

The armies of the east will march to Armageddon by crossing the dried-up Euphrates River (16:12). But the Lord will appear, and the earth will shake.

Some Christians believe that the battle of Armageddon will be a spiritual rather than a physical conflict. Others believe that the battle is being fought now.

Dispensational premillennialists believe that the battle of Armageddon begins when the king of the north and the king of the south converge on Israel to attack the Antichrist and his troops. After these armies are defeated, the kings of the east invade Israel (16:16). Then Christ will intervene and demonstrate his power by destroying all remaining foes (19:19-21).

Amillennialists and *historic premillennialists* believe that evil and destruction will increase in the last days. Christians will be present on earth during this period of Tribulation. Both amillennialists and historic premillennialists believe that the vision of Armageddon in Revelation figuratively portrays the final rebellion against God. As a result, they pay more attention to Christ's second coming than to the battle itself.

Postmillennialists believe that evangelists and Christians who try to spread God's word will always face obstacles. Postmillennialists don't believe that wickedness and persecution will significantly increase as the world draws to a close. Instead, because they think the church is gradually transforming society, they believe that Armageddon is a picture of Christ's victory over evil forces throughout church history. God's word will triumph over all opposition and establish the millennial kingdom.

While interpretations differ, all believers agree that Jesus has already defeated both Satan and death (1:18; Matthew 12:25-29). At some point, Christ will decisively demonstrate his power over Satan and his evil forces.

THE WINNING SIDE
Sinful people will unite to fight against God in a final display of rebellion. Many have already joined forces against Christ and his people—those who stand for truth, peace, justice, and morality. Your personal battle with evil foreshadows the great battle pictured here, where God will meet evil and destroy it once and for all. Be strong and courageous as you battle against sin and evil: you are fighting on the winning side.

16:17-18 **Then the seventh angel poured out his bowl into the air. And a mighty shout came from the throne of the Temple in heaven, saying, "It is finished!" Then the thunder crashed and rolled, and lightning flashed. And there was an earthquake greater than ever before in human history.**[NLT] This verse echoes 11:15-19, where we saw the seventh trumpet sounding, followed by voices in heaven shouting that Christ's kingdom had come (11:15). Then there was lightning, thunder, a hailstorm, and an earthquake (11:19; see also 4:5; 8:5). Here, when *the seventh angel poured out his bowl,* he did so *into the air,* which was followed by a *mighty shout.* The shout *came from the throne of the Temple* and it announced that *it is finished.* This also was followed by *thunder, lightning,* and *an earthquake* (the hailstorm is described in 16:21). The earthquake would be *greater than ever before in human history.*

History was finished; the end had come—proleptically speaking. With the bowl, God's wrath was completed. The reason for the creation of mankind was coming to fruition.

16:19-20 **The great city split into three parts, and the cities of the nations collapsed. God remembered Babylon the Great and gave her the cup filled with the wine of the fury of his wrath. Every island fled away and the mountains could not be found.**[NIV] In Revelation, the phrase "the great city" (here also called "Babylon the Great"), refers both to an evil city and an immoral empire, a world center for idol worship. Just as Babylon had been an enemy of the Jews (by conquering Jerusalem and taking many of the people into captivity, 2 Kings 25), so Rome was the enemy of the Christians. The name Babylon, the "great city," is used to describe the focal point of anti-Christian activity. John's readers would immediately have identified this great city as Rome, and they would have been correct. Yet they did not know, nor did John, that many years would pass before this event occured, nor did they know that both Babylon and Rome were models of the future and the ultimate collapse of the entire world system that would reject God. The great city's division into *three parts* symbolizes its complete destruction. This foreshadows what John would describe in more detail in chapters 17 and 18.

Not only that, but also *the cities of the nations collapsed.* So great is this earthquake that every city in the world will be destroyed—New York, Chicago, Mexico City, Hong Kong, Paris, London, Tokyo, Sydney—all will be flattened by this worldwide earthquake. This will indeed be an earthquake "greater than ever before in human history" (16:18), for places that had never had earthquakes will be destroyed.

In 14:8, an angel had described the fall of Babylon, and in
14:9, another angel spoke of the Beast's followers drinking the
undiluted wine of God's wrath. This is a further description of
God giving the city *the cup filled with the wine of the fury of his
wrath.* Babylon had seduced the nations (see 17:2) and so
deserved punishment.

The earthquake will be so severe that *every island* will disappear. The earth will have such an upheaval that it will flatten the
mountains so that they cannot even be found (see also 6:12-14).
Other earthquakes have occurred in Revelation, but this will be
the last and worst.

**16:21 And huge hailstones, each weighing about a hundred pounds,
dropped from heaven on people, until they cursed God for
the plague of the hail, so fearful was that plague.**NRSV Along
with the lightning, the thunder, and the earthquake, there was a
hailstorm so severe that *huge hailstones* fell from heaven onto the
people on earth. These stones weighed about *a hundred pounds.*
The Old Testament records God using hail to punish Israel's enemies (Joshua 10:11), and Ezekiel described a hailstorm (Ezekiel
38:18-22). Even golf-ball sized hail will cause severe damage.
Imagine the horrible destruction and death caused by these hun-
dred-pound hailstones. The cities had already been destroyed by
the earthquake, but anything left standing was smashed by the
hail. But still, the people on earth *cursed God.* After each of these
three final plagues, the inhabitants of the earth continued to blas-
pheme God (16:9, 11, 21).

Revelation 17

The destruction of Babylon mentioned in 16:17-21 is now described in greater detail (see the commentary at 16:19-20). Verses 1-6 describe John's vision of the prostitute and the scarlet beast; the remainder of the chapter describes the interpretation of the symbols.

17:1-2 **One of the seven angels who had poured out the seven bowls came over and spoke to me. "Come with me," he said, "and I will show you the judgment that is going to come on the great prostitute, who sits on many waters. The rulers of the world have had immoral relations with her, and the people who belong to this world have been made drunk by the wine of her immorality."**NLT One of the angels *who had poured out* the bowls came to John *and spoke* to him. The angel wanted to show John what those seven bowls had been directed against. The angel would show John *the judgment that is going to come on the great prostitute.* The "great prostitute" is also called "Babylon" in 17:5 and "the great city that rules over the kings of the earth" in 17:18. To the early Christians, this great prostitute represented the early Roman Empire with its many gods and the blood of Christian martyrs on its hands.

Rome was the capital city of the vast and mighty Roman Empire, an empire that stretched from Britain to Arabia. Truly, all roads led to Rome. Founded in 753 B.C., Rome was strategically located on the Tiber River at a ford that was indispensable for traveling between northern and southern Italy. In John's day, Rome was the largest city in the world, with a population of approximately one million. Wealthy and cosmopolitan, it was the diplomatic and trade center of the world. But for all its power, it was exceedingly immoral. During the period of the Roman Republic (527–509 B.C.), the Romans adopted and "Romanized" Greek gods. For example, Zeus, the king of the gods, became Jupiter. Idol worship flourished, and often involved temple prostitutes and homosexuality as part of the "worship rites." There were about 60 million slaves in the

Empire, which probably led to sexual exploitation by slave owners. Emperor worship was also enforced in varying degrees, depending on the emperor. There was much treachery in the government—in one year there were three different emperors due to assassinations.

Christians ran afoul of Roman society and values and thus found themselves severely persecuted. With Rome's backdrop of paganism and persecution, it is no wonder that Rome was seen as the epitome of evil. Like Babylon, Rome became a symbol of paganism and opposition to Christianity.

But the prostitute represents far more than just the Roman Empire. This "great prostitute," Babylon, symbolizes any economic, political, or military system that is hostile to God (see 17:5) and an eventual worldwide system that will encompass more evil than has been seen thus far in the world. Babylon had been a huge empire in its day; Rome was even larger as the Caesars took over many countries and gained their allegiance. In the end, the Antichrist will set up a final worldwide empire that will encompass all the nations and will be immoral and completely anti-God. At this time will occur the great apostasy—many will turn away from God, leave the churches, and follow the Beast. The prostitute *sits on many waters,* described in 17:15 as "masses of people of every nation and language" (NLT). The great prostitute, therefore, represents all the forces in the end who will come together to oppose God.

The Old Testament uses "prostitute" (or harlot) to describe a nation's religious apostasy. (The following verses are quoted from NLT.)

- "See how Jerusalem, once so faithful, has become a prostitute" (Isaiah 1:21).
- "Tyre . . . will come back to life and sing sweet songs like a prostitute" (Isaiah 23:15).
- "I am keenly aware of your adultery and lust, and your abominable idol worship" (Jeremiah 13:27).
- "You thought you could get along without me, so you trusted instead in your fame and beauty. You gave yourself as a prostitute to every man who came along" (Ezekiel 16:15).
- "Go and marry a prostitute. . . . This will illustrate the way my people have been untrue to me, openly committing adultery against the Lord by worshiping other gods" (Hosea 1:2).
- "Nineveh, the beautiful and faithless city, mistress of deadly charms, enticed the nations with her beauty. She taught them all to worship her false gods, enchanting people everywhere" (Nahum 3:4).

The great prostitute, rather than being described as any particular city of any particular time period, exists where there is satanic deception and resistance to God. This was true in many ancient kingdoms, such as Babylon, Egypt, Tyre, Nineveh, and Rome. The "prostitute" represents the seductiveness of any governmental system that uses immoral means to gain its own pleasure, prosperity, and advantage. This worldwide kingdom of the Beast will draw in all *the rulers of the world.* The immorality and drunkenness describe the actions of people who have completely turned away from the true God and have been lured into evil and idolatry. The Beast will deceive many people—drawing them into this immorality.

God is completely in control, even as this evil, worldwide apostasy takes place. The angel will show John *the judgment that is going to come* on this great prostitute. The judgment is described in chapter 18.

THE DAY WILL COME
The angel showed John the judgment to come. It is very difficult to convince unbelievers that God will judge the world for sin. Because God gives people free will and has not yet judged the earth, people do not immediately experience the consequences for their sins. Some get rich who oppress others and disregard God's claim on their lives. But the Bible is clear that judgment will come: "But no, you won't listen. So you are storing up terrible punishment for yourself because of your stubbornness in refusing to turn from your sin. For there is going to come a day of judgment when God, the just judge of all the world, will judge all people according to what they have done" (Romans 2:5-6 NLT, see also Matthew 16:27; 25:46; Revelation 20:12). God does not take pleasure in punishing sin. We must thank God and proclaim to others that he extends his mercy to us.

17:3 So the angel took me in spirit into the wilderness. There I saw a woman sitting on a scarlet beast that had seven heads and ten horns, written all over with blasphemies against God.^{NLT} The angel promised to show John the judgment on the "great prostitute" (17:1-2); here, John was taken *in spirit into the wilderness* where he would see this great prostitute. Four times in Revelation, John is described as being "in the spirit" or carried away in the spirit (1:10; 4:2; 17:3; 21:10). This means that the Holy Spirit transformed and elevated John's mind and spirit so that he could see prophetic visions. These could have been in the form of a trance or an ecstatic experience.

In chapter 12, another "woman" (symbolizing God's faithful

people) had been protected by God when she had fled into the wilderness away from the dragon (12:5-6). Here the "wilderness" has been taken over by evil, for here in the wilderness, John saw *a woman sitting on a scarlet beast.* This woman is, of course, the great prostitute described in 17:1. Most likely, this "scarlet beast" is Satan, for he is described in 12:3 as a "large red dragon," but this Beast is also identified as the beast out of the sea (13:1). All three have the same source—and all are described as having *seven heads and ten horns* (as noted in 12:3; 13:1). These heads and horns are further described by John in verses 9-18.

The Beast from the sea is further described as having names on each head that blasphemed God. This scarlet beast also was *written all over with blasphemies against God.* This Beast—the Antichrist controlled by Satan—is the supreme enemy of the church and God's people. The woman represents the world system of evil; the Beast represents the power supporting that world system. The blasphemous names are probably the names the Beast takes upon himself in calling himself God. One king of Babylon was described as being severely punished for thinking himself to be God (Daniel 3:1-6; 4:28-37). The Roman emperors called themselves gods, divine, saviors, lords, etc. These self-deifying names are blasphemous to God.

17:4 The woman wore purple and scarlet clothing and beautiful jewelry made of gold and precious gems and pearls. She held in her hand a gold goblet full of obscenities and the impurities of her immorality.[NLT] This *woman,* the great prostitute, was dressed in *purple and scarlet clothing,* signifying royalty and luxury. The purple and scarlet dyes were extremely expensive in the first century; no common person ever wore purple or scarlet. She was also wearing *beautiful jewelry made of gold and precious gems and pearls,* signifying wealth and materialism.

The woman was holding *a gold goblet full of obscenities and the impurities of her immorality.* In a sense, that was her inner person—she was extremely immoral. She was a prostitute—beautifully clothed but obscene and impure. Her veneer could not hide what was in her goblet. Jeremiah had described the destruction of the ancient empire of Babylon: "Flee from Babylon! Save yourselves! Don't get trapped in her punishment! It is the Lord's time for vengeance; he will fully repay her. Babylon has been like a golden cup in the Lord's hands, a cup from which he made the whole earth drink and go mad" (Jeremiah 51:6-7 NLT). The word for "obscenities" was also used by Jesus when referring to Daniel's "sacrilegious object that causes desecration" (Mark 13:14; Daniel 9:27; 11:31; 12:11).

AWAY FROM IT ALL
This woman pictures the evil power that will envelop the world.
It will look attractive and glorious on the outside—wealthy, pros-
perous, beautiful, luxurious—but the inside will be nothing but
rebellion against God, leading to total impurity. This is part of
Satan's deception—to draw people to live for the external and
ignore the internal.

    The angel took John into the desert (17:3) to see the prostitute
in her reality. Sometimes we have to step back from the involve-
ments of our daily lives to see the patterns of evil and all the
complicities of sin around us. Retreats, conferences, and days
of prayer and fasting can help us extricate ourselves from jobs,
newspapers, and television and bring us to new spiritual heights.
Take time to evaluate your life's directions and activities. Do they
glorify God and renew you to serve others?

17:5 This title was written on her forehead:

**MYSTERY
BABYLON THE GREAT
THE MOTHER OF PROSTITUTES
AND OF THE ABOMINATIONS OF THE EARTH.**[NIV]

The further description of the woman on the beast focuses on the
title that *was written on her forehead.* The first word, *mystery,*
may be part of the title or may indicate that the following words
were a mystery that was now being revealed. The word "mystery" has two meanings in Hellenistic Greek. One meaning
referred to something secret and known to only a select few. The
word described heathen religions or "mystery religions" with
their secret rites and practices. As used in the Septuagint (a Greek
version of the Jewish Old Testament writings), a second meaning
of the word describes what God reveals (as in Daniel 2:19). The
Jews used the word to describe some secret plan that God would
reveal at the end of the age. In the New Testament, the word
refers to a truth formerly hidden but now made known to people
(see Romans 11:25; Ephesians 3:3-4, 9; 5:32; 6:19; Colossians
1:26-27; 2:2; 4:3). Here in Revelation, the "mystery" is that the
true source and nature of evil is being shown.

    The title "Babylon the Great" describes an entire world system
(such as Babylon, Rome, and many other great powers) that will
be the culmination of all evil, leading people away from God (see
commentary on 17:1-2). This woman is a picture of Babylon,
which had taken God's people into captivity; she also is a picture
of Rome with its luxury and decadence. But she is far more than
just one particular city or empire in history. She is actually the
"mother" of them all. She is the source of all evil, the source of

all rebellion against God throughout history, of which various nations have taken part. She is *the mother of prostitutes and of the abominations of the earth.* For all her great finery (17:4), she is no more than a prostitute rebelling against God.

17:6 I could see that she was drunk—drunk with the blood of God's holy people who were witnesses for Jesus. I stared at her completely amazed.^{NLT} The woman riding the beast *was drunk,* certainly a pastime in the city of Rome and in the cult worship. However, this woman was *drunk with the blood of God's holy people.* She had gorged herself with this drink—meaning that she lived to hurt and to slaughter the people of God. This was her reason for being. This world power had the authority of the Beast "to wage war against God's holy people and to overcome them" (13:7). The woman had become intoxicated with the slaughter of God's followers.

Throughout history, people have been killed for their faith. Over the last century, millions have been killed by oppressive governments, and many of those victims have been believers. The woman's drunkenness shows her pleasure in her evil accomplishments and her false feeling of triumph over the church. But every martyr who has fallen before her sword has only served to strengthen the faith of the church. Those who have been threatened for their faith by any power on earth must realize that they are facing the "mother prostitute" whom God will judge once and for all.

John's reaction at the sight was total amazement. The woman and beast present a horrifying picture of the true nature of evil.

PERSECUTION TODAY
According to David Barrett of the World Evangelization Research Center, "Martyrdom is a regular, ongoing feature of church life in the 25 percent of global Christianity that we call the 'underground church.' In one part of the globe, over ten thousand Christians have been killed every year since 1950, due to clashes with anti-Christian mobs, infuriated relatives, state-organized death squads, and so on." Martyrdoms have increased from 35,000 in 1900 to an estimated 260,000 this year (Courtesy of *Christian History* magazine, Issue 27, page 37).
   Persecution is by no means a thing of the past. Christians in many parts of the world know that faith in Christ amounts to a death sentence. Believers who live in places free of such persecution must not forget to pray for their brothers and sisters in Christ in those difficult parts of the world.

17:7-8 Then the angel said to me: "Why are you astonished? I will explain to you the mystery of the woman and of the beast she

rides, which has the seven heads and ten horns. The beast, which you saw, once was, now is not, and will come up out of the Abyss and go to his destruction. The inhabitants of the earth whose names have not been written in the book of life from the creation of the world will be astonished when they see the beast, because he once was, now is not, and yet will come."NIV The *angel* had brought John into the wilderness (17:3) to witness the scarlet beast and the great prostitute. John had "stared at her completely amazed" (17:6). The angel asked, *"Why are you astonished?"* This is the true nature of evil, so perhaps believers should not be surprised at its sheer ugliness. The angel said that he would explain to John *the mystery of the woman and of the beast she rides.* John had seen the word "mystery" on the forehead of the woman (17:5), and that mystery would be explained. The remainder of this chapter interprets the beast; chapter 18 explains more about the prostitute.

The Beast, as noted in 17:3, signifies the Antichrist and his power source, Satan. The phrase, *once was, now is not, and will come up* is a parody of the description of Christ as "the one who always was, who is, and who is still to come" (4:8 NLT). Regarding the Beast, this could refer to Satan as he exercised power ("once was"), was bound when Christ died on the cross ("is not"), and then will have a time at the end of history during which to exercise great authority on the earth and to go into battle with God at Armageddon ("is still to come") before he is finally destroyed. This also could describe the Beast in 13:3 who had "seemed wounded beyond recovery—but the fatal wound was healed! All the world marveled at this miracle and followed the beast in awe" (NLT).

> Man does not like the religion of the cross, of faith, of self-denial, and each age has witnessed some false system from which all these objectionable elements are eliminated. Surely a false system has revelated itself successively in Babylon, Jerusalem, Rome, London, New York, and other great centers. Fashion smiles on it, wealth adorns it, human power unites with it, and in every age it has been intoxicated with the blood of martyrs.   *F. B. Meyer*

The Beast was alive, then dead, and then came back to life. The Beast's resurrection symbolizes the persistence of evil. His source is *the Abyss*—the abode of the demonic forces, the eternal destination of the wicked, the place of the Beast's final *destruction* (see 9:1, 11; 11:7; 20:1-3; Luke 8:31; 2 Peter 2:4; Jude 6).

This resurgence of evil power will convince many to join forces with the Beast. Those to join him will be *the inhabitants of the earth* who *will be astonished when they see the beast, because he once was, now is not, and yet will come.* They will be so astonished by his resurrection (a copy of Christ's true resurrection) that they will fol-

ROMAN EMPERORS

Name	Dates of Rule
Augustus	27 B.C.–A.D. 14
Tiberius	A.D. 14–37
Caligula	A.D. 37–41
Claudius	A.D. 41–54
Nero	A.D. 54–68
Galba	A.D. 69
Otho	A.D. 69
Vitellius	A.D. 69
Vespasian	A.D. 69–79
Titus	A.D. 79–81
Domitian	A.D. 81–96

low him. These people have received the Beast's mark (13:16); these people's *names have not been written in the book of life from the creation of the world.* The same description of these people is in 13:8, "All inhabitants of the earth will worship the Beast—all whose names have not been written in the book of life belonging to the Lamb that was slain from the creation of the world" (NIV). The book of life is a register in heaven of those who believe in Christ and have been saved. Only those whose names are in the book will be saved. These people on earth who worship the Beast have not been saved, and, therefore, their names are not written in the book of life. (For a discussion of the meaning of the phrase "from the creation of the world," see the commentary at 13:8.)

17:9-10 **"This calls for a mind with wisdom. The seven heads are seven hills on which the woman sits. They are also seven kings. Five have fallen, one is, the other has not yet come; but when he does come, he must remain for a little while."**[NIV] Many scholars think that, in this explanation, the angel was referring to Rome, the city famous for its *seven hills.* Rome symbolized all evil in the world—any person, religion, group, government, or structure that opposed Christ. John was writing during a time of persecution of believers, with Rome at the focal point. His original readers may have immediately associated the "seven hills" with Rome. Certainly Rome portrays the power and corruption that those final evil days will encompass. If the association with the seven hills of Rome seems obvious, however, why would the angel preface these

words by saying, *"This calls for a mind with wisdom"?* John may
have been telling the readers something not readily apparent. In
addition, because the hills are *also seven kings,* some have linked
the seven kings with seven of Rome's emperors counting from
Tiberius to Domitian (however, three emperors are omitted from
their list—see the chart "Roman Emperors," page 202). All of those
attempts are problematic, for there are arbitrary omissions that must
be made in order to make them fit with the formula given: *five have
fallen, one is, the other has not yet come, he must remain for a little
while.*

Others connect the seven kings to seven world kingdoms. The
first five would be Egypt, Assyria, Babylon, Persia, and Greece
(they had already fallen), the one that *is* would be Rome (present-
tense for John's day), and the one yet to come would be the final
kingdom of the Antichrist (although this theory has its problems
at 17:11). While this fits fairly well, it again depends on arbitrary
omissions in order to make the numbers work.

It is also possible that the number seven is used here as it is
everywhere else in Revelation as symbolic of completeness (seven
seals, seven trumpets, seven bowls). The seven heads could indicate complete blasphemy, with the seven kings referring to the complete number of kings who will rule until the end, with the end
coming when the complete number has been reached (similar to the
complete number of the martyrs in 6:11). The question then arises
why John included the numeric formula. Some scholars point to
an ancient seal showing the seven-headed monster of chaos being
killed. In the seal, four of the heads are dead, but the creature is still
living with three active heads. But it is being defeated and obviously faces imminent death. John could be describing the evil as
being progressively destroyed. The battle has been fought and won
in the past; the battle is presently being fought; and the battle will
continue to be fought until the Beast is completely defeated. John's
numeric formula also could simply mean that he is declaring the
imminent end of history. Time is passing (five sevenths have
passed) and has a definite end point which is all in God's plan.

Whatever the interpretation, Rome was indeed a preview of that
final thrust of evil and hatred of all who love God. While God has
chosen to keep this vague, believers ought to be careful about
attempting to decipher what God has chosen not to make clear. It is
far more important to realize that, even as the power of evil gains
control of the whole world, God is in charge. Evil will only have
the upper hand "for a little while."

**17:11 "The scarlet beast that was alive and then died is the eighth
king. He is like the other seven, and he, too, will go to his**

doom."^{NLT} The seven heads are seven hills, which are interpreted as seven kings, but here an *eighth king* is introduced who *was alive and then died.* This eighth king is *the scarlet beast* himself—identified elsewhere as Satan or the Antichrist (see commentary at 17:3). As the seventh seal leads into the first trumpet, and the seventh trumpet into the first bowl, so the seven kings lead into the final king who actually embodies all of them. This eighth king, then, *is* the Antichrist himself. He is not simply another evil ruler; he is evil itself. He will become a human being—a leader, a king. But again, God's sovereignty shows itself—the Antichrist *will go to his doom.*

17:12 **"The ten horns you saw are ten kings who have not yet received a kingdom, but who for one hour will receive authority as kings along with the beast."**^{NIV} With this verse, John returned to the future in his vision, describing the Antichrist and what would occur during his rule. If the previous verses were describing emperors of Rome or empires up through the Roman Empire, then this verse skips over all of intervening history and returns to the Antichrist still to come. John could hardly have imagined that over two thousand years would pass from the time that he wrote these words, and that the Antichrist and the end still would not have come. Surely he could hardly have imagined anything worse than what the believers had experienced under the emperors Nero or Domitian.

The *ten horns* are *ten kings* who will be the Antichrist's minions and will rule under him (see also Daniel 7:7, 24). The ten horns represent kings of nations yet to arise. Some have suggested that these ten kings who *have not yet received a kingdom* are ten future kings who will reign over the world under the Antichrist or even the ten nations of the European Common Market. The number ten may be literal, or, more likely, it symbolizes the totality of the powers on earth that will serve the Antichrist and war against Christ. Rome will be followed by other powers. Rome is a good example of how the Antichrist's system will work, demanding complete allegiance, and ruling by raw power, oppression, and slavery. Whoever the ten kings are, they will give their power to the Antichrist and will make war against the Lamb.

They *will receive authority as kings along with the beast.* Again, the passive voice is used—they "will receive." Their authority will have been given by Satan and simply allowed by God. But their authority will only last *one hour.* The Beast was given authority for forty-two months (13:5), but these kings will have only "one hour"—a figurative number highlighting the brevity of their time of power.

John's readers would have understood the authority given to these kings by the Beast as similar to the authority the emperors gave to local governors or kings. When Rome conquered a country, the empire allowed local kings, such as Herod the Great in Palestine, to continue to rule as long as they gave allegiance to the Empire.

AN EASY TARGET

As we ponder the identity of the seven kings and the emergence of the ten kings, we must see John's theme of worldly power and its ultimate ineffectiveness against God and his people. Their authority only lasts for "one hour," symbolizing its brevity and ultimate destruction. As Christians, have we become infatuated with the worldly power of movie stars and sports celebrities, political coalitions, and world economic forces? Are you craving the power and prestige that position, wealth, and connections offer? If so, you are an easy target for Satan's great deception. Worldly power is Satan's trap; the desire for it can turn us away from God. Worship only God and make it your strongest desire to serve him.

17:13-14 **"They have one purpose and will give their power and authority to the beast. They will make war against the Lamb, but the Lamb will overcome them because he is Lord of lords and King of kings—and with him will be his called, chosen and faithful followers."**[NIV] These "ten kings" (which may be an actual or symbolic number) will *give their power and authority to the beast.* These human kings will allow themselves to be completely possessed by Satan (or his demons). The Beast will have one job for these kings—*one purpose*—to *make war against the Lamb.*

The outcome, however, is guaranteed: *the Lamb will overcome them.* The outcome of the war has already been determined. Even as Satan will seem to gain the upper hand in the final days, the end is already known. Christ will win because *he is Lord of lords and King of kings* (see 19:16; Deuteronomy 10:17; Daniel 2:47). He is above all the kings of the earth; he is the final authority. When Christ comes for that final victory over Satan, *his chosen and faithful followers* will be *with him.* When the believers arrive with Christ at the battlefield, they will not need to fight. The battle will be over at the very appearance of Christ (see 19:11-21).

"Called" *(kletoi)* means to be invited. Christians have been called with a purpose to be part of God's kingdom. "Chosen" *(eklektoi)* means those whom God has selected or drawn to himself. Christians have been drawn to God for salvation in Christ. "Faithful" *(pistoi)* means those who show themselves trustworthy, dependable, and loyal. These words stress not only God's choice of these people but also their continued perseverance and loyalty to him (12:11; 13:8; see also the chart "Persevere to the End" at 14:12, page 172).

THEN . . . AND NOW
The Lamb will overcome and be victorious. The King of kings will bring his chosen ones with him. We will be with Christ *then* but we are also with him *now*. The battle will be won against Satan then, but with Christ in us, we can win the battles against Satan every day. If we accept compromise and defeat, we surrender to Satan. But if we trust Christ, claim his victory, and live by his power, we can defeat Satan.

17:15 **And the angel said to me, "The waters where the prostitute is sitting represent masses of people of every nation and language."**[NLT] The *angel* continued his description of the vision that John was seeing (17:7). The *prostitute* is described as one "who sits on many waters" (17:1 NLT). The great prostitute is called "Babylon" (17:5) and the imagery of the waters comes from Jeremiah's prophecy to Babylon whose water source was the Euphrates River: "You are a city rich with water, a great center of commerce, but your end has come" (Jeremiah 51:13 NLT). Although Babylon and Rome are in view, again this great prostitute represents a far-reaching, anti-God power that will encompass the world. The angel explained that *the waters . . . represent masses of people of every nation and language.* The Antichrist will influence (or even possess) the leaders across the world, but his influence will extend to all people. The "masses" also will be overtaken by the great prostitute and will be enamored by her. In doing so, they will become hostile to God. The leaders and the people will be joined in their adoration of the Antichrist.

17:16 **"The beast and the ten horns you saw will hate the prostitute. They will bring her to ruin and leave her naked; they will eat her flesh and burn her with fire."**[NIV] This verse describes the nature and outcome of evil. In a dramatic turn of events, the *beast* on whom the prostitute rides will turn on her and destroy her. In fact, the Beast has hated the prostitute all along. This is how evil operates. Destructive by its very nature, it turns on itself. The Beast and the ten kings (Satan and the leaders) will end up destroying what they have made. The very evil of the culture they have created will leave it in shambles. They will bring that culture *to ruin.* Despite the great beauty and luxury of the prostitute's clothing and jewels (17:4), the Beast will *leave her naked.* She will be completely destroyed—her flesh eaten and her remains burned. The horror of her demise parallels the penalty in the Old Testament for prostitution (Leviticus 21:9), the end of the wicked queen Jezebel (2 Kings 9:30-37), and the fate of the allegorical Oholibah, who represented the apostate Israelites in Ezekiel's prophecy (Ezekiel 23:11-35).

SELF-DESTRUCTION
The vivid picture of evil that the angel showed John—Beast, kings, prostitute—also displays the destructive nature of selfishness. Past and future kings give their authority and power to the Beast with greedy desire for even greater power. The prostitute depends (sits on) the Beast. The Beast, the kings, and the prostitute are allies until the Beast and kings turn on the prostitute and betray, humiliate, sacrifice, and consume her. Faced with doom, they turn on each other.

Evil proves to be vicious and destructive. It hates everything good that God has made. Evil people may profess values such as loyalty and unity, but in the end, they will destroy their allies to preserve themselves.

Compromises and alliances with evil, in order to accomplish a "greater good," also prove to be deceptions. Satan uses an effective tactic. He tried it with Jesus himself (Matthew 4:1-11) by tempting him to use his power to make a "shortcut" to a good goal. The temptations were real. Jesus could have gained the whole world in a moment, but he would have also abandoned God's plan. Christians face the same kinds of temptations today. But "good ends" accomplished by evil means serve Satan, not Christ. Only what we do for Christ and by his power will last.

17:17 **"For God has put it into their hearts to carry out his purpose by agreeing to give their kingdom to the beast, until the words of God will be fulfilled."**[NRSV] In an ironic twist, John wrote that *God has put it into* the hearts of the ten kings *to carry out his purpose by agreeing to give their kingdom to the beast* (17:13). God will bring about the destruction of the great prostitute (17:16) by allowing the evil to run its course. Even as Satan overruns the world and finally destroys his own kingdom and followers, God still rules. All of these events will be completely under God's control. His *words . . . will be fulfilled.* God's plans will happen just as he says. God even uses people opposed to him as tools to carry out his will. God even allows Satan to further deceive the people who have already completely rejected God. Nothing will stop their destruction of the

What do we mean by this expression "the sovereignty of God"? We mean the supremacy of God, the kingship of God, the godhood of God. To say that God is sovereign is to declare that God is God. He is the Most High, doing according to his will, so that none can stay his hand, defeat his counsels, or thwart his purpose.   *Arthur W. Pink* "prostitute." This will carry out God's purpose of final judgment for all who have refused his offer of salvation.

17:18 **"And this woman you saw in your vision represents the great city that rules over the kings of the earth."**[NLT] The angel explains John's vision further, describing the *woman* (the "great prostitute" in 17:1, 3) as *the great city that rules over the kings of the earth.* As noted in the commentary on 17:1, John's original readers would have identified this immediately with Rome—the capital of an empire that had spread across much of the known world, a city filled with immorality and idolatry and famous for its active persecution of Christians. The vision surely represents that, but it also means far more. Like Rome, and Babylon before her, this "woman" is the worldwide system of power and influence that will be completely rebellious against God and subservient to the Antichrist. Babylon and Rome were forerunners of what will be far bigger and more horrible than anything John or his readers could have imagined.

Revelation 18:1–19:5

Chapter 17 describes the "great prostitute," called "Babylon the Great," (17:5) and why she would need to be destroyed (17:1). She was evil, immoral, and drunk with the blood of the martyrs. This section describes that destruction—how it occurred and its effect upon the inhabitants of the world. First, an angel proclaimed judgment on the great city (18:1-8). The rulers of the world lament the destruction of the city (18:9-10), as do the merchants who have become rich through trade (18:11-16), the ship owners, and the captains of the merchant ships (18:18-20).

18:1 **After this I saw another angel coming down from heaven. He had great authority, and the earth was illuminated by his splendor.**NIV John saw *another angel coming down from heaven.* This angel had *great authority,* which probably made him even more glorious than the previous angels described in Revelation (and those angels were powerful as well!). This angel was so glorious that *the earth was illuminated by his splendor*—he was like the sun, reflecting the glory of God himself from whose presence the angel had come. This angel would be bringing the final message of destruction upon the evil world system of the Antichrist. This important and world-changing message was entrusted to this angel who carried great authority.

18:2 **He gave a mighty shout, "Babylon is fallen—that great city is fallen! She has become the hideout of demons and evil spirits, a nest for filthy buzzards, and a den for dreadful beasts."**NLT As described in the commentary in 17:1, the name "Babylon" (also known as the "great prostitute") was immediately assumed by John's readers to be Rome. While they would have been correct, the symbol goes far beyond Rome to a world-encompassing system of religion and economics that will be under the control of the Antichrist and completely against God and his people.

The glorious angel *gave a mighty shout* that *Babylon is fallen—the great city is fallen.* Babylon is John's metaphorical name for the evil world power and all it represents. Described in 17:1 as a "great prostitute," this city had great wealth and luxury. The

Babylon of ancient days had been a world empire—the empire that had invaded Judah, burned down Solomon's Temple, destroyed Jerusalem, and took people into captivity (2 Kings 25:8-21). It was the empire that Daniel had served, under Nebuchadnezzar and Belshazzar (Daniel 1–5).

The angel described the city as *the hideout of demons and evil spirits, a nest for filthy buzzards, and a den for dreadful beasts.* The "hideout of demons and evil spirits" is literally a prison or watchtower, like a haunt, from which the evil beings watch over the desolate ruins. This is an image of desperate desolation. "Buzzards" are carrion birds, considered "unclean," also found in desolate places. The Old Testament records many prophecies against the ancient city of Babylon, which are appropriate parallels to the total destruction described by John for this metaphorical "Babylon" to come.

- "Babylon, the most glorious of kingdoms, the flower of Chaldean culture, will be devastated like Sodom and Gomorrah when God destroyed them. Babylon will never rise again. Generation after generation will come and go, but the land will never be lived in. Nomads will refuse to camp there, and shepherds will not allow their sheep to stay overnight. Wild animals of the desert will move into the ruined city. The houses will be haunted by howling creatures. Ostriches will live among the ruins, and wild goats will come there to dance. Hyenas will howl in its fortresses, and jackals will make their dens in its palaces. Babylon's days are numbered; its time of destruction will soon arrive" (Isaiah 13:19-22 NLT).
- "I see an awesome vision: I see you plundered and destroyed. . . . Babylon will fall. Babylon is fallen! All the idols of Babylon lie broken on the ground!" (Isaiah 21:2, 9 NLT).
- "You are a pleasure-crazy kingdom, living at ease and feeling secure, bragging as if you were the greatest in the world! You felt secure in all your wickedness. So disaster will overtake you suddenly" (Isaiah 47:8, 10, 11 NLT).
- "Because of the Lord's anger, Babylon will become a deserted wasteland. All who pass by will be horrified and will gasp at the destruction they see there. Soon this city of Babylon will be inhabited by ostriches and jackals. It will be a home for the wild animals of the desert. Never again will people live there; it will lie desolate forever" (Jeremiah 50:13, 39 NLT).

The angel announced that the formerly great, luxurious city had become a total wasteland, filled with everything evil and unclean. It is a haunt of evil spirits.

18:3 "For all the nations have drunk the wine of her passionate immorality. The rulers of the world have committed adultery with her, and merchants throughout the world have grown rich as a result of her luxurious living."NLT The reason that Babylon had fallen is described here—*all the nations have drunk the wine of her passionate immorality* (see also 17:2). Babylon personifies everything that is evil—sexual immorality, idolatry, greed, and oppression. The people of the world have turned completely away from God and have enjoyed the seductiveness of what she was offering through her immorality and idolatry. The Old Testament uses adultery to describe spiritual apostasy (see, for example, Jeremiah 3:2; Hosea 4:10). In the last days, apostasy will reach a pinnacle in the worship of the Beast (13:15).

First, *the rulers of the world have committed adultery with her,* meaning that they have committed shameful sins—giving up what is most important for what is gratifying. This "adultery" probably refers to both sinful alliances and the total abandoning of God's morality. The rulers were living immorally and had turned away from God. The rulers' lament over the city is recorded in 18:9-10.

Also, the *merchants throughout the world have grown rich as a result of her luxurious living.* They were seduced by the great riches that could be gained by their relationship with her. Isaiah 47:8 describes the great luxury of Babylon and God's judgment of it. Their luxury led to pride and self-sufficiency. Part of this adultery was in taking the mark of the Beast because these merchants could not buy or sell without it (13:17). The merchants' lament over the city is recorded in 18:11-16.

18:4-5 Then I heard another voice from heaven say: "Come out of her, my people, so that you will not share in her sins, so that you will not receive any of her plagues; for her sins are piled up to heaven, and God has remembered her crimes."NIV Jeremiah had prophesied regarding the ancient city of Babylon, "Flee from Babylon! Save yourselves! Don't get trapped in her punishment! It is the Lord's time for vengeance; he will fully repay her" (Jeremiah 51:6 NLT, also 51:45). So *another voice from heaven* warned about this future evil system and called to God's people, *"Come out of her,"* warning the people not to *share in her sins* nor in her *plagues.* This is reminiscent of the problems Christ pointed out to the churches in Pergamum and Thyatira—both were compromising with evil (2:14-15, 20). Just as God had brought vengeance upon the ancient city because of her cruelty to others, so God *has*

HOW CAN A PERSON KEEP AWAY FROM THE EVIL SYSTEM?

Here are some suggestions:

1. Know that people are always more important than products.

2. Keep away from pride in programs, plans, and successes.

3. Remember that God's will and Word must never be compromised.

4. Always consider people above making money.

5. Do what is right, no matter what the cost.

6. Be involved in businesses that provide worthwhile products or services—not just things that feed the world's desires.

---

remembered the crimes of all nations who have fought God and persecuted his people—resulting in sins that *are piled up to heaven.* God remembers, and he will punish. As an answer to all the questions of why wicked people prosper, God points out here that he knows it all and will punish it all.

God's people are called to separate themselves—to "come out"—for two reasons: (1) not to share in society's sins, and (2) not to eventually share in that society's punishment by God. Believers must always be aware of when they must not compromise with a godless society. To compromise will mean facing punishment. Although "come out" can refer to a physical separation from the places of evil, it always refers to a spiritual, mental, and emotional separation from the sins that plague the current society. The church must always stand firm on the foundations of the faith, never swaying at the whims of society.

VALUED VALUES
Roman merchants often grew rich by exploiting the sinful pleasures of their society. Many business people today do the same thing. Businesses and governments are often based on greed, money, and power. Many bright individuals are tempted to take advantage of an evil system to enrich themselves. Christians are warned to stay free from the lure of money, status, and the good life. We are to live according to the values that Christ exemplified: service, giving, self-sacrifice, obedience, and truth.

18:6-7 **"Do to her as she has done to your people. Give her a double penalty for all her evil deeds. She brewed a cup of terror for others, so give her twice as much as she gave out. She has lived in luxury and pleasure, so match it now with torments and sorrows. She boasts, 'I am queen on my throne.**

I am no helpless widow. I will not experience sorrow.'"[NLT]
The people of Babylon had lived in luxury and pleasure. The
city was boasting, *"I am a queen on my throne. I am no helpless widow. I will not experience sorrow."* Isaiah had prophesied of Babylon, "You are a pleasure-crazy kingdom, living at
ease and feeling secure, bragging as if you were the greatest in
the world! You say, 'I'm self-sufficient and not accountable to
anyone! I will never be a widow or lose my children'" (Isaiah
47:8 NLT).

Rome also had great luxury and pride, as have other powerful kingdoms. In the end, this great kingdom would receive
what it had meted out. The Roman law, *lex talionis,* was that a
person's punishment should match his or her crime. During this
judgment, however, the angel asked God to *give her a double
penalty for all her evil deeds.* She had given *terror* (making
war against the believers and spilling their blood, 13:7; 17:6)
and should receive *twice as much* terror in return. She had *lived
in luxury and pleasure*—this should be matched with *torments
and sorrows.*

Jeremiah had written of ancient Babylon, "King Nebuchadnezzar of Babylon has eaten and crushed us and emptied out
our strength. He has swallowed us like a great monster and
filled his belly with our riches. May Babylon be repaid for
all the violence she did to us. May the people of Babylonia
be paid in full for all the blood they have spilled" (Jeremiah
51:34-35 NLT).

ATTITUDE ADJUSTMENT
John described Babylon's attitude as, "I am invincible." The
powerful, wealthy people of this world are susceptible to this
same attitude. A person who is financially comfortable often
feels invulnerable, secure, and in control, feeling no need for
God or anyone else. This kind of attitude defies God and brings
God's harsh punishment. We are told to avoid Babylon's sins.
If you are financially secure, don't become complacent and
deluded by the myth of self-sufficiency. Use your resources
to help others and advance God's kingdom.

**18:8 "Therefore in one day her plagues will overtake her: death,
mourning and famine. She will be consumed by fire, for
mighty is the Lord God who judges her."**[NIV] For all of Babylon's self-sufficiency, pride, and power (18:6), the ugliness of
her evil will eventually overtake her. She will be brought down
by *her plagues*—her own sin will destroy her. The timing will be
God's, of course, but her own plagues will become her snare. All

the sins of luxurious, prideful, and self-centered living that have been "piled up to heaven" (18:5) will come crashing down and destroy her. The most beautiful, powerful, and evil city in the world will not be able to stand when the holy God intervenes and allows the evil to run its course to destruction. *In one day* (possibly figurative, but signifying a very short time; see 17:12 on "one hour"), she will face *death, mourning and famine.* In one day she will face what she had been able to avoid thus far through her wealth and power.

In the end, the city *will be consumed by fire,* unable to escape the destruction, unable to stop the raging fire as it sweeps and destroys. Jeremiah had prophesied of ancient Babylon, "The wide walls of Babylon will be leveled to the ground, and her high gates will be burned. The builders from many lands have worked in vain, for their work will be destroyed by fire!" (Jeremiah 51:58 NLT).

18:9-10 **"When the kings of the earth who committed adultery with her and shared her luxury see the smoke of her burning, they will weep and mourn over her. Terrified at her torment, they will stand far off and cry: 'Woe! Woe, O great city, O Babylon, city of power! In one hour your doom has come!'"**NIV Those who control various parts of the economic system will mourn at Babylon's fall. Verses 9-20 are a funeral dirge for the fall of Babylon, sung by three different groups: the rulers of the world (18:9-10), the merchants (18:11-16), and the ship owners (18:17-20). These have all grown rich because of the evil economy represented by Babylon. They will sing songs of mourning because they will lose everything when the economy collapses. The political leaders will mourn because they have been the overseers of Babylon's wealth and have been in a position to enrich themselves greatly. The merchants will mourn because Babylon, the greatest customer for their goods, will be gone. The sea captains will no longer have anywhere to bring their goods because the merchants will have nowhere to sell them. The fall of the evil world system will affect all who enjoyed and depended on it. No one will remain unaffected by Babylon's fall. The funeral dirge sung by the prophet Ezekiel over the city of Tyre (another evil city) forms a backdrop to John's vision of the horror of the fall of this coming "Babylon."

First, *the kings of the earth . . . will weep and mourn over her.* The kings had given over their power to the Beast, who controlled the economy, and had worshiped the Beast—thereby committing *adultery with her.* As a reward for their subservience, these kings *shared her luxury.* But when the city is destroyed, they will be *terrified at her torment* and *stand far off*. Most likely, the destruction is so great that they don't want to be caught up in it. They do not attempt to rescue the city because they realize it is futile.

Ezekiel had written of Tyre, "Was there ever such a city as Tyre? . . . The merchandise you traded satisfied the needs of many nations. Kings at the ends of the earth were enriched by your trade. All who live along the coastlands are appalled at your terrible fate. Their kings are filled with horror and look on with twisted faces" (Ezekiel 27:32-33, 35 NLT).

These rulers will be terrified because, without Babylon, they will be nothing. They are terrified for Babylon, but more important, they are terrified for themselves.

> Have you given your time and energy to get those things that go with living in Babylon so that, when it falls, all that you have ever worked for will fall with it? Or have you so invested your life in the Kingdom of God that, even if heaven and earth shall pass away, what is important to you will endure?
>
> *Tony Campolo*

LASTING REWARDS
When Babylon collapses, all those who depend on her wealth will be left destitute. Those tied to the world's system will lose everything when it collapses. What they have worked for a lifetime to build up will be destroyed in one hour. Those who work only for material rewards will have nothing when they die or when their possessions are destroyed. What can we take with us to the new earth? Our faith, our Christian character, and our relationships with other believers. These are more important than any amount of money, power, or pleasure. Guide your life toward receiving God's lasting rewards, not toward what will pass away.

18:11-13 **"And the merchants of the earth weep and mourn for her, since no one buys their cargo anymore, cargo of gold, silver, jewels and pearls, fine linen, purple, silk and scarlet, all kinds of scented wood, all articles of ivory, all articles of costly wood, bronze, iron, and marble, cinnamon, spice, incense, myrrh, frankincense, wine, olive oil, choice flour and wheat, cattle and sheep, horses and chariots, slaves—and human lives."**NRSV The next group to join the funeral dirge are the *merchants of the earth* (18:11-16). These people *weep and mourn* because *no one buys their cargo anymore*. The collapse of the economy will mean the end of their trade and income.

This list of various merchandise illustrates the extreme materialism of this society. Few of these goods are necessities—most are luxuries, including precious metals, jewels, and cloth, aromatic perfumes, and foods. Purple cloth would have been imported from Phoenicia. It was highly expensive and valued by royalty. Silk, cinnamon, and other spices would have come from faraway China. Ivory and certain types of wood probably would have come from North Africa. Wheat would have been imported from Egypt. The society had become so self-indulgent that people were willing to use evil means to gratify their desires. Even people had become no more than commodities—*human lives* were the *slaves* who would have been sold to Babylon.

Rome was a city of great luxury and extravagance. The Roman emperors were known for their sumptuous lifestyles, clothing, and banquets. This list of exotic commodities describes the breadth of the trade that usually would come into the port of Rome. Much of the list is identical to the types of trade mentioned in Ezekiel 27:12-22 when describing a former maritime trade power, the city of Tyre. Rome's luxury and extravagance led to decadence that eventually destroyed her. In the end, Tyre also had been destroyed: "The merchants of the nations shake their heads at the sight of you, for you have come to a horrible end and will be no more" (Ezekiel 27:36 NLT).

LIVING LIKE THE BABYLONIANS
The merchants wept at their loss of wealth and prosperity. The economy had collapsed and all their hopes with it. They had lived for their wealth and, when it was gone, they had nothing left.

God's people should not live for money, because money will be worthless in eternity. And they should keep on guard constantly against greed, a sin that is always ready to take over their lives. God wants us to work and to provide for our families, and he commands the proper use of money. But when the desire for money fills our lives, it becomes a false god. Don't be enslaved by the desire for wealth.

18:14 "'All the fancy things you loved so much are gone,' they cry. 'The luxuries and splendor that you prized so much will never be yours again. They are gone forever.'"NLT The *fancy things* refer to all the exotic imports that would come into cities like Tyre and Rome. People *love* these things, but when Babylon is destroyed, all will be *gone forever.* The luxury and splendor of this world will not last.

LAP OF LUXURY
The voice from heaven (18:4) continued to prophesy against the greedy merchants. "All the fancy things you loved" and "the luxuries and splendor that you prized" were gone. The desire for nonessential luxuries had driven these merchants. Yet, how many of these luxuries listed are in *your* home? Most people will find that they own almost everything on this list. We are people who truly live in great luxury. We, too, are in danger of being absorbed in possessions and pleasure. Make sure that your desires lead you in the right direction. Put boundaries on them. Don't go after everything you see. Keep your desires on serving God and building his Kingdom by helping others.

18:15-17a **"The merchants who sold these things and gained their wealth from her will stand far off, terrified at her torment. They will weep and mourn and cry out: 'Woe! Woe, O great city, dressed in fine linen, purple and scarlet, and glittering with gold, precious stones and pearls! In one hour such great wealth has been brought to ruin!'"**[NIV] Like the kings of the world (18:9-10), *the merchants* will also be *terrified* at the torment of the great city. They too will *weep* and *cry,* echoing the lament of the kings, *"Woe! Woe, O great city,"* a cry that describes utter and hopeless grief. Naming some of the items in their list of imports, the merchants will describe the city *"dressed in fine linen, purple and scarlet, and glittering with gold, precious stones and pearls."* The great prostitute, who was sitting on the scarlet beast, was described in identical terms as wearing "purple and scarlet clothing and beautiful jewelry made of gold and precious gems and pearls" (17:4 NLT). These merchants will be terrified at the swiftness and totality of the great city *brought to ruin.* With the economy collapsed, there will no longer be a market for the exotic and pricey goods that the merchants had traded and from which they had grown wealthy.

18:17b-19 **"Every sea captain, and all who travel by ship, the sailors, and all who earn their living from the sea, will stand far off. When they see the smoke of her burning, they will exclaim, 'Was there ever a city like this great city?' They will throw dust on their heads, and with weeping and mourning cry out: 'Woe! Woe, O great city, where all who had ships on the sea became rich through her wealth! In one hour she has been brought to ruin!'"**[NIV] The third group to join the funeral dirge will be the sea captains and sailors—*all who earn their living from the sea.* The vast amount of trade was carried on, at least partially, by ships arriving from far distant lands. As the merchants had become rich on the commodities, those who ran the ships had become rich delivering them. With the fall of the great city, their services will no longer be required. There will be no one to buy and nothing to trade. As the city goes up in smoke, *they will throw dust on their heads, weeping and mourning.* Ezekiel had written of Tyre, "All the oarsmen abandon their ships; the sailors and helmsmen come to stand on the shore. They weep bitterly as they throw dust on their heads and roll in ashes" (Ezekiel 27:29-30 NLT). In one moment, everything they know goes up in smoke.

The dirge of each group—the kings, the merchants, and the seamen—begins with "woe, woe," and then describes the city according to their own relationship with it. For the kings, it is power (18:10); for the merchants, it is the commodities (18:12-13); for the sea captains and sailors, it is their income from the vessels carrying the commodities. All will see the fate of the city and will be stunned by it.

18:20 **"But you, O heaven, rejoice over her fate. And you also rejoice, O holy people of God and apostles and prophets! For at last God has judged her on your behalf."**[NLT] In contrast to the weeping and mourning of the people at the fall of Babylon, the heavens will rejoice. The call to rejoice is extended to the *holy people of God and apostles and prophets*—the people who have been persecuted and killed because they refused to join Babylon's system and worship the Beast (17:6). Babylon's fall will be God's judgment on behalf of his people. God will avenge his people for all they have suffered. God will do "to her as she has done to [his] people" (18:6). She has been judged for her evil deeds. This is the promised judgment of the great prostitute (17:1). God had promised, "It is mine to avenge; I will repay" (Deuteronomy 32:35 NIV). This time, that is exactly what he will do.

18:21 **Then a mighty angel picked up a boulder the size of a large millstone and threw it into the sea, and said: "With such violence the great city of Babylon will be thrown down, never to be found again."**[NIV] This *large millstone* would be a stone about fifteen to twenty feet wide, a foot thick, and weighing thousands of pounds—heavier than any human being could even move. But *a mighty angel* picked up *a boulder* that size and *threw it into the sea.* As a huge boulder, hurtled through the air, sinks to the bottom of the sea, so would Babylon *be thrown down, never to be found again.*

Jeremiah had given a similar prophecy to the city of Babylon:

Jeremiah had recorded on a scroll all the terrible disasters that would soon come upon Babylon. He said to Seraiah, "When you get to Babylon, read aloud everything on this scroll. Then say, 'Lord, you have said that you will destroy Babylon so that neither people nor animals will remain here. She will lie empty and abandoned forever.' Then, when you have finished reading the scroll, tie it to a stone, and throw it into the Euphrates River. Then say, 'In this same way Babylon and her people will sink, never again to rise, because of the disasters I will bring upon her.'" (Jeremiah 51:60-64 NLT*)*

Babylon, Rome, and the future focal point of the Antichrist's reign will have great glory and power and then will disappear like a rock beneath the waves. This will happen with great *violence.* This is a picture of God's judgment. In describing all who would turn children away from him, Jesus said: "If anyone causes one of these little ones who trusts in me to lose faith, it would be better for that person to be thrown into the sea with a large millstone tied around the neck" (Mark 9:42 NLT).

> The promises of sin are fair but the payoff is cruel.   *Albert Nielsen*

All that the people had lived for—their great luxuries and power—will become a millstone around their necks and will drag them to the bottom of the sea.

18:22-23 **"Never again will the sound of music be heard there—no more harps, songs, flutes, or trumpets. There will be no industry of any kind, and no more milling of grain. Her nights will be dark, without a single lamp. There will be no happy voices of brides and grooms. This will happen because her merchants, who were the greatest in the world, deceived the nations with her sorceries."**NLT The mighty city, thrown like a boulder into the sea, will be destroyed and silenced. This city had been filled with music—*harps, songs, flutes,* and *trumpets.* There had been busy industry in its humming economy. The *milling of grain* had provided plenty of food. People had enjoyed life, and there had been wedding celebrations. But when it all collapses, there will be no more *music, no industry, no happy voices.* There will be complete darkness, *without a single lamp.* This will be total and utter destruction.

> In spite of what people often think, no one is getting away with anything. Payday someday! God's vengeance will be revealed, even against false religion in whose name and under whose influence millions have suffered and died. God's judgment will fall and vindicate His people.
> *David Hocking*

Why will this happen? *Because her merchants, who were the greatest in the world, deceived the nations with her sorceries.* The word "sorceries" probably does not refer to black magic, although that was certainly practiced in the Roman Empire and will certainly be a part of any worship of Satan. Instead, it pictures the "spell" under which Rome, and this flourishing economy, puts its people. They are so enamored by the greatness of their culture that they believe it will last forever. They willingly worship the Beast in order to partake in what they perceive as the peace and joy that they think the Beast has brought (13:14-17).

18:24 **"In her streets the blood of the prophets was spilled. She was the one who slaughtered God's people all over the world."**NLT This is the great sin of Babylon, of Rome, and of the Antichrist's kingdom. The inhabitants of the world enjoy the great prosperity that the Beast's economy brings them. However, in the *streets* of that great city, *the blood of the prophets was spilled. Babylon was the one who slaughtered God's people all over the world.* Certainly this was true of Rome, for being a Christian in the Roman Empire was tantamount to treason. The emperors considered themselves to be gods, and, of all their peoples, it was the Christians who refused to worship them. Persecution under the emperors Nero and Domitian reached the heights of horror.

Jesus had warned his followers about the end of the world, "There will be great distress, unequaled from the beginning of the world until now—and never to be equaled again" (Matthew 24:21 NIV). The prophet Daniel had written, "At that time Michael, the great prince who protects your people, will arise. There will be a time of distress such as has not happened from the beginning of nations until then. But at that time your people—everyone whose name is found written in the book—will be delivered" (Daniel 12:1 NIV). God's people will suffer greatly in the years ahead. Jeremiah described a similar future, "In all history there has never been such a time of terror. It will be a time of trouble for my people Israel. Yet in the end, they will be saved!" (Jeremiah 30:7 NLT). The time would be evil and filled with suffering. This language may sound like an exaggeration, but it is not unusual in Scripture when describing an impending disaster. The Jewish historian Josephus recorded that when the Romans sacked Jerusalem and devastated Judea, 100,000 Jews were taken prisoner and another 1.1 million died by slaughter and starvation.

Jesus' words in Matthew could be taken as referring to the destruction of Jerusalem by the Romans in A.D. 70, but they also point ultimately to the final period of tribulation at the end of the age because, as Jesus stated, nothing like it had ever been seen or would ever be seen again. Yet this prediction of great suffering is tempered by the great promise of hope for true believers, as well as by the promise that Babylon will be annihilated for what she has done.

19:1-3 **After this, I heard the sound of a vast crowd in heaven shouting, "Hallelujah! Salvation is from our God. Glory and power belong to him alone. His judgments are just and true. He has punished the great prostitute who corrupted the earth with her immorality, and he has avenged the murder of his servants." Again and again their voices rang, "Hallelujah! The smoke from that city ascends forever and forever!"**^{NLT} These first five verses of chapter 19 describe the end of the destruction of Babylon the Great (chapters 17–18). In contrast to the funeral dirges of the kings, merchants, and seamen (18:9-19), the crowd in heaven sings a great song of praise.

This *vast crowd in heaven* begins praising God for his victory (19:1-3). Then the twenty-four elders (identified in the commentary on 4:4) join the chorus (19:4). Finally, the great choir of heaven once again praises God—the wedding of the Lamb has come (19:6-8). In Matthew 25:1-13, Christ had compared the coming of his kingdom to a wedding for which his people must be prepared.

This is the only place in the New Testament where the word "hallelujah" is found, and it occurs in verses 1, 3, 4, and 6. The word is derived from a combination of two Hebrew words, *halal* and *Jah,* meaning "Praise Yahweh" or "Praise God." The word can be found in the Old Testament, especially in Psalms 113–118, known as the Hallelujah psalms.

The song in Revelation praises God for his just and true judgments (see also 15:3; 16:5, 7). He is praised for avenging the murders of his people. The punishment of the evil adversaries of God and his people is cause for praise in heaven. God *has punished the great prostitute who corrupted the earth with her immorality, and he has avenged the murder of his servants.* The identity of this "great prostitute" is explained in the commentary on 17:1. Her corruption of the earth is described in chapters 17–18. This "corruption" causes people to be separated from God, unable to worship him, and, in the Old Testament, unable to enter the Temple. The "murder of [God's] servants" is described as the great prostitute being "drunk with the blood of God's holy people who were witnesses for Jesus" (17:6 NLT). The Beast and his kingdom will be judged for deceiving the nations and for killing God's servants.

The *voices* in heaven ring out, *again and again,* the praise for God's final victory. The "great prostitute," the evil city, has been destroyed and *the smoke from that city ascends forever and forever* (see also 9:2; 14:11; 18:9, 18). Babylon's destruction will be final. She will never rise again. The eternally burning fires are reminders of *Gehenna* or hellfire.

This gruesome sight causes rejoicing in heaven because God's name and God's people have been vindicated. The people who are judged were those who had lived in total depravity against God, willingly rejecting his offer of salvation. Their sins "are piled as high as heaven" (18:5), and God justly judges.

PRAISE
Praise is the heartfelt response to God by those who love him. The more you get to know God and realize what he has done, the more you will respond with praise. Praise is at the heart of true worship. Let your praise of God flow out of your realization of who he is and how much he loves you.

19:4 Then the twenty-four elders and the four living beings fell down and worshiped God, who was sitting on the throne. They cried out, "Amen! Hallelujah!"[NLT] The identity of *the twenty-four elders and the four living beings* is explained in 4:4 and 4:6. These joined with the vast crowd (19:1) in praise to *God, who was sitting on the throne.* They *fell down* in worship, indicating a position of total humility and subservience to God (see also 4:10; 5:14; 7:11; 11:16). They cried out *Amen,* affirming what God had done. They then repeated *Hallelujah.* In essence, they were saying: "Your will be done! Praise God!"

SO BE IT!
John may have been overwhelmed by all that he saw, but everyone in this vision rejoiced! In Revelation, sin and its effects abound, but grace abounds even more. So, as the evil systems of earth explode, God's people exclaim in praise, "Amen! Hallelujah!"
How can this be? If we have trusted Jesus, we will be among the multitude who proclaim, "His judgments are right and true." We will recognize that all the accounts have been settled justly. We will all experience the fulfillment of our hope and the justice for which we have hungered and thirsted. In that moment, only two expressions will be necessary: Amen ("So be it!" or "I mean it!") and Hallelujah ("Praise the Lord!"). We can use the same two expressions today when we declare our anticipation and expectation of Christ's coming! Amen! Hallelujah!

19:5 And from the throne came a voice that said, "Praise our God, all his servants, from the least to the greatest, all who fear him."[NLT] The closing of this song of praise was given by *a voice* located near *the throne.* This was not God's voice, because the words "praise our God" would not have come from God. The voice came from one of the heavenly beings and called upon *all* of God's *servants, from the least to the greatest, all who fear him,* to praise him. "Fear" refers to reverence for God. These are all of God's redeemed people called to join in praise to the God who had saved them from the end brought by Satan and evil—the burning fires of Babylon.

These words recall the psalms of praise in the Old Testament: "Praise the Lord! Yes, give praise, O servants of the Lord. Praise the name of the Lord! . . . Everywhere—from east to west— praise the name of the Lord. He will bless those who fear the Lord, both great and small" (Psalms 113:1, 3; 115:13 NLT).

Revelation 19:6-21

Verses 6-10 describe the marriage supper of the Lamb, but the event does not occur at this point. This foreshadows the actual event, and its appealing description is meant to invite the readers to take part in the banquet.

19:6-8 **Then I heard what seemed to be the voice of a great multitude, like the sound of many waters and like the sound of mighty thunderpeals, crying out, "Hallelujah! For the Lord our God the Almighty reigns. Let us rejoice and exult and give him the glory, for the marriage of the Lamb has come, and his bride has made herself ready."**NRSV John heard *the voice of a great multitude* (see also 7:9), whose voices sounded like *many waters* and like *mighty thunderpeals.* All heaven sang this hymn—the heavenly hosts and God's redeemed people praise God. *Hallelujah* is a word of praise, as noted in 19:1-5. The title *God the Almighty* has been used several times in Revelation to describe God's absolute sovereignty (see 1:8; 4:8; 11:17; 15:3; 16:7, 14; 19:15; 21:22).

The multitude was singing, rejoicing, exulting, and giving glory to God in a time of celebration like nothing ever seen before, for it will celebrate *the marriage of the Lamb,* referring to Christ. This next great vision, the bride getting ready for her wedding, contrasts with the "great prostitute" of 17:1. *His bride has made herself ready*—the bride is the new Jerusalem (21:2, 9-10), the church, the believers, those redeemed by Christ's blood. This is the culmination of human history—the judgment of the wicked and the wedding of the Lamb and his bride, the church.

In the Old Testament, the figure of a wedding banquet, with the bride as God's people Israel, pictured God's eternal love and protection over them (Isaiah 24:6-8; 54:5-7; 61:10; 62:5; Hosea 2:19). In some of his parables about the Kingdom of God, Jesus used the imagery of a wedding banquet (Matthew 22:2-14; 25:1-13; Luke 14:15-24). John the Baptist spoke of Jesus as the bridegroom (John 3:29), and Jesus described himself that way (Matthew 9:15; Luke 5:34-35). Other New Testament writers described God's people—

all believers, both Jews and Gentiles—as Christ's bride (2 Corinthians 11:2; Ephesians 5:23-32).

In Jewish tradition, a wedding had three stages. First, the two families would agree to the union and negotiate a betrothal. Next, they would make a public announcement. At that point, the couple would be "pledged." This is similar to engagement today, except that it was much more binding in ancient times. At this point, even though the couple was not officially married, their relationship could be broken only through death or divorce. This second step lasted a year. During that time, the couple would live separately. This waiting period would demonstrate the bride's purity. In a sense, that betrothal time for the bride is like the present days for the bride of Christ, the church. The church is presently in that waiting period between the betrothal and the actual wedding banquet, described by John here. A fuller description of this is in chapters 21 and 22.

ALL DRESSED UP
In Old Testament times, it was customary for wedding guests to be given special clothes to wear to the banquet. It was unthinkable to refuse to wear these clothes. That would insult the host, who could only assume that the guest was arrogant and thought the clothes were unnecessary, or that he or she did not want to take part in the wedding celebration. The wedding clothes picture the righteousness needed to enter God's Kingdom—the total acceptance in God's eyes that Christ gives every believer. Christ has provided these clothes of righteousness, but each person must choose to put them on in order to enter the King's banquet (eternal life). This clothing also pictures "the righteous acts of the saints" (19:8). In addition to wearing what Christ has done for us, we will be wearing what we have done for Christ. How have you prepared to meet Christ? Have you accepted his gift of righteousness?

"Fine linen, bright and clean, was given her to wear." (Fine linen stands for the righteous acts of the saints.)[NIV] The bride's clothing stands in sharp contrast to the gaudy clothing of the great prostitute (17:4). The bride was *given* her clothing—*fine linen, bright and clean.* In John's day, linen was expensive—only the very wealthy wore clothing made with linen. Here the bride of Christ, the believers, were wearing "fine linen," explained as representing *the righteous acts of the saints*—the believers (see also 3:4-5, 18; 4:4; 6:11; 7:9, 14; 15:6; 19:14). These "righteous acts" were not religious deeds done by believers so that they could be saved; instead, the acts reflected the fact that the saints had been saved in order to do good works (Ephesians 2:10).

The bride wore this clothing that had been purchased for her by the blood of Christ; she made herself "ready" through her faithfulness to Christ until the day of the "wedding," when she would be joined with him.

19:9 And the angel said to me, "Write this: Blessed are those who are invited to the marriage supper of the Lamb." And he said to me, "These are true words of God."[NRSV] This verse includes the fourth of seven beatitudes in Revelation, *Blessed are those who . . .* (see also 1:3; 14:13; 16:15; 20:6; 22:7; 22:14). Each beatitude describes the "blessedness" of those who have remained faithful to Christ. In this case, the believers were "blessed" because they had been *invited to the marriage supper of the Lamb.* At this banquet will be all those who have trusted Christ for salvation; they will come from every nation. Jesus had stated, "I tell you this, that many Gentiles will come from all over the world and sit down with Abraham, Isaac, and Jacob at the feast in the Kingdom of Heaven" (Matthew 8:11 NLT).

> How far away is heaven? It is not so far as some imagine. It wasn't very far from Daniel. It was not so far off that Elijah's prayer, and those of others, could not be heard there. Christ said when ye pray say, "Our Father, who art in heaven." Men full of the Spirit can look right into heaven.
>
> *Dwight L. Moody*

In the parable of the wedding feast (Matthew 22), Jesus described a king who prepared a great banquet and, while many guests had been invited, at the time of the banquet they all refused to come. They had taken on other commitments that they decided were more important. So the king filled his banquet hall with others who *did* come when invited. The point is that God has invited people to join him at this great feast. Blessed are those who have accepted the invitation to the marriage supper.

As an assurance to the readers of the absolute truth of the wedding banquet of Christ in which they would take part, the angel told John, *"These are true words of God."* God's true words stand forever.

R.S.V.P.
The traditional invitation response formula is "R.S.V.P.," which stands for a French phrase meaning "respond if you please." This response applies to the grandest invitation of all—the invitation to participate at the wedding feast of the Lamb. God awaits our response. Our presence at the celebration will be neither earned nor deserved. The angel declared that those invited to the wedding feast would be "blessed" because they had accepted the invitation. They simply responded to the invitation! From the angel, through John, to the written page, the invitation goes out to us. Tell others that there is still time to respond.

19:10 **Then I fell down at his feet to worship him, but he said,
"No, don't worship me. For I am a servant of God, just like
you and other believers who testify of their faith in Jesus.
Worship God. For the essence of prophecy is to give a clear
witness for Jesus."**[NLT] Whether John had mistaken this heavenly being for Christ, or whether he was simply overcome with
the emotion of the promise he had just foreseen, John *fell down*
at the angel's *feet to worship him.* But the angel stopped him,
"No, don't worship me." The Bible forbids worship of angels,
for, as the angel said, *"I am a servant of God, just like you and
the other believers who testify of their faith in Jesus."* The powerful angelic beings thus far described in Revelation—despite
their amazing strength and glory—were simply faithful servants of God, as are all believers who tell about their faith in
Jesus.

These servants of Christ had testified of their faith in Jesus,
and the angel said that *the essence of prophecy is to give a
clear witness for Jesus.* "Clear witness" also means "testimony" (1:9; 6:9; 12:11, 17; 17:6; 20:4). All believers are, in
a sense, prophets because they testify of their faith. For many
of the believers mentioned here, it had meant testifying to their
own deaths. The word "prophecy" means more than seeing
and foretelling the future, although in some cases that is true
(especially in the Old Testament prophets and in John's case
here). The main purpose of prophecy is to communicate God's
message.

ULTIMATE VICTORY
The angel did not accept John's homage and worship because
only God is worthy of worship. Like John, it would be easy for
anyone to become overwhelmed by this prophetic pageant.
But Jesus and his redemptive plan (as announced by the prophets) are the central focus of God's revelation. As you read the
book of Revelation, don't get bogged down in all the details
of the spectacular visions; remember that the overarching
theme in all the visions is the ultimate victory of Jesus Christ
over evil.

THE RIDER ON THE WHITE HORSE / 19:11-21

The vision shifts again. Heaven opened and Jesus appeared,
this time not as a Lamb but as a warrior on a white horse
(symbolizing victory). Jesus had come first as a Lamb to be
a sacrifice for sin, but he will return as a Conqueror and King

to execute judgment (2 Thessalonians 1:7-10). Jesus' first coming brought forgiveness; his second will bring judgment. The battle lines had been drawn between God and evil, and the world was waiting for the King to ride onto the field.

19:11-12 **I saw heaven standing open and there before me was a white horse, whose rider is called Faithful and True. With justice he judges and makes war. His eyes are like blazing fire, and on his head are many crowns. He has a name written on him that no one knows but he himself.**NIV This verse describes the second coming of Christ—the moment God's people had been waiting for:

- Christ said, "You will see me, the Son of Man, sitting at God's right hand in the place of power and coming back on the clouds of heaven" (Mark 14:62 NLT).
- Christ said, "The Son of Man will appear in the sky, and all the nations of the earth will mourn. They will see the Son of Man coming on the clouds of the sky, with power and great glory" (Luke 24:30 NIV).
- An angel told the disciples, "Jesus has been taken away from you into heaven. And someday, just as you saw him go, he will return!" (Acts 1:11 NLT).
- Paul wrote, "God will provide rest for you who are being persecuted and also for us when the Lord Jesus appears from heaven. He will come with his mighty angels, in flaming fire, bringing judgment on those who don't know God and on those who refuse to obey the Good News of our Lord Jesus. They will be punished with everlasting destruction, forever separated from the Lord and from his glorious power when he comes to receive glory and praise from his holy people" (2 Thessalonians 1:7-10 NLT).

Christ's return will be unmistakable. *Heaven* will be *standing open,* as Christ, the *rider* on a *white horse,* makes his entrance. The white horse symbolizes victory. (Some think this is the same rider as mentioned in 6:2, who was also on a white horse. They suggest that the rider symbolized Christ and the spread of the Good News across the world. See commentary at 6:2 for more information.) This rider is called *Faithful and True,* in contrast with the faithless and deceitful Babylon described in chapter 18 (see also 3:14). Christ, the great warrior, comes *with justice,* and with that justice *he judges and makes war.* The order of words indicates that the warfare is a result of God's judgment on the inhabitants of the earth who have completely rejected him. Although Jesus is called

THE RAPTURE

When Christ returns as the rider on the white horse, is this the point where he "raptures" the church, or has that already happened? There is much discussion regarding the rapture of the church (never specifically mentioned in Revelation) and the second coming of Christ. Listed below are three passages that many people believe describe the Rapture.

- "No one knows the day or the hour when these things will happen, not even the angels in heaven or the Son himself. Only the Father knows. When the Son of Man returns, it will be like it was in Noah's day. . . . People didn't realize what was going to happen until the Flood came and swept them all away. That is the way it will be when the Son of Man comes. Two men will be working together in the field; one will be taken, the other left. Two women will be grinding flour at the mill; one will be taken, the other left. So be prepared, because you don't know what day your Lord is coming" (Matthew 24:36-37, 40-42 NLT).

- "Listen, I tell you a mystery: We will not all sleep, but we will all be changed—in a flash, in the twinkling of an eye, at the last trumpet. For the trumpet will sound, the dead will be raised imperishable, and we will be changed" (1 Corinthians 15:51-52 NIV).

- "For the Lord himself will come down from heaven with a commanding shout, with the call of the archangel, and with the trumpet call of God. First, all the Christians who have died will rise from their graves. Then, together with them, we who are still alive and remain on the earth will be caught up in the clouds to meet the Lord in the air and remain with him forever" (2 Thessalonians 4:16-17 NLT).

At the Rapture, Christ will bring his people to be with him. Some Christians think that the Rapture will be a separate event from the Second Coming; others believe they are two names for the same event.

Dispensational premillennialists (and pretribulationists) think that the Rapture and the Second Coming are two separate and distinct events. They believe that the church will be raptured before the Tribulation begins. Then, at the end of the Tribulation (seven years later), Christ will return, and this will be the Second Coming. At that time, Christ will bring judgment

---

"Faithful and True," "Word of God" (19:13), and "King of kings and Lord of lords" (19:16), these verses imply that no name can do him justice. He is greater than any description or expression the human mind can devise.

His eyes are like blazing fire (see also 1:14; 2:18). Christ's *many crowns* symbolize his ultimate authority (contrast this with the seven crowns on the dragon in 12:3 and the ten crowns on the Beast in 13:1). He has *a name written on him that no one knows but he himself.* Although many possibilities have been proposed, most likely this is a name that the believers were not meant to know, at least not yet.

and set up the millennial kingdom (19:11-21). Those who believe this way separate the Rapture and the Second Coming by saying:

1. The Rapture can occur at any time and will affect only true believers, while the Second Coming will affect the entire world.

2. At the Rapture Christ won't completely descend to earth; instead, believers will meet the Lord in the air. At the Second Coming, Christ will descend to earth.

3. The Rapture will remove believers from the earth; the Second Coming will remove the wicked from the earth so that only believers enter the millennial kingdom.

Midtribulationists believe that the Rapture of all believers will occur halfway through the Tribulation (after three and a half years) so that believers will not be a part of the bowl judgments. These believers will return with Christ at his second coming.

Posttribulationists (along with historic premillennialists and amillennialists) think that believers will go through the Tribulation and that the Rapture and Second Coming are the same event. Believers will meet the Lord in the air; then they will immediately accompany Christ on his descent to earth as the rider on the white horse.

Postmillenialists also view the Rapture and the Second Coming as the same event; however, they place these events at the end of the Millennium, the thousand-year reign of Christ. After Satan is released from the bottomless pit to deceive the nations and wage war on God's people (20:7-10), Christ will call his people to him; then Christ's people will accompany him as he descends to earth, defeats his enemies, and establishes a new heaven and new earth.

Whenever the Rapture of the church occurs, it is already certain that the rider on the white horse will come in victory and that believers will be with him in heaven. While the various views on these topics can be difficult to understand, it is far more important that every believer know on which side of the battle he or she is. Those who remain faithful to Christ, no matter what, will receive all that God has promised.

19:13 He is dressed in a robe dipped in blood, and his name is the Word of God.^{NIV} The believers who had come out of the Great Tribulation had "washed their robes in the blood of the Lamb and made them white" (7:14 NLT). Christ himself, when he rides to the earth on the white horse, will be *dressed in a robe dipped in blood*. Some suggest that this is the blood of the martyrs; some think it is the blood of Christ's enemies (referring to a similar passage in Isaiah 63:1-6); others think that this is the Lamb's own blood which, ultimately, brings about this final day of victory.

Another name is given for Christ, *the Word of God.* In Greek, the word for "Word" is *logos,* also used in John's Gospel, "In the beginning was the Word, and the Word was with God, and the Word was God" (John 1:1 NIV; see also John 1:14; 1 John 1:1). Jesus is the final word of God, the voice of God himself, the revealer of God.

19:14 And the armies of heaven, wearing fine linen, white and pure, were following him on white horses.NRSV Accompanying Christ are *the armies of heaven,* referring to all believers who have been taken to heaven (in the Rapture, which will have occurred at some point prior to this although believers are divided as to when this will happen). Here the believers will be returning to earth with Christ as part of his vast army. They will be *wearing fine linen, white and pure,* as noted also in 19:8. Some suggest that this army will be angels because Christ had spoken of returning with his angels (Matthew 24:30-31). Most likely, however, this army will be believers because 17:14 says, "They [the Beast and the false prophet] will make war against the Lamb, but the Lamb will overcome them . . . and with him will be his called, chosen and faithful followers" (NIV).

The believers will come with Christ *on white horses.* They will not come to fight, however, for there will not need to be a battle. Christ will conquer with his potent word (19:15).

19:15 From his mouth came a sharp sword, and with it he struck down the nations. He ruled them with an iron rod, and he trod the winepress of the fierce wrath of almighty God.NLT Christ is described as having a *sharp sword* coming from his mouth. This is also seen in 1:16 and 2:12. The word for "sword" used here, however, is not the small two-edged sword but a mighty sword that is four or five feet long. This was the sword used by cavalry soldiers. Christ's words of judgment are as sharp as swords. With that sword, he *struck down the nations.* Isaiah had prophesied of Christ, "He will rule against the wicked and destroy them with the breath of his mouth" (Isaiah 11:4 NLT).

The picture of Christ ruling *with an iron rod* (or scepter) describes him beating down the nations (see also 2:27). This is not a king's scepter that is merely symbolic of power; instead, it is a club with which he will destroy them. The psalmist had written of the Messiah, "You will break [the nations] with an iron rod and smash them like clay pots" (Psalm 2:9 NLT).

Lastly, Christ is pictured as treading *the winepress of the fierce wrath of almighty God.* The winepress image appeared in 14:19-20; it describes God's great wrath against those who had rejected him. Here, God's fierce anger is directed at all of sin personified. At this point, God will totally destroy sin and evil. A winepress is a large vat where grapes are collected and then crushed. It is often used in the Bible to symbolize judgment (Isaiah 63:3-6; Lamentations 1:15; Joel 3:12-13).

MERCY . . . AND JUDGMENT
This scene provides a graphic display of the wrath of God. It shows God's anger and judgment against sin and against those who have constantly rejected Christ as the means of forgiveness and reconciliation. God's wrath exists alongside his mercy. In each generation, there must be balanced preaching and teaching about God's grace and his anger against sin. In Martin Luther's day, God had been presented as so wrathful that grace and forgiveness needed to be reemphasized and taught to the people.

In our day, however, teaching about God's love and tolerance have become so predominant that God's anger seems to be mythical. Such a portrayal of God hardly warns people away from sin. Teaching about God's wrath may be watered down by some, but it is nevertheless real and will be terrible for those who have steadfastly refused him (1 Thessalonians 1:10). In your study and teaching, do not emphasize God's mercy to the exclusion of his wrath.

19:16 **On his robe and on his thigh he has a name inscribed, "King of kings and Lord of lords."**^{NRSV} Most of the world will be worshiping the Beast, the Antichrist, whom they believe has all power and authority. Then suddenly out of heaven Christ and his army will appear. *On his robe and on his thigh* (easily seen, for he is on a horse), *he has a name inscribed.* This title indicates God's sovereignty—*King of kings and Lord of lords.* This title is used elsewhere in Scripture, always indicating God's absolute sovereignty over all other kings and lords (see 17:14; Deuteronomy 10:17; Daniel 2:47; 1 Timothy 6:15).

19:17-18 **Then I saw an angel standing in the sun, and with a loud voice he called to all the birds that fly in midheaven, "Come, gather for the great supper of God, to eat the flesh of kings, the flesh of captains, the flesh of the mighty, the flesh of horses and their riders—flesh of all, both free and slave, both small and great."**^{NRSV} John saw another *angel;* this one described as *standing in the sun* and calling out *to all the birds that fly in midheaven*—referring to the eagles and the vultures, birds of carrion. This will be the most gruesome single act of carnage ever in the history of mankind; the entire army will come to do battle and, with the word of Christ, they will be totally annihilated. Their *flesh* will be left for the birds to eat, for there will be no one left to bury the dead. A previous description of this battle included how "the blood flowed from the winepress in a stream about 180 miles long and as high as a horse's bridle" (14:20 NLT). This *great supper of God* is a grim contrast to the wedding supper of the Lamb (19:9). Both will be provided by God—but one will be a celebration, the other will be devastation.

The angel called the birds together before the battle. Again, the picture is clear of the certainty of the final outcome. Ezekiel had written God's words to him in a prophecy of this final battle, "'And now, son of man, call all the birds and wild animals,' says the Sovereign Lord. 'Say to them, "Gather together for my great sacrificial feast. Come from far and near to the mountains of Israel, and there eat the flesh and drink the blood. . . . Feast at my banquet table—feast on horses, riders, and valiant warriors" (Ezekiel 39:17, 20 NLT).

19:19 Then I saw the beast and the kings of the earth with their armies gathered to make war against the rider on the horse and against his army.^NRSV This *beast* is the same one that had risen out of the sea (chapter 13; see commentary there). The phrase "kings of the earth" refers to the "ten horns" that John had seen on the Beast (see 13:1), and, most likely, their number symbolizes all the kings of the earth who pledge allegiance to the Antichrist. At the pouring out of the sixth bowl of God's wrath, "miracle-working demons caused all the rulers of the world to gather for battle against the Lord . . . to a place called *Armageddon*" (16:14-16 NLT). Chapter 16 gave a preview of what was to come and how; chapter 19 describes the event itself. Here, verse 19 tells of the assembly for the battle of Armageddon. (For further information on this battle and the various viewpoints regarding it, see commentary at 16:16.)

The Beast and the kings of the earth and their armies gathered *to make war against the rider on the horse* (Christ) *and against his army* (the redeemed). The battle lines had been drawn, and the greatest confrontation in the history of the world was about to begin. The enemy armies believed they had come of their own volition; in reality, God had summoned them to battle in order to defeat them. That they would even presume to fight against God shows how pride and rebellion had perverted their thinking.

19:20 But the beast was captured, and with him the false prophet who had performed the miraculous signs on his behalf. With these signs he had deluded those who had received the mark of the beast and worshiped his image. The two of them were thrown alive into the fiery lake of burning sulfur.^NIV The two armies sat facing each other—the Beast and all the kings of the earth versus the rider on the white horse and his redeemed people. Suddenly, the battle was over. There was no fight, for, in a second, the end had come. There was no need for a battle because the victory had been won centuries earlier when the rider on the white horse, Christ, had died on a cross. At that time, Satan had been defeated; here at Armageddon, he is finally stripped of all his power. Satan's *beast* (the Antichrist, described in 13:1-10) *was captured.* In addition, his *false prophet who had performed the miraculous signs on his behalf* was also captured, for *he had deluded those who had received the mark of the beast and worshiped his image.* This is described in 13:11-18.

The Beast and the false prophet were captured and *thrown alive into the fiery lake of burning sulfur.* This is the final destination of all evil. At this point, however, only these two evil beings received this punishment. This lake is different from the Abyss (bottomless pit) referred to in 9:1; it is the *Gehenna* of 14:10-11 and 19:3 (see commentary there). There are several statements concerning both spiritual powers and people being thrown into the lake of fire. Here, the Antichrist and the false prophet were thrown into the fiery lake. Next, their leader, Satan himself, will be thrown into that lake (20:10), and finally death and Hades (20:14). Afterward, everyone whose name is not recorded in the Book of Life will be thrown into the lake of fire (20:15).

THE END OF EVIL
Evil's final destination will be a fiery lake. Throughout Scripture, fire portrays God's searing holiness, and burning sulfur reflects his awful judgment as he exacts retribution for evil (Genesis 19:24; Ezekiel 38:22; Hebrews 10:30). Hell is a horrible reality, a place of endless torment, but hell was designed for Satan and his demons. The people sent there will be those who viciously attack God and join Satan in his rebellion against God. In *The Problem of Pain,* C. S. Lewis wrote that "the doors to hell are locked on the inside" to keep God and goodness out. The warnings of Revelation were given to keep believers faithful to Christ and active in his service. Keep your trust in him strong, and be vigilant in withstanding evil.

19:21 Their entire army was killed by the sharp sword that came out of the mouth of the one riding the white horse. And all the vultures of the sky gorged themselves on the dead bodies.[NLT] With the two leaders captured (the Beast and the false prophet), the army was left to be destroyed. Christ, with *the sharp sword* of his *mouth* (19:15), kills the entire army of rebellious kings and soldiers in one fell swoop. His sword of judgment falls and destroys everything. The *vultures* who had been called ahead of time by the angel (19:17-18) *gorged themselves on the dead bodies.* With no one left on the planet to bury these dead, they were abandoned to the carrion birds to devour.

Revelation 20

Chapter 20 has probably engendered more argument, discussion, and books than any other section of Revelation. Much of how a person understands this chapter will depend on the approach taken in the other sections of the book. There are three main views of the Millennium, and these are described below (see the chart "Views of the Millennium," in 20:2-3). The views differ over: (1) whether the millennial reign of Christ is an earthly historical reign of peace or a spiritual reign in the hearts of God's people; (2) whether this millennial reign is a literal one thousand years or another length of time.

Whether the one thousand years is a literal or figurative number, most likely, the Millennium will occur in history; it will probably be an earthly reign of Christ that follows his second coming.

20:1 And I saw an angel coming down out of heaven, having the key to the Abyss and holding in his hand a great chain.^{NIV} The end of chapter 19 describes the Beast, the false prophet, and all their followers thrown into the lake of fire. This vision at the beginning of chapter 20 describes Christ's dealings with Satan. John saw another *angel coming down out of heaven.* This angel had *the key to the Abyss* (also called the bottomless pit). In 9:1-12, an angel had arrived with the key to the Abyss and had released the locusts as part of the fifth trumpet judgment. This may be the same angel. When that angel opened the Abyss, "smoke poured out as though from a huge furnace, and the sunlight and air were darkened by the smoke" (9:2 NLT). The "Abyss" pictures the abode of the demonic forces, as well as the place from which the Beast comes (11:7; 17:8). The angel was also carrying *a great chain* that he would use to bind Satan. (For more information on the Abyss, see the commentary at 9:1-2.)

20:2-3 He seized the dragon, that ancient serpent, who is the devil, or Satan, and bound him for a thousand years. He threw him into the Abyss, and locked and sealed it over him, to keep him from deceiving the nations anymore until the thousand years were ended. After that, he must be set free for a short time.^{NIV}

HOW SATAN IS ACTIVE IN THE PRESENT AGE

New Testament example	Application for today
"Then Satan entered Judas Iscariot." (Luke 22:3)	Satan can cause willing people to do his bidding.
"Peter said, 'Ananias, why has Satan filled your heart?'" (Acts 5:3)	Satan leads people to deceive others.
"Satan, the god of this evil world, has blinded the minds of those who don't believe." (2 Corinthians 4:4)	Satan prevents people from accepting the gospel.
"Satan can disguise himself as an angel of light." (2 Corinthians 11:14)	Satan counterfeits goodness and truth to trap people.
"Satan, the mighty prince of the power of the air . . . is at work in the hearts of those who refuse to obey God." (Ephesians 2:2)	Satan inflames the evil desires of those who reject God.
"We wanted very much to come . . . but Satan prevented us." (1 Thessalonians 2:18)	Satan attempts to block evangelistic efforts.
"Then they will come to their senses and escape from the Devil's trap. For they have been held captive by him to do whatever he wants." (2 Timothy 2:26)	Satan uses church controversies and quarrels to lead people astray.
"Be careful! Watch out for attacks from the Devil, your great enemy. He prowls around like a roaring lion, looking for some victim to devour." (1 Peter 5:8)	Satan attacks the weak, suffering, or lonely Christian who then withdraws from the church.

Several names are used here for the same being—the *dragon,* the *ancient serpent,* the *devil,* and *Satan* (see also 12:9 for another list of these names). The angel *seized* Satan, *bound him,* and *threw him into the Abyss,* locking and sealing the door *over him.* Satan was put away and could not get out until God would decide to let him out. God's sovereignty is emphasized again.

This describes a different situation than that in 12:7-13. Chapter 12 describes Satan's fall from heaven and his freedom to roam the earth where he "declared war against . . . all who keep God's commandments and confess that they belong to Jesus" (12:17 NLT). Chapter 20 describes Satan being removed from the earth for a time in order that he would be kept *from deceiving the nations anymore.* God did not bind the dragon as punishment— that would occur later (20:10)—but to stop him from deceiving the nations. But who are "the nations"? It appears that, at the battle of Armageddon (16:14-16; 19:19), only the Beast, the false prophets, the kings of the nations, and their armies were destroyed. The battle at Armageddon did not kill the entire population of the earth. Therefore, some unbelievers would still be alive (the believers would be with Christ, for they had been part of his army, 19:14). Satan will be bound *during this thousand year period.* Whether symbolic or literal, this time period of Satan's imprisonment matches the time period of Christ's reign (20:4-6). After a thousand years, Satan will be freed to build an army; the people in it will be "as numerous as the sands of the sea" (20:8 NRSV).

Those who propose that this Millennium time period is not limited to a thousand years (the amillennialists) and believe that it is the time between the first and second comings of Christ interpret this binding as referring to Satan being kept from working in the lives of believers and from stopping the gospel's advance. Others explain, however, that the word "nations" is always used in Revelation to describe unbelievers. It seems clear, therefore, that Satan will be bound and locked away from deceiving the unbelievers (still alive after Armageddon), while Christ rules during this period. The words describing how Satan is locked and sealed away indicate that his activity on earth will be completely stopped for this period of time. During this time, the unbelievers will experience true justice and God's perfect rule over the earth.

Why is there a Millennium? Why doesn't God go straight from Armageddon to eternity? Why this interim and then another final battle—Gog and Magog? We don't know, but it appears that unbelievers on earth are given the opportunity to experience what the rule of God is like. However, as shown in the following verses, even though unbelievers will experience the reign of Christ, they will continue to rebel against God even without Satan's deceptive influence. And the moment that Satan is let out of the prison, these people will flock after Satan and go to war against Christ. This will prove their absolute depravity, their true allegiance, and the necessity of the final punishment in the lake of fire.

20:4-6 **"Then I saw thrones, and the people sitting on them had been given the authority to judge. And I saw the souls of those who had been beheaded for their testimony about Jesus, for proclaiming the word of God. And I saw the souls of those who had not worshiped the beast or his statue, nor accepted his mark on their foreheads or their hands. They came to life again, and they reigned with Christ for a thousand years."**NLT
Satan has been bound and thrown into the Abyss so that for a thousand years he will not be able to deceive the nations. Here Revelation describes who will take part in that thousand-year reign of Christ, free from the influence of evil.

VIEWS ON THE MILLENNIUM

The one thousand years are often referred to as the Millennium (Latin for one thousand). There are three major views about the Millennium, commonly called premillennialism, amillennialism, postmillennialism.

Premillennialism
Premillennialism says that the one thousand years is a literal time period. Christ's second coming will begin the Millennium before the final removal of Satan. (The pre-, mid-, and post-Tribulation views are all "premillennial" in that they all agree that Christ will return at some point around the Tribulation, but before this thousand-year reign.)

Under this view are two types of understandings:

1. Dispensational premillennialists say that at the end of the Tribulation will come the battle of Armageddon, the imprisonment of Satan, and Jesus' reign over Israel (19:19–20:6). During that thousand-year reign, the Old Testament promises for Israel will be fulfilled (such as Isaiah 2:4; 9:6-7; 11:6-9; 35:5-6; 42:1). Dispensationalists believe the Millennium will end with Satan leading a brief rebellion against Christ and then being thrown into the lake of fire. Then God will re-create the heavens and earth.

2. Historic premillennialists believe that Christ's second coming will occur after the Tribulation to bring believers into his millennial kingdom. He will defeat the Antichrist's forces at Armageddon and kill the Antichrist, ending a first stage in Christ's defeat of evil. The believers will accompany Christ as he establishes his millennial kingdom on earth. Satan will be chained during that time. Premillennialists believe that the establishment of Christ's millennial reign on earth will cause the nation of Israel to turn to Jesus, thus fulfilling many of the Old Testament prophecies for Israel. Historic premillennialists contend that only believers will be raised from the dead to reign with Christ in the Millennium. The remaining unbelieving dead will be raised to life when the Millennium ends—they will be raised for judgment. At that point, God will bring into existence the new heaven and new earth.

First, John saw *thrones*. The people *sitting* on the thrones *had been given authority to judge*. Who are those sitting on the thrones? The Scripture does not identify them specifically. Many interpreters believe that these are those who had been martyred for their faith, but the problem with this theory is that the martyrs are not mentioned until the last part of the verse. Some suggest that this is only the twenty-four elders (4:4) or that this forms an angelic court of some kind. In Matthew 19:28, the apostles are promised that they will judge from twelve thrones. First Corinthians 6:2-3 says that the saints will judge the world. What we can determine is that this is a court in heaven composed of those whom God wants to assist in judgment (see also Daniel 7:26).

Next, he saw *the souls of those who had been beheaded for their testimony about Jesus, for proclaiming the word of God.*

Amillennialism

Amillennialism understands the one-thousand-year period to be symbolic of the time between Christ's ascension and his second coming; thus, the Millennium is the reign of Christ in the hearts of believers and in his church and is another way of referring to the church age. This period will end with the second coming of Christ. Amillennialists do not believe in a literal period of Tribulation because they view the Tribulation as including various events during the history of the church. To them, the events of the Millennium described in Revelation 20:1-6 are actually occurring now! Amillennialists believe that as the last days approach, the forces of evil will climax with the Antichrist and the great tribulation he will bring (2 Thessalonians 2:1-3). They believe that the wicked will continue to gather strength, persecuting believers more and more. Only when Christ returns will wickedness be stopped once and for all. After judging both the living and dead, Christ will establish his everlasting reign of peace.

Postmillennialism

Postmillennialism looks for a period of peace on earth ushered in by the church. At the end of this time, Satan will be released, but Christ will return to defeat Satan and reign forever. Postmillennialists believe that Jesus will return to a world that has been "Christianized" by the work of the church. Thus, the Millennium will be established by the efforts of Christians, and Christ will only return to the earth after the Millennium. They believe that the church is now gradually transforming society (Matthew 13:31-33). Postmillennialists believe that the Tribulation symbolizes the constant conflict between good and evil which has existed throughout history.

Postmillennialists believe that the Millennium will end when Satan is released from the bottomless pit. Then Christ will return to judge all people and establish a new heaven and new earth. Postmillennialists believe the church bears the responsibility for spreading the Good News to all the world.

Then a problem arises with the translation. Between the sentence describing the martyrs and the sentence that says they *had not worshiped the beast . . . nor accepted his mark,* the Greek includes the words "and who," which can be taken as a further description of the martyrs, or as a description of an entirely different group. If the latter is the case, John saw the martyrs, whom he had described in 6:9-11, as well as others who were martyred during the Great Tribulation. Then he saw a separate group, those who "had not worshiped the beast or his statue, nor accepted his mark on their foreheads or their hands."

If "those who had not worshiped the beast" is merely a further description of the martyrs, then it appears that only the martyrs *came to life again, and they reigned with Christ for a thousand years*—a reward for their ultimate faithfulness to Christ by giving up their lives. However, John continued, **(The rest of the dead did not come to life until the thousand years were ended.) This is the first resurrection. Blessed and holy are those who have part in the first resurrection. The second death has no power over them, but they will be priests of God and of Christ and will reign with him for a thousand years.**NIV This *first resurrection,* then, could be a resurrection only of the martyrs and those who had not worshiped the Beast. If so, then the rest of the believers along with the unbelievers are described as *the rest of the dead* who do *not come to life until the thousand years* are over. At this point, God will separate the unbelievers from the believers, sending the former to the lake of fire and granting the latter eternal life. However, some commentators think that all believers partake of the *first resurrection* because all believers have been freed from the *second death*—that is, the lake of fire. The phrase "come to life" refers to a physical resurrection of their bodies. These believers will have new bodies, as described in 1 Corinthians 15:51-53.

Those who do not believe in a literal thousand-year reign of Christ say that this first resurrection is spiritual (in believers' hearts at salvation), and that the Millennium is their spiritual reign with Christ on earth between his first and second comings. During this time, believers are priests of God because Christ reigns in their hearts. In this view, the second resurrection is the bodily resurrection of all people for judgment. Others believe that the first resurrection occurs after Satan is set aside. It is a physical resurrection of believers who then reign with Christ on the earth for a literal one thousand years. The second resurrection will occur at the end of this Millennium when God will judge unbelievers who have died.

These believers are "blessed," the fifth of seven beatitudes in Revelation (1:3; 14:13; 16:15; 19:9; 22:7, 14; see the chart at 14:13).

THE DESTRUCTION OF SATAN / 20:7-10

At Armageddon, the Beast and the false prophet had been thrown into the lake of fire. Then Satan was locked away for a thousand years. Upon his release, he immediately goes on the offensive against Christ and his people. But his end will be like his followers—he too will be cast into the lake of fire.

20:7-8 **When the thousand years are ended, Satan will be released from his prison and will come out to deceive the nations at the four corners of the earth, Gog and Magog, in order to gather them for battle; they are as numerous as the sands of the sea.**NRSV Satan had been locked up for a thousand years so

that he could no longer deceive the nations (20:2-3). But at the
end of that thousand years, *Satan will be released from his prison*
(this is planned for by God, see 2:3). Immediately, Satan will
deceive the nations at the four corners of the earth. The unbelievers still on the earth after the battle of Armageddon will have
lived through the thousand-year reign of Christ, but as soon as
Satan is set free, they will be deceived and ready to *gather . . .
for battle.* This reaction demonstrates that Satan will not repent.
It also shows that people rebel against God no matter how long
or how many chances they are given to repent. The source of
rebellion against God comes not from the
environment or even from Satan himself but
from within the human heart.

> A thousand years of
> confinement does not
> alter Satan's plans, nor
> does a thousand years
> of freedom from the
> influence of wickedness
> change man's basic
> tendency to rebel against
> his Creator. . . . Neither
> the designs of Satan
> nor the waywardness of
> the human heart will
> be altered by the mere
> passing of time.
>   *Robert Mounce*

The names *Gog and Magog* symbolize all
the nations of the earth that join together to
battle God. Noah's son, Japheth, had a son
named Magog (Genesis 10:2). Ezekiel presented Gog, of the land of Magog, as a
leader of forces against Israel (Ezekiel 38–
39). This comparison is used in Revelation,
as is so much other Old Testament prophecy, because of the similarity of evil forces
battling against God's people and God's cataclysmic victory. In Ezekiel 37, Ezekiel
revealed how Israel (God's people) would
be restored to their land from many parts of
the world. Once Israel became strong, a con-
federacy of nations from the north would
attack, led by Gog, of the land of Magog (Ezekiel 38:1). Their
purpose would be to destroy God's people. It might be that Gog
will be a person, or Gog might also symbolize all the evil in the
world. Whether symbolic or literal, Gog represents the aggregate
military might of all the forces opposed to God. Many say that
the battle Ezekiel described will occur at the end of human history, but there are many differences between the events described
in Ezekiel and the final battle of Revelation 20. Regardless of
when this battle will occur, the message is clear: God will deliver
his people. No enemy (even an enemy from *the four corners of
the earth* and *as numerous as the sands of the sea*) will be able
to stand against his mighty power.

20:9 **And I saw them as they went up on the broad plain of the
earth and surrounded God's people and the beloved city. But
fire from heaven came down on the attacking armies and consumed them.**[NLT] This vast army of people, led by Satan himself,

THE CERTAINTY OF THE RESURRECTION

The resurrection is a certainty based on God's Word. The following verses are quoted from the NLT.

Author	Quote
Job	"I know that my Redeemer lives . . . And after my body has decayed, yet in my body I will see God." (Job 19:25-26)
David	"When I awake, I will be fully satisfied, for I will see you face to face." (Psalm 17:15)
Descendants of Korah	"But as for me, God will redeem my life. He will snatch me from the power of death." (Psalm 49:15)
Isaiah	"Yet we have this assurance: Those who belong to God will live; their bodies will rise again! Those who sleep in the earth will rise up and sing for joy. For God's light of life will fall like dew on his people in the place of the dead!" (Isaiah 26:19)
Daniel	"Many of those whose bodies lie dead and buried will rise up, some to everlasting life and some to shame and everlasting contempt. . . . You will rise again to receive the inheritance set aside for you." (Daniel 12:2, 13)
Jesus	"He will even raise from the dead anyone he wants to, just as the Father does." (John 5:21)
Jesus	"And this is the will of God, that I should not lose even one of all those he has given me, but that I should raise them to eternal life at the last day." (John 6:39)
Jesus	"I am the resurrection and the life. Those who believe in me, even though they die like everyone else, will live again." (John 11:25)
Paul	"I have hope in God . . . that he will raise both the righteous and the ungodly." (Acts 24:15)
Paul	"The Spirit of God, who raised Jesus from the dead, lives in you. And just as he raised Christ from the dead, he will give life to your mortal body by this same Spirit living within you." (Romans 8:11)
Paul	"And God will raise our bodies from the dead by his marvelous power, just as he raised our Lord from the dead." (1 Corinthians 6:14)
Paul	"Christ was raised first; then when Christ comes back, all his people will be raised." (1 Corinthians 15:23)
Paul	"When we die and leave these bodies—we will have a home in heaven, an eternal body made for us by God himself." (2 Corinthians 5:1)

went up on the broad plain of the earth and surrounded God's people and the beloved city. The unbelievers attacked the believers. "Beloved city" probably refers to Jerusalem. Or the "beloved city" could simply be a way of describing God's people. These people will be surrounded by this great evil army.

Before a battle can even ensue, however, *fire from heaven came down on the attacking armies and consumed them* (see also Ezekiel 38:22; 39:6). God totally destroyed this entire army that was "as numerous as the sands of the sea" (20:8). All of Satan's followers were destroyed in an instant.

TREMENDOUS VICTORY
Two mighty forces of evil—first, those of the Beast (19:19) and second, those of Satan (20:8)—attempt to do battle against God on two different occasions. Unlike typical battles where the outcome is in doubt during the heat of the conflict, here there is no contest. The Bible uses just two verses to describe each battle—the evil Beast and his forces were captured and thrown into the fiery lake (19:20-21), and fire from heaven devours Satan and his attacking armies (20:9-10). For God, it is as easy as that. There will be no doubt, no worry, no second thoughts for believers about whether they have chosen the right side.

If you are with God, you will experience this tremendous victory with Christ. This power is available now for those who believe. This mighty display of God's power is foretold here so Christians will trust God now. Let this victory fill you with hope and rekindle your desire to live for God and not give in to sinful desires. Above all, let it produce eager anticipation for Christ's reign.

20:10 And the devil, who deceived them, was thrown into the lake of burning sulfur, where the beast and the false prophet had been thrown. They will be tormented day and night for ever and ever.[NIV] The *devil,* Satan, the one who had been let free and had *deceived* all the nations, received his just punishment. He was *thrown into the lake of burning sulfur, where the beast and the false prophet had been thrown* (19:20). The evil trinity was gone forever (for more on the Beast and the false prophet, see chapter 13). Satan's power is not eternal—he will meet his doom. He began his evil work in mankind at the beginning (Genesis 3:1-6) and continues it today, but he will be destroyed when he is thrown into the lake of burning sulfur. The devil will be released temporarily from the Abyss (20:7), but he will never be released from the fiery lake. He will never be a threat to anyone again (for more information on the lake of burning sulfur, see commentary at 19:3 and 19:20). Those in that place will face torment *day and night for ever and ever.*

The description of the torment in this lake of burning sulfur has caused a debate regarding the true nature of this place. Some

DON'T FORGET TO DO GOOD

We are saved by faith in Jesus Christ, but faith ought to result in a changed life and a willingness to do good to others.

What Jesus said . . .	Matthew 5:14-16
	Matthew 6:1
	John 3:21
What Paul said . . .	2 Corinthians 9:8
	Ephesians 2:10; 4:12
	2 Thessalonians 2:16-17
	1 Timothy 6:17-19
	2 Timothy 3:16-17
	Titus 3:14
What James said . . .	James 1:22
	James 2:14-26
	James 3:13
What Peter said . . .	1 Peter 1:14
	1 Peter 2:12
What John said . . .	1 John 2:6
	Revelation 14:13; 21:13
What Hebrews said . . .	Hebrews 13:16

believe in a doctrine of "annihilationism"—meaning that after death, the wicked are utterly obliterated and consumed through God's judgment. Their "torment" is knowing that they will never come to life again; they will be dead "for ever and ever." This view is based on the fact that much of the biblical imagery of hell—a consuming fire, destruction, and perishing—may imply eternal death. Another view is that this lake of burning sulfur (and its implication of the fires of hell) may be symbolic of a certain kind of horror that will be appropriate punishment. The exact nature of this lake of fire is unknown, but certainly it is not a place one would desire to go. (For more information on the lake of fire, see commentary at 14:9-11.)

THE FINAL JUDGMENT / 20:11-15

20:11 And I saw a great white throne, and I saw the one who was sitting on it. The earth and sky fled from his presence, but they found no place to hide.NLT Next, John saw *a great white throne,* a large and majestic throne. He saw *the one who was sitting on it,* but he did not identify the one on the throne. Throughout Revelation, it is God who is pictured as sitting on a throne (see, for example, 4:2; 7:10; 19:4). Daniel had a similar vision:

As I looked, thrones were set in place, and the Ancient of Days took his seat. His clothing was as white as snow; the hair of his head was white like wool. His throne was flaming with fire, and its wheels were all ablaze. A river of fire was flowing, coming out from before him. Thousands upon thousands attended him; ten thousand times ten thousand stood before him. (Daniel 7:9-10 NIV)

Some suggest that the one sitting on the great white throne is Jesus, citing Matthew 25:31, "When the Son of Man comes in his glory . . . he will sit upon his glorious throne" (NLT); John 5:22, "And the Father leaves all judgment to his Son" (NLT); and 2 Corinthians 5:10, "For we must all stand before Christ to be judged" (NLT). Most likely, the little verse that solves the mystery is found in Jesus' statement, "The Father and I are one" (John 10:20 NLT); thus, the one throne is occupied by the Father and the Son as one.

With the appearance of this one on the throne, *the earth and sky fled from his presence, but they found no place to hide.* This poetic imagery could describe the dissolution of everything material and corrupt in the presence of God as Judge; it could also depict the end of the old earth and old heavens—in preparation for the creation of the new (21:1). No one could "hide" from God, for there is no place from which anything can flee from God's presence (Psalm 139:7). Other verses picture a disappearance of the heavens and the earth (quoted from NIV):

- "Lift up your eyes to the heavens, look at the earth beneath; the heavens will vanish like smoke, the earth will wear out like a garment and its inhabitants die like flies. But my salvation will last forever, my righteousness will never fail" (Isaiah 51:6).
- "Heaven and earth will pass away, but my words will never pass away" (Matthew 24:35).
- "But the day of the Lord will come like a thief. The heavens will disappear with a roar; the elements will be destroyed by fire, and the earth and everything in it will be laid bare. Since everything will be destroyed in this way, what kind of people ought you to be? You ought to live holy and godly lives as you look forward to the day of God and speed its coming. That day will bring about the destruction of the heavens by fire, and the elements will melt in the heat" (2 Peter 3:10-12).

20:12-13 And I saw the dead, great and small, standing before the throne, and books were opened. Also another book was opened, the book of life. And the dead were judged according to their works, as recorded in the books. And the sea gave up

THE COMING JUDGMENT

Other places in Scripture describe this judgment (quoted from NLT).

"The Ancient One sat down to judge . . . the court began its session, and the books were opened." (Daniel 7:9-10)

"For I, the Son of Man, will come in the glory of my Father with his angels and will judge all people according to their deeds." (Matthew 16:27)

"For there is going to come a day of judgment when God, the just judge of all the world, will judge all people according to what they have done." (Romans 2:5-6)

"The day will surely come when God, by Jesus Christ, will judge everyone's secret life." (Romans 2:16)

"Each of us will stand personally before the judgment seat of God. . . . Each of us will have to give a personal account to God." (Romans 14:10, 12)

"For we must all stand before Christ to be judged. We will each receive whatever we deserve for the good or evil we have done in our bodies." (2 Corinthians 5:10)

"Christ Jesus . . . will someday judge the living and the dead when he appears to set up his Kingdom." (2 Timothy 4:1)

"It is destined that each person dies only once and after that comes judgment." (Hebrews 9:27)

"But just remember that you will have to face God, who will judge everyone, both the living and the dead." (1 Peter 4:5)

"The Lord knows how to rescue godly people from their trials, even while punishing the wicked right up until the day of judgment." (2 Peter 2:9)

"And God has also commanded that the heavens and the earth will be consumed by fire on the day of judgment, when ungodly people will perish." (2 Peter 3:7)

"And as we live in God, our love grows more perfect. So we will not be afraid on the day of judgment, but we can face him with confidence." (1 John 4:17)

"Look, the Lord is coming with thousands of his holy ones. He will bring the people of the world to judgment. He will convict the ungodly of all the evil things they have done in rebellion." (Jude 14-15)

---

the dead that were in it, Death and Hades gave up the dead that were in them, and all were judged according to what they had done.[NRSV] The phrase "dead, great and small" probably refers to all people—believers and nonbelievers. No one will escape God's scrutiny. Why they are called "the dead" is uncertain. Some suggest that this is only the judgment of unbelievers because they would be the ones still dead who would take part in the second resurrection (20:5). However, it most likely stands for everyone, for God "will judge everyone, both the living and the dead" (1 Peter 4:5 NLT). *The throne* before which they were standing is the great white throne described in 20:11. The picture that Christ gave of this judgment scene seems to indicate the judgment of all people:

> *When the Son of Man comes in his glory, and all the angels with him, then he will sit upon his glorious throne. All the nations will be gathered in his presence, and he will separate them as a shepherd separates the sheep from the goats. He will place the sheep at his right hand and the goats at his left. . . . and they [the unrighteous—the goats] will go away into eternal punishment, but the righteous [the sheep] will go into eternal life."* (Matthew 25:31-33, 46 NLT)

This is the great and final judgment, the place where the *books* will be *opened,* including *another book* called *the book of life.* As noted in 3:5, the Book of Life is the heavenly registry of those who have accepted Christ's gift of salvation (see commentary there). All believers' names are written in the Book of Life. All people will be *judged according to their works, as recorded in the books. . . according to what they had done.* The idea of judgment by works is a theme throughout the Old and New Testaments (Psalm 62:12; Jeremiah 17:10; Daniel 7:10; Romans 2:6; 14:10-12; 1 Corinthians 3:12-15; 2 Corinthians 5:10; 1 Peter 1:17). No one will be forgotten at this final gathering— those who had drowned in *the sea* will return, even *Death and Hades gave up the dead that were in them.* In 6:8, Death and Hades were inseparable as riders of the pale horse, representing the realm of the dead.

> Hell was not prepared for man. God never meant that man would ever go to hell. Hell was prepared for the devil and his angels, but man rebelled against God and followed the devil. . . . Hell is essentially and basically banishment from the presence of God for deliberately rejecting Jesus Christ as Lord and Savior.   *Billy Graham*

Believers will be judged—not to see if they merit eternal life, for their names will already be in the Book of Life. This will be a judgment for rewards. Believers' works cannot save them, but their deeds are important to God. Although "no one can lay any other foundation than the one we already have—Jesus Christ" (1 Corinthians 3:11 NLT), the deeds with which believers build their lives *do* matter. "Now anyone who builds on that foundation may use gold, silver, jewels, wood, hay, or straw. But there is going to come a time of testing at the judgment day to see what kind of work each builder has done. Everyone's work will be put through the fire to see whether or not it keeps its value. If the work survives the fire, that builder will receive a reward. But if the work is burned up, the builder will suffer great loss. The builders themselves will be saved, but like someone escaping through a wall of flames" (1 Corinthians 3:12-15 NLT).

Unbelievers also will be judged according to their works, but, of course, no works, no matter how good, will be able to save them.

BY THE BOOK

At the judgment, the books will be opened. These books contain the recorded deeds of everyone, good or evil. Everyone's life will be reviewed and evaluated. No one is saved by deeds, but deeds are seen as clear evidence of a person's actual relationship with God. Jesus will look at how we have handled gifts, opportunities, and responsibilities. God's gracious gift of salvation does not free us from the requirement of faithful obedience and service. Each of us must serve Christ in the best way we know and live each day knowing the books will be opened.

20:14-15 Then death and Hades were thrown into the lake of fire. The lake of fire is the second death.^{NIV} Death and Hades, here personified, were thrown into the lake of fire. God's judgment was finished. Paul had written, "The last enemy to be destroyed is death" (1 Corinthians 15:26 NIV). John exclaimed that in heaven, "there will be no more death" (21:4 NLT). Isaiah had foreseen this day, "He will swallow up death forever!" (Isaiah 25:8 NLT). (For more on the lake of fire, or the lake of burning sulfur, see commentary at 19:3; 19:20; and 20:10.)

The lake of fire is the ultimate destination of everything wicked—Satan, the beast, the false prophet, the demons, death, Hades, and anyone whose name was not found recorded in the Book of Life was thrown into the lake of fire.^{NLT} Those whose names were not found recorded in the Book of Life are those who did not place their faith in Jesus Christ. This is the second death. They died the first time physically; this time their death was spiritual (see also 20:6). John's vision does not permit any gray areas in God's judgment. Jesus, when describing this final judgment scene, spoke to unbelievers, "Away with you, you cursed ones, into the eternal fire prepared for the Devil and his demons" (Matthew 25:41 NLT). Those who do not, by faith, accept Christ as Savior and confess him as Lord, will find that they have been cast away with no hope, no second chance, no appeal.

Revelation 21

John watched as this gigantic city descended to the new earth created by God. The city was a 1,400-mile square with 200-foot high walls. Made of pure gold, it was decorated with all kinds of beautiful gems. Its gates opened in every direction, as evidence of the church's success in proclaiming Christ to every nation (5:9; 21:13). At the very center of this city was God, the enthroned Lamb. The light from his throne illumined the entire city. From his throne, a crystal-clear river of life was flowing. At the river's bank, the tree of life was flourishing, producing twelve different kinds of fruit for the healing of the nations. "Nothing unclean . . . will ever enter" the city (21:27), for this is where God will reign!

21:1 Then I saw a new heaven and a new earth, for the old heaven and the old earth had disappeared. And the sea was also gone.^{NLT} John sees *a new heaven and a new earth, for the old heaven and the old earth had disappeared.* The earth and sky had fled from God's presence (see 20:11), and this new heaven and earth had taken their place. When sin entered the human race, it and all creation were corrupted. That's why Paul wrote, "Everything on earth was subjected to God's curse. All creation anticipates the day when it will join God's children in glorious freedom from death and decay. For we know that all creation has been groaning as in the pains of childbirth right up to the present time" (Romans 8:20-22 NLT). All of this "newness" is not merely physical but also spiritual and moral. Everything will be "new" because "God is now among his people" (21:3 NLT).

That *the sea was also gone* could refer to evil being gone, for the sea was associated with evil (the Beast had come out of the sea, 13:1). This could mean that there will be no oceans in the new earth. It probably means, however, that all evil will be banished, "for the old world and its evils are gone forever" (21:4 NLT).

The Old Testament prophets had predicted that God would create a brand-new earth and heaven. Isaiah described this:

THE BEGINNING AND THE END

The Bible records the beginning of the world and the end of the world. The story of mankind, from beginning to end—from the fall into sin to redemption and God's ultimate victory over evil—is found in the pages of the Bible.

Genesis	*Revelation*
The sun is created.	The sun is not needed.
Satan is victorious.	Satan is defeated.
Sin enters the human race.	Sin is banished.
People run and hide from God.	People are invited to live with God forever.
People are cursed.	The curse is removed.
Tears are shed, with sorrow for sin.	All sin, tears, and sorrow are gone.
The garden and earth are cursed.	God's city is glorified, the earth is made new.
Paradise is lost.	Paradise is regained.
People are doomed to death.	Death is defeated, believers live forever with God.

Look! I am creating new heavens and a new earth—so wonderful that no one will even think about the old ones anymore. Be glad; rejoice forever in my creation! And look! I will create Jerusalem as a place of happiness. Her people will be a source of joy. I will rejoice in Jerusalem and delight in my people. And the sound of weeping and crying will be heard no more." (Isaiah 65:17-19 NLT)

Peter also encouraged believers to "look forward to that day and hurry it along—the day when God will set the heavens on fire and the elements will melt away in the flames. But we are looking forward to the new heavens and new earth he has promised, a world where everyone is right with God" (2 Peter 3:12-13 NLT).

The earth as we know it will not last forever, but after God's great judgment, he will create a new earth (see Romans 8:18-21; 2 Peter 3:7-13). God had also promised Isaiah that he would create a new and eternal earth (Isaiah 65:17; Isaiah 66:22). The sea in John's time was viewed as dangerous and changeable. It was also the source of the Beast (Revelation 13:1). We don't know how the new earth will look or where it will be, but God and his followers—those whose names are written in the Book of Life—will be united to live there forever.

THE REAL WORLD
Christians see the world as it is—physically decaying and
spiritually infected with sin. But faced with these conditions,
Christians do not need to be pessimistic because they have hope
for future glory. They look forward to the new heaven and new
earth that God has promised, and they wait for God's new order
that will free the world of sin, sickness, and evil. In the meantime,
Christians should go with Christ into the world to heal people's
bodies and souls and to fight the evil effects of sin.

**21:2 And I saw the holy city, the new Jerusalem, coming down out
of heaven from God, prepared as a bride adorned for her husband.**^{NRSV} In addition to a new heaven and a new earth is a new
city. *The holy city, the new Jerusalem* descends out of heaven *from
God.* The "new Jerusalem" is where God lives among his people.
God had become man in Jesus Christ and had lived among sinful
people in a broken world (John 1:14). At the end of time, God will
come down to his new heaven and new earth to be with his
renewed people. The church in Philadelphia was promised "all who
are victorious . . . will be citizens in the city of my God—the new
Jerusalem that comes down from heaven from my God" (3:12 NLT).

That this city is called "the new Jerusalem" indicates a relationship to the "old Jerusalem," the capital of Israel. As the old creation had been corrupted by sin, so the old Jerusalem had been
the city where prophets were killed and where Christ himself was
crucified. Jesus had lamented over the city, "O Jerusalem, Jerusalem, you who kill the prophets and stone those sent to you, how
often I have longed to gather your children together, as a hen
gathers her chicks under her wings, but you were not willing"
(Matthew 23:37 NIV). Yet throughout the Old Testament are rich
promises for the future restoration of Israel—God's people. This
new Jerusalem will be God's dwelling place among his people
(see commentary at 21:3).

God's people, all believers, will live in this magnificent city,
described as a *bride adorned for her husband*—pure and radiant,
ready to join the one she loves (see also 21:9). In 19:7-9, God's
people, the church, are described as a bride making herself ready
for the marriage feast (see commentary there); here, the new Jerusalem is also described as a bride. Whether Jerusalem is an actual
city, or symbolic of the community of God's people, is unknown.
But we are certain that there will be relationships in the new Jerusalem—first between God and his people, and second among
God's people. The image of individuals floating on their own fluffy
clouds is incorrect. God's people will corporately worship him; all

will be together, and it will be so beautiful that it defies description. The details of the bride's adornment are given in verses 11-21.

The remainder of the chapter gives a fuller picture, yet the new Jerusalem is surely beyond anything words can describe:

- It is the home of God among his people. Those who had never seen the one they loved will see him face-to-face and behold his glory (21:3; 22:4).
- It has no more death, sorrow, crying, or pain. Anything that caused sadness in life on earth will be gone; this will be a place of eternal and unimaginable joy that nothing will ever cloud (21:4, 26-27).
- It is a place for those who trusted Christ, regardless of what it cost them. Its blessings are an inheritance for them, and they will be called God's children (21:7).
- It is filled with the glory of God and gleams like a very rare jewel (21:11). This is nothing but the best and finest and most precious—given to God's people as their inheritance.
- It is in the shape of a perfect cube, symbolizing perfection and completeness (21:15-16).
- It has no temple, for God and the Lamb are its temple (21:22).
- Worship of God will be a foundational aspect of daily life (22:3).
- It has no need of the sun or the moon (21:23). There will never be any darkness (symbolic or otherwise, 21:25; 22:5), for the people will experience God's glory constantly; there will be no need for the sun to mark the days, for time will cease to be.
- It has the river of life coursing through it with many trees of life growing there, giving constant refreshment and meeting every need (22:1-2).

21:3 I heard a loud shout from the throne, saying, "Look, the home of God is now among his people! He will live with them, and they will be his people. God himself will be with them."NLT A *loud shout from the throne* (not from God, but probably an angel near the throne) announced the words all of creation had been waiting to hear: *"Look, the home of God is now among his people! . . . God himself will be with them."* God had promised that one day, "I will live among you, and I will not despise you. I will walk among you; I will be your God, and you will be my people" (Leviticus 26:11-12 NLT). What has been foreshadowed in God's presence in the Tabernacle (Exodus 40:34-35), in the Temple (1 Kings 8:10-11), and in the bodily presence of God himself in Jesus (John 1:14) will become a reality in the new Jerusalem. As God had walked with Adam and Eve in the Garden (Genesis 3:8), so *he will live with* his people. God's people will live within the *shekinah* glory of God.

The presence of God among his people fulfills all the longing of the entire Bible. The Old Testament prophets had foreseen this great day:

- "I will make you my own special people, and I will be your God" (Exodus 6:7 NLT).
- "I will live among you, and I will not despise you. I will walk among you; I will be your God, and you will be my people" (Leviticus 26:11-12 NLT).
- "For you are a holy people, who belong to the Lord your God. Of all the people on earth, the Lord your God has chosen you to be his own special treasure" (Deuteronomy 7:6 NLT).
- "I will put my laws in their minds, and I will write them on their hearts. I will be their God, and they will be my people. . . . Everyone, from the least to the greatest, will already know me" (Jeremiah 31:33-34 NLT).
- "My dwelling place will be with them; I will be their God, and they will be my people" (Ezekiel 37:27 NIV).
- "I will bring them back to live in Jerusalem; they will be my people, and I will be faithful and righteous to them as their God" (Zechariah 8:8 NIV).

This desire to be in the presence of God should be our strongest desire here on earth and the focus of all our worship.

21:4 "He will wipe every tear from their eyes. There will be no more death or mourning or crying or pain, for the old order of things has passed away."[NIV] The utter joy of living in God's presence is indescribable; Revelation explains what will not be there. There will be no more tears. *There will be no more death or mourning or crying or pain.* All that has caused sadness and suffering will be taken away. All sin that has been the source of sorrow will be gone. God himself will wipe away the tears, and they will never return. Isaiah had seen a future day when "the ransomed of the Lord will return. They will enter Zion with singing; everlasting joy will crown their heads. Gladness and joy will overtake them, and sorrow and sighing will flee away" (Isaiah 35:10 NIV). Believers' physical bodies will have been transformed (1 Corinthians 15:35-57), and they will have been made perfect. John wrote in another place, "Dear friends, we are already God's children, and we can't even imagine what we will be like when Christ returns. But we do know that when he comes we will be like him, for we will see him as he really is" (1 John 3:2 NLT).

> Has this world been so kind to you that you should leave it with regret? There are better things ahead than any we leave behind.
>
> *C. S. Lewis*

There can be no evil in God's glorious presence; therefore, *the old order of things has passed away.* The "old order" where Satan ran free and sin ran rampant will be replaced by God's order.

NO MORE TEARS
The "Holy City, the new Jerusalem" is described as the place where God will "wipe every tear from their eyes." Forevermore, there will be no death, pain, sorrow, or crying. What a wonderful truth! No matter what you are going through, it's not the last word—God has written the final chapter, and it is about true fulfillment and eternal joy for those who love him. We do not know as much as we would like, but it is enough to know that eternity with God will be more wonderful than we could ever imagine. When you face daily uncertainties, take courage from the promise of eternal life with God.

21:5 And the one who was seated on the throne said, "See, I am making all things new." Also he said, "Write this, for these words are trustworthy and true."NRSV This time, God himself, *the one who was seated on the throne,* spoke (see also 1:8). His words describe the reality of what was happening: *"See, I am making all things new."* God is the Creator. The Bible begins with the majestic story of God creating the universe, and it concludes with his creating a new heaven and a new earth. This is a tremendous hope and encouragement for believers. God told John to *write this* so that believers across the generations, awaiting this glorious future, can be encouraged to know that *these words are trustworthy and true.* Because God has spoken, believers can know of the absolute certainty that these events will one day occur. God's word never changes.

21:6 Then he said to me, "It is done! I am the Alpha and the Omega, the beginning and the end. To the thirsty I will give water as a gift from the spring of the water of life."NRSV Just as God finished the work of creation (Genesis 2:1-3) and Jesus finished the work of redemption (John 19:30), so they will finish the entire plan of salvation by inviting the redeemed into a new creation and proclaim, *"It is done!"*

God said, *"I am the Alpha and the Omega, the beginning and the end."* This repeats 1:8 (see also 1:17; 2:8), where Christ had said this to John. *Alpha* and *Omega* are the first and last letters of the Greek alphabet. The Lord God is the "beginning and the end." God is sovereign over history and in control of everything.

God promised that he would *give water as a gift from the spring of the water of life,* to all who are thirsty. This water is also described in 22:1, and it symbolizes eternal life. Jesus had told the Samaritan woman: "People soon become thirsty again after drinking this water. But the water I give them takes away thirst altogether. It becomes a perpetual spring within them, giving them eternal life" (John 4:13-14 NLT). "If you are thirsty, come to me! If you believe in me, come and drink! For the Scriptures declare that rivers of living water will flow out from within" (John 7:37-38 NLT). Those "Scriptures" to which Jesus was referring include Isaiah 55:1; 58:11; Jeremiah 2:13; Ezekiel 47:1-10; Joel 3:18. Water is pictured as salvation, and God's gracious offer is to anyone who "thirsts." Here in Revelation, water pictures the reward of those who have been "victorious" (21:7). They will no longer have any needs, for their needs will be completely met by God throughout all eternity.

> In the great Day of the Lord some will be stoical, some will whimper, some will turn in search of human sympathy. Let God answer the question, "What shall be the end of them that obey not the Gospel of God?"
>
> *Billy Sunday*

WELL-WATERED
God promised the "water of life" (21:6). Those reading God's words knew the importance of water. They knew that water is essential for life and crops. And they did not take water for granted.

All the water anyone used in their homes had to be carried from nearby springs or wells. People handled water carefully and conserved it. Because much of the country in the Bible lands was arid, the survival of the crops was determined by rain. Late rains could cause the planted seeds not to germinate. In the cultivation of grapes, for instance, the vines require at least one hundred gallons of water in order to produce one gallon of wine.

Symbolically, water came to represent Israel's deliverance in the wilderness when they were actually dying of thirst. In the new Jerusalem, God promises the water of life so that thirst will be no more. It is pitiful not to respond to God's offer. We do this when:

- we discount God's blessings instead of depending on Christ's constant provision,
- we foolishly crave what we do not need instead of trusting Christ to determine what we really need,
- we lean on the comforts of this life and our personal gratification instead of looking to the eternal destiny that Christ has promised.

21:7-8 "All who are victorious will inherit all these blessings, and I will be their God, and they will be my children. But cowards who turn away from me, and unbelievers, and the

corrupt, and murderers, and the immoral, and those who practice witchcraft, and idol worshipers, and all liars—their doom is in the lake that burns with fire and sulfur. This is the second death."ᴺᴸᵀ Verses 7 and 8 form an interlude; they are directed to the readers who must make a choice whether they will be part of the *victorious* ones who *will inherit all these blessings* (21:7) or the *cowards who turn away from* God and face *their doom* in *the lake that burns with fire and sulfur* (21:8). That lake is described in 19:20 and 20:10 as the place of torment and punishment for the Beast, the false prophet, Satan, and all who followed them. Because they stubbornly refused to drink from the water of life and receive salvation in Christ, their doom will be *the second death*—the lake of fire. The "first death" is physical death. But all the dead will be raised to be judged, and those who are sent away to punishment will face the "second death," which is spiritual.

John described the Beast's followers as *unbelievers, and the corrupt, and murderers, and the immoral, those who practice witchcraft, and idol worshipers, and all liars.* This list is not meant to be exhaustive, but is representative of all sin and rebellion against God. Those who refuse to believe (the "unbelievers"), no matter how good or moral they are, will join those whose sins are more blatant, as recorded in this list. All unbelievers will face the same punishment. This is a warning to those who may be Christians in name only to be certain of their salvation. Which will they choose? The water of life, or the fire of the second death?

The "cowards" are those who turn back from following God, not those who are fainthearted in their faith or who sometimes doubt or question. They are not brave enough to stand up for Christ; they are not humble enough to accept his authority over their lives. In contrast, the "victorious" are those who overcome and "stand firm to the end" (Mark 13:13 NIV). They will receive the blessings that God promised:

- eating from the tree of life (2:7),
- escaping the lake of fire (the "second death," 2:11),
- receiving a special name (2:17),
- having authority over the nations (2:26),
- being included in the Book of Life (3:5),
- being a pillar in God's spiritual temple (3:12),
- sitting with Christ on his throne (3:21).

Those who can endure the testing of evil and remain faithful will be rewarded by God.

THE COWARD'S CHOICE
God warned John and all who read Revelation that cowards
will be in a godless eternity. The cowards are the fearful ones
who abandon Christ at the threats of the Beast. They fear persecution so badly that they choose temporary personal safety
over eternal life with God. To follow Christ requires boldness
and bravery to stand for him when oppression occurs. Pray for
courage to do what is right no matter what pressure you face.
Keep clearly in mind the heavenly reward of Christ so that you
won't be tempted to turn away.

THE NEW JERUSALEM / 21:9-27

The remainder of the chapter is a stunning description of the new
city of God. The vision is symbolic and shows that the believers'
new home with God will defy description. They will not be disappointed by it in any way.

**21:9 Then one of the seven angels who held the seven bowls con-
taining the seven last plagues came and said to me, "Come
with me! I will show you the bride, the wife of the Lamb."**[NLT]
John was addressed by *one of the seven angels who held the
seven bowls containing the seven last plagues* (see 15:1). Also,
in 17:1, one of the seven angels had taken John to see the great
prostitute. Here, one of the seven angels told John that he would
show him *the bride, the wife of the Lamb*—referring to the
church (the believers, 19:7-8) and the new Jerusalem (21:2) all
rolled into one in this awesome vision. (For
more on the imagery of the bride as the wife
of the Lamb, see commentary at 19:7-8 and
21:2.) In contrast to the great prostitute, who
symbolizes the evil system and the people
who rebeled against God, the bride represents those who remained faithful to Christ
and now are prepared to join him.

> Jesus is preparing the
> New Jerusalem for us
> now. . . . For all eternity
> He will be with us and we
> will know and see Him.
> *David Jeremiah*

**21:10-11 And in the spirit he carried me away to a great, high mountain
and showed me the holy city Jerusalem coming down out of
heaven from God. It has the glory of God and a radiance like a
very rare jewel, like jasper, clear as crystal.**[NRSV] When John had
been taken to see the great prostitute, he had been taken "in spirit
into the wilderness" (17:3 NLT). When John was taken to see the
bride, he once again was *in the spirit*—this time carried away *to a
great, high mountain.* From that vantage point, the angel showed
John *the holy city Jerusalem coming down out of heaven from God.*

This is a further description of what John had written in 21:2—this time describing the city itself. Verses 10-14 describe the beauty of this city: *It has the glory of God and a radiance like a very rare jewel, like jasper, clear as crystal.* These descriptions are not meant to be taken literally, but the fact that this is a symbolic vision does not diminish the glory of what John was attempting to describe. As the great prostitute, dragon, Beast, and false prophet symbolized evil, so the vision of a bride and a beautiful city provide the opposite picture. Often John drew upon Old Testament imagery (as from Ezekiel's prophecies) in his attempt to describe the indescribable. As with the imagery of the bride, this city pictures the future, glorious dwelling place of the believers. John has already described eternal life in the new heaven and new earth (21:3-6); here he described heaven's physical characteristics—absolute and incomparable beauty.

This city had no lights in it; instead, it radiated with the glory of God. John did not have electric or neon lights to describe, so he used the picture of a clear jewel, perhaps cut with many facets, radiating and reflecting light. "Jasper" had been used earlier in describing the appearance of God himself (4:3) and is used again in 21:11, 18-19.

21:12-13 **It has a great, high wall with twelve gates, and at the gates twelve angels, and on the gates are inscribed the names of the twelve tribes of the Israelites; on the east three gates, on the north three gates, on the south three gates, and on the west three gates.**^{NRSV} Next, John described the *wall* of the city. In John's day, most cities had walls around them, so in this part of the vision John described what would be the ideal city to his audience. This is a *high wall with twelve gates,* three on each side of the city. Each gate was *inscribed* with the name of one of the *twelve tribes of the Israelites.* Ezekiel had seen a similar vision (see Ezekiel 48:30-34). Each gate had twelve angels, once again describing for John's audience the ideal city with high walls (and watchmen at every gate).

The gates would always be open (21:25)—allowing people from every nation to come into the city. These open gates indicate that all of God's people will be there; no one will be missed or forgotten.

21:14 **The wall of the city had twelve foundation stones, and on them were written the names of the twelve apostles of the Lamb.**^{NLT} The great, high wall of the city *had twelve foundation stones.* Ancient city walls would have huge stones as their foundations. This city had only twelve foundation stones—these were indeed huge stones. While the gates had the names of the twelve tribes, these stones had the *names of the twelve apostles of the Lamb.* Jesus told the apostles that they would rule the twelve tribes (Matthew 19:28; Luke 22:30). The term "twelve apostles" could refer to the original twelve disciples, but other believers had been called "apostles" (such as Paul and Barnabas). It is more important to understand the symbolism that the church rests on the work of the apostles—the first followers of Jesus. Paul had written, "We are [God's] house, built on the foundation of the apostles and the prophets. And the cornerstone is Christ Jesus himself. We who believe are carefully joined together, becoming a holy temple for the Lord" (Ephesians 2:20-21 NLT).

21:15-16 The angel who talked with me had a measuring rod of gold to measure the city, its gates and its walls. The city was laid out like a square, as long as it was wide. He measured the city with the rod and found it to be 12,000 stadia in length, and as wide and high as it is long.^{NIV} In chapter 11, an angel had told John to "measure the Temple of God and the altar" (see comments on 11:1). This time, the angel *had a measuring rod of gold,* and with it *he measured the city, its gates and its walls.* The city's measurements are symbolic of a place that will hold all God's people. These measurements are all multiples of 12, the number for God's people: there were 12 tribes in Israel and 12 apostles who started the church. The walls are 144 (12 x 12) cubits (200 feet) thick; there are 12 layers in the walls, and 12 gates in the city; and the height, length, and breadth are all the same: 12,000 stadia. It is interesting to note that the 12,000 stadia converts to 1,400 miles, roughly the length of the Roman Empire. The new Jerusalem is a perfect cube, the same shape as the Most Holy Place in the temple (1 Kings 6:20). This act of measuring shows its completeness as noted in 11:1 and in Ezekiel 40–41.

21:17 He also measured its wall, one hundred forty-four cubits by human measurement, which the angel was using.^{NRSV} The measurement of the city's wall is *one hundred forty-four cubits* (about 200 feet), another multiple of 12 and another symbol of the perfection and completeness of this city. If it were an actual wall, it would be far thicker than the walls of any city in the ancient world, even thicker than the Great Wall of China. The phrase that John adds, "by human measurement, which the angel was using," is a parenthetical note that the angel's cubit was no different than the cubit measurement with which his readers were familiar.

21:18 The wall was made of jasper, and the city was pure gold, as clear as glass.^{NLT} That *the wall was made of jasper* and that God himself is described as appearing like jasper (4:3) indicates that everything in the city would radiate the presence of God. This holy city, in the shape of a perfect cube, is reminiscent of the Most Holy Place in the tabernacle and in the temple. In Solomon's Temple, the Most Holy Place was splendid, with its interior overlaid with pure gold (1 Kings 6:21-22). So this entire city is *pure gold, as clear as glass.* Its clearness indicates its lack of impurity; nothing will impede its ability to transmit God's glory.

21:19-20 The foundations of the wall of the city are adorned with every jewel; the first was jasper, the second sapphire, the third agate, the fourth emerald, the fifth onyx, the sixth carnelian, the seventh chrysolite, the eighth beryl, the ninth topaz, the tenth chrysoprase, the eleventh jacinth, the twelfth amethyst.^{NRSV} *The foundations of the wall* were adorned with twelve precious stones. The significance of each stone has been debated. Some have suggested that this imagery comes from the breastplate of the high priest, which had twelve precious stones on it (Exodus 28:17-20), even though the identifications of the stones are different. This is the most likely source of the imagery, indicating that what had once been the high priest's privilege alone had become part of the very foundation of the city of God, made available to all people. The high priest would enter the Most Holy Place (again, this is the same shape as the city—a cube) only once each year on the Day of Atonement to make a sacrifice for the sins of the entire nation. The Most Holy Place was the place of God's presence. In the new Jerusalem, all of God's people will constantly be in his presence. Nothing will ever again separate them from him.

The names of the various stones indicate jewels of various colors—all of them rare and beautiful. The picture John gives of this city indicates beauty beyond description.

21:21 The twelve gates were made of pearls—each gate from a single pearl! And the main street was pure gold, as clear as glass.^{NLT} Each of the *twelve gates* (21:11) was made *from a single pearl.* Pearls were very valuable in ancient times (see Matthew 13:45-46), so a pearl large enough to make a gate for this great city would be beyond imagining. In addition, *the main street was pure gold, as clear as glass,* just like the rest of the city (21:18). Again the emphasis is on its purity and transparency in order to radiate the glory of God.

21:22 **No temple could be seen in the city, for the Lord God
Almighty and the Lamb are its temple.**^{NLT} This beautiful city,
like any other city in the ancient world, would be expected to
have a temple—a central place of worship. Many ancient cities
would have several temples for the various gods the people worshiped. The focal point of worship in Jerusalem was God's
temple. That temple, the center of God's presence among his
people, was the primary place of worship. In the new Jerusalem,
however, *no temple could be seen* because God's presence would
be everywhere. He would be worshiped throughout the city. *The
Lord God Almighty and the Lamb are its temple.* Their presence
would be enough.

21:23 **And the city has no need of sun or moon to shine on it, for the
glory of God is its light, and its lamp is the Lamb.**^{NRSV} God had
remade the heavens (21:1). Perhaps, when he did so, he didn't re-
create a sun or a moon. The new city *has no need of sun or moon
to shine on it,* for the radiance of God's glory *is its light.* Isaiah
had written, "No longer will you need the sun or moon to give
you light, for the Lord your God will be your everlasting light,
and he will be your glory. The sun will never set; the moon will
not go down. For the Lord will be your everlasting light" (Isaiah
60:19-20 NLT). Isaiah continued by describing that "all your
people will be righteous" (Isaiah 60:21 NLT), so perhaps the same
reality is being described here. God and the Lamb impart the
"light" of their righteousness to the city (the people). John, in
his Gospel, had recorded Jesus' statement, "I am the light of the
world" (John 8:12).

GOD IS ITS LIGHT
God will be the light in the new Jerusalem. Light represents
what is good, pure, true, holy, and reliable. Darkness represents what is sinful and evil. The statement "God is its light"
means that the city will be enveloped by God, who is perfectly
holy and true. Light is also related to truth in that it exposes
whatever exists. Just as darkness cannot exist in the presence
of light, so sin cannot exist in the presence of a holy God. The
city will be completely without sin and evil.
　　If we want to have a relationship with God, we must put
aside our sinful ways of living. To claim that we belong to
God but then to go out and live for ourselves is hypocrisy. To
prepare to live with him in eternity, we must love the light and
let it chase out any darkness in our lives.

21:24-25 **The nations will walk by its light, and the kings of the earth
will bring their splendor into it. On no day will its gates**

ever be shut, for there will be no night there.^{NIV} Elsewhere in Revelation, the word "nations" referred to the nations of the earth that joined the Antichrist (see 11:2, 18; 18:3, 23; 19:15). Here, however, the term refers to God's people. This shows the culmination of the conversion offered to all nations (5:9; 11:18; 14:6-7). This does not mean universal salvation, as some have suggested, but that God has chosen from every tribe, nation, people, and language who will come to be part of his great city. The city will be lit by the glory of God and the Lamb (21:23), and the people *will walk by its light.* All people on earth, even the *kings of the earth* who experienced power and glory in this world, will simply *bring their splendor* to God's throne, casting down their crowns before him. Their splendor will be nothing compared to what they will experience in eternity.

The city's gates will never be shut. This does not imply that outside of the New Jerusalem, unsaved people are still roaming around. Instead, this pictures a city with open gates on a new earth where believers will dwell throughout. Ancient cities shut their gates at night for security purposes. However, since *there will be no night there,* and since all evil will have been eradicated, these gates will stay open constantly. Revelation seems to picture great activity coming and going from the city.

THE REAL INTERNATIONAL CITY
Once the glittering diversity of the construction gems of the New Jerusalem have been described and the gates have been variously named, the inhabitants are introduced. They are "all the nations." They will bring splendor, glory, and honor into the city. The peace and harmony we have longed for but only glimpsed in this world will be our way of life in the next. The eradication of sin will remove the barriers that separate people here. Somehow, even differences like language and customs will be translated into shared praise before God's throne. The city will be God's city, and we will be God's people.

Meanwhile, we continue to live in a fractured world. But Jesus commands us and enables us to be peacemakers. Every day we live on earth as temporarily misplaced citizens of God's Kingdom, we can begin to demonstrate our true citizenship by offering our splendor, glory, and honor to the Lord each day. Praise God for the peace he brings you now and pray for the fulfillment of his reign on earth.

21:26-27 **And all the nations will bring their glory and honor into the city. Nothing evil will be allowed to enter—no one who practices shameful idolatry and dishonesty—but only those whose names are written in the Lamb's Book of Life.**^{NLT} In contrast to

HEAVENLY REWARDS

Reference	What It Says about Heaven
Matthew 16:24-27	To follow Christ, take up the cross. To save life, lose it. For Christ will come in glory with his angels and reward each person according to what he or she has done.
Matthew 19:28-30	If we give up material rewards on this earth for the sake of Christ and his kingdom, we are promised a hundred times as much, as well as eternal life with Christ.
Romans 6:8	If we died with Christ, we will also live with him.
Romans 8:17	If we are children of God, then we are his heirs (and coheirs with Christ) of all the riches of his glory. We share in suffering; we also share in glory.
1 Corinthians 15:42-58	We will be changed—at the sounding of the last trumpet we will receive imperishable bodies. Christ has the victory!
Colossians 3:3-4	Our lives are hidden with Christ in God. When Christ appears, we will appear with him in glory.
1 Thessalonians 4:13-18	The Lord will come down from heaven with a loud command, with the voice of the archangel, and with a trumpet call. The dead in Christ will rise first. Those who are still alive at his return will be caught up to meet him in the clouds. Then we will all be with the Lord together forever.
Revelation 3:21	To the one who overcomes, Christ will give him the right to sit with him on his throne in heaven.
Revelation 21:1–22:21	There will be a new heaven and a new earth. There will be no more death or mourning or crying or pain. The Holy City will be beautiful beyond imagination, and only those whose names are written in the Lamb's Book of Life will be allowed to enter. There will be no sun or light, for the Lord himself will be the light. And God's kingdom will remain forever.

the worldly nations' trade with evil Babylon (chapter 18), the nations (again describing God's people) *will bring their glory and honor into the city.* John again made the point that *nothing evil will be allowed to enter.* This does not indicate that evil would still be present in some realm outside the great city. All evil will be gone. Instead, in 20:7-8, John was warning his contemporary readers that they would not be in this glorious place unless their names *are written in the Lamb's Book of Life.* (For more on the Book of Life, see 3:5 and 20:12-15).

CITIZENS OF HEAVEN
Not everyone will be allowed into the new Jerusalem, but "only those whose names are written in the Lamb's Book of Life." Don't think that you will get in because of your background, personality, or good behavior. Eternal life is available to you only because of what Jesus, the Lamb, has done. Trust him today to secure your citizenship in his new creation.

Revelation 22

This section describes what could be called the "new Eden."
What the first Garden of Eden was supposed to be is fulfilled
here. What Adam and Eve would have had if they had not fallen
is what is given to God's people. Adam and Eve lost Paradise;
here, God has remade it.

22:1-2 **Then the angel showed me the river of the water of life, as
clear as crystal, flowing from the throne of God and of the
Lamb down the middle of the great street of the city. On each
side of the river stood the tree of life, bearing twelve crops of
fruit, yielding its fruit every month. And the leaves of the tree
are for the healing of the nations.**^{NIV} *The angel* showed John *the
river of the water of life, as clear as crystal, flowing . . . down the
middle of the great street of the city.* The water of life is a symbol
of eternal life. Jesus used this same image with the Samaritan
woman (John 4:7-14). It pictures fullness of life with God and the
eternal blessings that come when people believe in him and allow
him to satisfy their spiritual thirst (see 22:17). The Garden of
Eden also had a river running through it that watered it (2:10). In
both the Old and New Testaments, water pictures salvation and
the refreshment of the Holy Spirit. Ezekiel's vision also had a
river with trees growing along it (Ezekiel 47:1-12). The water in
the new Jerusalem flows *from the throne of God and of the Lamb.*
God in Christ, who is the water of life (John 7:37-38), is the
source of this constant stream of blessing and refreshment for his
people. This river flows down the middle of the main street of the
city and is accessible to everyone.

This *tree of life* can be compared to the tree of life in the Garden of Eden (Genesis 2:9; see also Ezekiel 47:12.) After Adam
and Eve sinned, they were forbidden to eat from the tree of life.
But because of the forgiveness of sin through the blood of Jesus,
there will be no evil or sin in the new Jerusalem. Believers will
be able to eat freely from the tree of life when sin's control is
destroyed and eternity with God is secure. This tree (one tree or
many trees) grows *on each side of the river* and bears *twelve*

WHAT WE KNOW ABOUT ETERNITY

The Bible devotes much less space to describing eternity than it does to convincing people that eternal life is available as a free gift from God. Most of the brief descriptions of eternity would be more accurately called hints, since they use terms and ideas from present experience to describe what we cannot fully grasp until we are there ourselves. These references hint at aspects of what our future will be like if we have accepted Christ's gift of eternal life.

Description	Reference
We will have a place prepared for us.	John 14:2-3
We will be unlimited by physical properties (1 Corinthians 15:35-49).	John 20:19, 26
We will be like Jesus.	1 John 3:2
We will have new bodies.	1 Corinthians 15
It will be a wonderful experience.	1 Corinthians 2:9
It will be a new environment.	Revelation 21:1
It will be a new experience of God's presence (1 Corinthians 13:12).	Revelation 21:3
We will have new emotions.	Revelation 21:4
There will be no more death.	Revelation 21:4

crops of fruit, with a new crop *every month.* Adam and Eve had been cut off from the tree of life because of their sin (Genesis 3:22-24); now the tree has fruit available for everyone—fresh fruit, not just once a year with a dry time in between, but new fruit every month.

In addition to the fruit, *the leaves of the tree are for the healing of the nations.* Why would the nations need to be healed if all evil has been eliminated? John was alluding to Ezekiel 47:12, where water flowing from the temple produced trees with healing leaves. He was not implying that there would be illness in the new earth; he was emphasizing that the water of life would produce health and strength wherever it would go. God's people in his kingdom will have no physical or spiritual needs. All the hurts of the nations will have been healed.

22:3-4 **No longer will there be any curse. The throne of God and of the Lamb will be in the city, and his servants will serve him. They will see his face, and his name will be on their foreheads.**[NIV] The phrase "no longer will there be any curse" could mean that nothing accursed will be in God's presence. This would fulfill Zechariah 14:11. More likely, this refers to God lifting the curse that had been placed in Eden (Genesis 3:17-18). The phrase "the throne of God and of the Lamb" indicates the oneness of God and the Lamb, as well as God's presence right among his people. *His servants will serve him.* This indicates that our relationship to God in eternity will involve service. While most translations say, "worship him," there may be more service to do in our worship. While all of our service will be focused on worshiping God, there may be ongoing caretaking responsibilities given to us as we reign with him (22:5).

God's people will *see his face.* The face of God had not been seen by anyone since Adam and Eve sinned. Even Moses, the great lawgiver who went up on the mountain to meet with God, had only been able to see God from the back. God had told him, "You may not look directly at my face, for no one may see me and live" (Exodus 33:20 NLT). Here in heaven, however, God's people will see him face-to-face. Jesus had promised, "Blessed are the pure in heart, for they will see God" (Matthew 5:8 NIV). John, in another of his books, wrote, "Dear friends, now we are children of God, and what we will be has not yet been made known. But we know that when he appears, we shall be like him, for we shall see him as he is" (1 John 3:2 NIV). To be able to see God's face suggests intimate personal relationship. God will not be a king on a throne in a remote castle; he will be among his people.

In addition, God's people will have *his name* written *on their foreheads.* This points out God's ownership. God's people had been "sealed" (7:3), and this seal previously had been described as being in the form of the Father's name (14:1). The point is that this is the same group—God will bring his own safely to his eternal kingdom.

22:5 And there will be no more night; they need no light of lamp or sun, for the Lord God will be their light, and they will reign forever and ever.^{NRSV} The point that *there will be no more night* was noted in 21:25. This indicates that there will be no more evil, no more darkness, and no more time (for God had created day and night, along with the sun and the moon, to mark the passage of time—Genesis 1:14-15). The people in the city will *need no light of lamp or sun, for the Lord God will be their light,* as was also noted in 21:23 (see commentary there). Zechariah had prophesied, "On that day, the sources of light will no longer shine, yet there will be continuous day" (Zechariah 14:7).

The result of the entire book of Revelation is in this verse: God's people, those who have been redeemed by the blood of Jesus, *will reign forever and ever* (see also Daniel 7:18, 28). It is interesting to note that 22:3 and 22:5 are parallel in the participle verb form, translated "they will serve" (22:3) and "they will reign" here. This identifies the nature of our reigning.

Those who believe in Christ will become rulers, reigning in his kingdom of life, where there is no death (see also 1:6; 5:10; 11:17; 20:6; 22:5; Romans 5:17, 21; 2 Timothy 2:12). What a promise this is to those who love Christ! We can reign over sin's power, over death's threats, and over Satan's attacks. Eternal life is ours now and forever. Though this promise has its greatest fulfillment in the future, it also has a significant immediate impact. In Christ, death loses its sting (see 1 Corinthians 15:50-57). We are still subject to the physical suffering and death brought by sin in the world, but we are free from the eternal spiritual separation that we would experience outside of Christ. Also, in the power and protection of Jesus Christ, we can overcome temptation.

THE PROMISE OF JESUS' RETURN / 22:6-21

These verses form the epilogue to this book. An angel expressed the authenticity of the prophecy, and at the very end, Jesus warned that the end would indeed come soon.

22:6 Then the angel said to me, "These words are trustworthy and true: 'The Lord God, who tells his prophets what the future holds, has sent his angel to tell you what will happen soon.'"NLT John referred to *the angel* (as opposed to "an" angel), so this is probably the same angel who had shown him the heavenly city (21:9; 22:1). At the beginning of this prophecy, "an angel was sent to God's servant John, so that John could share the revelation with God's other servants" (1:1 NLT). John's report is "the word of God and the testimony of Jesus" (1:2 NLT). The revelation closes with an angel explaining that what John has written is *trustworthy and true.* Throughout the ages, God had been telling his prophets *what the future holds,* and he did so again in this prophecy to John. Revelation describes *what will happen soon* (see also 1:1). The word "soon" means imminent—and implies certainty.

22:7 "Look, I am coming soon! Blessed are those who obey the prophecy written in this scroll."NLT From Jesus himself come the words of assurance: *"Look, I am coming soon!"* The word "soon" *(taxu)* means that his coming will be quick and without delay. It may not be "soon" according to human timing (after all, John wrote this two thousand years ago), but it *is* certain to occur; it is imminent. Jesus clearly told his followers, "So be prepared, because you don't know what day your Lord is coming. You also must be ready all the time. For the Son of Man will come when least expected" (Matthew 24:42, 44 NLT).

Then follows the sixth of seven beatitudes in the book:
"Blessed are those who obey the prophecy written in this scroll."
(The other beatitudes are found in 1:3; 14:13; 16:15; 19:9; 20:6;
22:14; see the chart at 14:13.) Like the beatitude at 1:3, the one
listed here promises a blessing to those who obey God by heed-
ing the warnings of this prophecy.

REMAIN FAITHFUL
Jesus announced a blessing for those who obey the prophecy.
What is the Christian's work of obedience as detailed in Revelation? We are to be faithful to Christ. God commended the Philadelphians for keeping Christ's words and not denying his name
(3:8). We are to be morally clean and prepared for his return
(7:14; 22:14). We are to endure patiently (14:12). We are neither to add nor detract from Revelation's words. Serving God
begins with our faithful service to him now.

22:8-9 **I, John, am the one who saw and heard all these things. And
when I saw and heard these things, I fell down to worship the
angel who showed them to me. But again he said, "No, don't
worship me. I am a servant of God, just like you and your
brothers the prophets, as well as all who obey what is written in
this scroll. Worship God!"**^{NLT} Next, John signed his name, so to
speak, as *the one who saw and heard all these things.* John did not
imagine what he had written; he had actually seen and heard everything he had recorded. He understood that he had been given an
awesome privilege. Once again overwhelmed, John wrote that he
fell down to worship the angel who had given him the inspired
glimpse of the future. *But again* (as at 19:10), the angel prohibited
John's worship, saying, *"Don't worship me,"* and he repeated the
words he had said earlier (19:10) regarding his being a *servant of
God,* just like everyone else—the *prophets* and *all who obey.*

The first of the Ten Commandments is "You shall have no
other gods before me" (Exodus 20:3 NIV). Jesus said that the
greatest command of Moses' laws was "Love the Lord your God
with all your heart and with all your soul and with all your mind"
(Matthew 22:37 NIV). Here, this truth is reiterated. The angel
told John to *worship God.* God alone is worthy of worship and
adoration. He is above all creation, even the angels.

22:10 **And he said to me, "Do not seal up the words of the prophecy
of this book, for the time is near."**^{NRSV} The angel told John
what to do after his vision had ended. Instead of sealing up what he
had written, as Daniel had been commanded to do (Daniel 12:4-
12), John was told, *"Do not seal up the words of the prophecy of*

this book, for the time is near." John's prophecy was to be left open so that all could read and understand. This message was needed immediately by the churches of John's day, as well as believers across the years until Christ's return. Daniel's message had been sealed because it was not a message for Daniel's time. But the book of Revelation was a message for John's time and is relevant today. As Christ's return approaches, there is an increased polarization between God's followers and Satan's followers. We must read the book of Revelation, hear its message, and be prepared for Christ's certain return.

SEEING GOD
The angel told John to worship God, and worship is a major emphasis in Revelation. The first step toward meaningful worship is a desire to know God. If we thirst for him, the Bible promises that he will provide for us and satisfy our needs. Would you like your worship to be completely transformed? Confess any sins that might be hindering your fellowship with God. Then ask God to stir your heart, to instill within you an unquenchable thirst to know him. Meditate upon how God has revealed himself in the Bible, and ask him to reveal himself to you again. When you see God in a new way, worship will be your only fitting response.

22:11 **"Let the one who is doing wrong continue to do wrong; the one who is vile, continue to be vile; the one who is good, continue to do good; and the one who is holy, continue in holiness."**[NLT] The angel was not recommending evil living in this verse. Instead, this note follows on the heels of the angel's words that "the time is near" (22:10). Indeed, it may be so near that there would be no time for people to alter their lifestyles. The angel is showing how our choices lead to consequences. Like a train running down a track, the consequences will ultimately come for the choices we make. God is always calling people to repent, but when Christ returns, the opportunity will have passed. This is a call to the readers to make up their minds now and live for God. People will reap the consequences for the kinds of lives they have led; those who have done *wrong* and who have been *vile* will face that in eternity, and those who have done *good* and have been *holy* will be rewarded accordingly, as noted in 22:12.

22:12-13 **"Behold, I am coming soon! My reward is with me, and I will give to everyone according to what he has done. I am the Alpha and the Omega, the First and the Last, the Beginning and the End."**[NIV] Christ here spoke, reiterating that he would be *coming soon* (22:7). He would bring a *reward* that would be given to his

people, *according to what* each had done. (For more on these
rewards, see commentary at 20:12-13.) Our reward will be a place
in God's kingdom (see Matthew 25:34-40; Mark 9:47; 10:29-30),
not on the basis of merit (good deeds) but because of God's gracious promise to people of faith (Luke 12:31-32). The Bible
records God rewarding his people for good works according to his
justice. In the Old Testament, obedience often was rewarded in this
life (Deuteronomy 28), but obedience and immediate reward are
not always linked. If they were, good people would always be rich,
and sin would always lead to pain and suffering. The believer's true
reward is God's presence and power through the Holy Spirit. Later,
in eternity, believers will be rewarded for their faith and service. If
material rewards in this life were to come to us for every faithful
deed, we would be tempted to boast about our achievements and
to act out of wrong motivations. No act of mercy will be forgotten;
no true believer will be abandoned. (For more on rewards, see
Matthew 16:27; 19:27-30; Luke 6:23, 35; 1 Corinthians 3:8, 13-15;
9:25; James 1:12.)

Although all God's people will be saved and will enjoy the
reward of eternity with him, a number of rewards seem to be
given to individuals, according to what they have done. God will
look at each individual's heart; thus, it may be that a quiet saint
praying daily beside her bed will receive even greater reward
than a flamboyant, well-known preacher. It may be that the
woman who used her gifts to the fullest extent will be rewarded
more greatly than the one who believed but was too afraid to
reach her potential. God will not bestow his rewards in ways that
we humans might. Each believer's job is to serve God to his or
her fullest potential with a heart that is right with him.

Next, Christ repeated the words he had spoken at the beginning of the Revelation: *"I am the Alpha and the Omega, the First
and the Last, the Beginning and the End"* (see 1:8, 17 and commentary there). The Creator began and will end time itself. *Alpha*
and *Omega* are the first and last letters of the Greek alphabet; it's
like saying he is the A and the Z, or even A-to-Z.

22:14 **Blessed are those who wash their robes so they can enter
through the gates of the city and eat the fruit from the tree of
life.**NLT This verse includes the seventh and final beatitude in Revelation (the others were in 1:3; 14:13; 16:15; 19:9; 20:6; 22:7; see
the chart at 14:13): *Blessed are those who wash their robes.* This
picture symbolizes those who seek to purify themselves from a
sinful way of life. Previously in the vision, John had seen God's
people dressed in white robes, and the angel had explained that
"these are they who have come out of the great tribulation; they

have washed their robes and made them white in the blood of the Lamb" (7:14 NIV). These people had been dirty with sin, but Christ had cleansed them through his death on the cross. They had accepted his salvation by "washing their robes." The verb in 7:14 was aorist, indicating an action in a specific time in the past. Here, the verb is present tense, indicating continuous action. This verse is a call to the believers to strive daily to remain faithful and ready for Christ's return. They do not need to be saved over and over; but they should continue to "wash their robes" and so remain clean and ready.

Those who do so *can enter through the gates of the city and eat the fruit from the tree of life.* Entering the city indicates joining the redeemed people in eternity (the "city" is described in 21:10-27). In Eden, Adam and Eve had been barred from any access to the tree of life because of their sin (Genesis 3:22-24). In the new earth, God's people will eat from the tree of life because their sins have been removed by Christ's death and resurrection. Those who eat the fruit of this tree will live forever.

KEEP ON WORKING
Christ said that he would reward his followers for their deeds. This means that we will give an account of our faithfulness. Jesus is coming back—we know this is true. Does this mean we must quit our jobs in order to serve God? No, it means we are to use our time, talents, and treasures diligently in order to serve God completely in whatever we do. For a few people, this may mean changing professions. For most, however, it means doing daily work out of love for God. Be faithful in what you have been given.

22:15 Outside the city are the dogs—the sorcerers, the sexually immoral, the murderers, the idol worshipers, and all who love to live a lie.^{NLT} Verse 14 describes those who will live in the kingdom of God for eternity; those who cannot be there are described in this verse. This is not meant to be an exhaustive list of sins, nor does it indicate that, somehow, sinners will surround the holy city. Instead, as in 21:8, this symbol pictures that those who have washed their robes and have been cleansed of sin will be in the city, but those who are *sorcerers, sexually immoral, murderers, idol worshipers,* or *love to live a lie* will not be in the city; instead, they will be in the lake of fire, as described in 20:15 and 21:8. They are characterized as "dogs"—a term used in Scripture for something impure or unclean. The emphasis is that nothing evil and no sinner will be in God's presence to corrupt or harm any of the faithful.

LIVING A LIE
Jesus will exclude from the holy city those "who love to live a lie."
These are people whose lives have gone so wrong that they
resemble Satan, who deceived the whole world (12:9; 13:13-15;
16:14). They are hypocrites, trying to live one way while believing
another. They are like the Nicolaitans, mentioned in 2:15, who
were among the believers but compromised their faith in order to
also include worship of the Roman emperor. John records Jesus'
statement that Satan is the father of lies (John 8:44).

Today we see politicians and civic and business leaders who
twist the truth to serve their purposes. Many people have lost
the ability to distinguish what's true from what they wish was
true. Dishonest people soon begin to believe the lies they
construct around themselves. Then they lose the ability to tell
the difference between truth and lies. By believing your own
lies, you deceive yourself, you alienate yourself from God, and
you lose credibility in all your relationships. In the long run,
honesty wins out.

**22:16 "I, Jesus, have sent my angel to give you this testimony for
the churches. I am the Root and the Offspring of David, and
the bright Morning Star."**NIV Jesus again spoke (as he had previously, 22:12-13), describing himself as the ultimate fulfillment
of everything that had been promised. Christ had sent his *angel* to
show John all that would come to pass (see 1:1), so that the *testimony* could be given to the churches (all churches, but especially
those mentioned in chapters 2–3 who would receive this letter).

Jesus is both David's *Root* and *Offspring.* As the Creator of all,
he existed long before David. As a human, however, Jesus was
one of David's direct descendants (see Isaiah 11:1-5; Matthew
1:1-17). As the Messiah, he is the *bright Morning Star,* the light
of salvation to all (see 2:28; 2 Peter 1:19). In Numbers 24:17,
Balaam declared, "I see him, but not in the present time. I perceive him, but far in the distant future. A star will rise from
Jacob; a scepter will emerge from Israel" (NLT). The "star" may
have referred both to King David and David's greater descendant, Jesus Christ. As the morning star is the first star to be seen
in the darkness before the dawn, so Christ, the morning star,
promises that the night of tribulation will soon be over and the
new kingdom is about to dawn.

**22:17 The Spirit and the bride say, "Come." And let everyone who
hears say, "Come." And let everyone who is thirsty come. Let
anyone who wishes take the water of life as a gift.**NRSV Both the
Holy *Spirit* and the *bride,* the church, extend the invitation to all
the world to come to Jesus and experience the joys of salvation
in Christ. *Everyone who hears* the message is invited to *come.*

Everyone who is thirsty is invited to *come* and *take the water of life as a gift.* When Jesus had met the Samaritan woman at the well, he had told her of the living water that he could supply (John 4:10-15; see also Isaiah 55:1; John 7:37). This image is used again here, as Christ invites anyone to come and drink of the water of life. The gospel is unlimited in scope—all kinds of people everywhere may come. Salvation cannot be earned, but God gives it freely. This evil world is desperately thirsty for living water, and many are dying of thirst. But it's still not too late. One day it will be too late, as Revelation has clearly shown, but the invitation is still being offered.

HAVE A DRINK
Jesus invites all who are thirsty to come to the water of life (22:17), and he gave his people the privilege and opportunity to continue to extend that glad invitation. There is no doubt that people around the world thirst for life, but there is no shortage of God's life-giving water. The challenge is to let those thirsty ones hear the word. Consider today what part God wants you to play in giving water to a thirsty world. You can pray, share the gospel with a friend, feed the poor in Christ's name, support missionaries and mission organizations, and even become an international emissary yourself. People are dying of thirst—and we have the water!

22:18-19 And I solemnly declare to everyone who hears the prophetic words of this book: If anyone adds anything to what is written here, God will add to that person the plagues described in this book. And if anyone removes any of the words of this prophetic book, God will remove that person's share in the tree of life and in the holy city that are described in this book.^{NLT} This warning is given to anyone who might purposefully distort the message in this book. Moses gave a similar warning (Deuteronomy 4:1-4). People must handle the Bible with care and great respect, so that its message is not distorted. No human explanation or interpretation of God's Word should be elevated to the same authority as the text itself.

This warning is given *to everyone who hears the prophetic words of this book*—not just future scribes who might recopy the text, but everyone who even hears the revelation must be careful not to add or remove anything. To do so carries a severe warning that *God will remove that person's share in the tree of life and in the holy city that are described in this book.* Many have taken this verse to refer to the Bible in its entirety, but it is actually focused on this book of Revelation. Yet all of God's Word should be handled with such care. It is a serious matter to tamper with God's Word, carrying a punishment with eternal consequences.

22:20-21 He who testifies to these things says, "Yes, I am coming soon." Amen. Come, Lord Jesus. The grace of the Lord Jesus be with God's people. Amen.^{NIV} Jesus testified to the truth of this entire revelation to John in 22:7, 12, 16; then he added one final message, *"Yes, I am coming soon."* No one knows the day or the hour, but Jesus is coming soon and unexpectedly. This is good news to those who trust him, but a terrible message for those who have rejected him and stand under judgment. "Soon" means at any moment, and his people must be ready for him, always prepared for his return.

John ended by saying, *Amen,* let it be so, two times. With him, God's people across the world say, *Come, Lord Jesus.* Then John pronounced a benediction on those who had read or listened to the words of this book: *The grace of the Lord Jesus be with God's people.* People need that grace in order to become God's children; God's children need that grace daily as they seek to be overcomers for him. In the end, his grace, and nothing else, brings his people to be with him forever.

THE END . . . THE BEGINNING
Revelation closes human history as Genesis had opened it—in paradise. But Revelation has a distinct difference—evil is gone forever. Genesis describes Adam and Eve walking and talking with God; Revelation describes people worshiping God face-to-face. Genesis describes a garden with an evil serpent; Revelation describes a perfect city with no evil. The Garden of Eden was destroyed by sin; but paradise is re-created in the new Jerusalem.

The book of Revelation ends with an urgent request: "Come, Lord Jesus." In a world of problems, persecution, evil, and immorality, Christ calls us to endure in our faith. Our efforts to better our world are important, but their results cannot compare with the transformation that Jesus will bring about when he returns. He alone controls human history, forgives sin, and will re-create the earth and bring lasting peace.

Revelation is, above all, a book of hope. It shows that no matter what happens on earth, God is in control. It promises that evil will not last forever. And it depicts the wonderful reward that is waiting for all who believe in Jesus Christ as Savior and Lord.

BIBLIOGRAPHY

Aune, David E. *Revelation 1–5.* Word Biblical Commentary Series, Vol. 52. Dallas: Word Books, 1997.

Brown, Robert K. and Philip W. Comfort, trans. *The Greek English Interlinear New Testament.* Wheaton, Ill.: Tyndale House Publishers, 1990.

Douglas, J. D., and Philip W. Comfort, eds. *New Commentary on the Whole Bible: New Testament Volume.* Wheaton, Ill.: Tyndale House Publishers, 1990.

Guthrie, Donald. *New Testament Introduction: Hebrews to Revelation.* Downers Grove, Ill.: InterVarsity Press, 1962.

Johnson, Alan F. Revelation. *The Expositor's Bible Commentary.* Grand Rapids: Zondervan, 1996.

Love, Julian Price. *1 John, 2 John, 3 John, Jude, Revelation.* The Layman's Bible Commentary Series, Vol. 25. Atlanta: John Knox Press, 1960.

Martin, Ralph P. and Peter H. Davids, eds. *Dictionary of the Later New Testament and Its Developments.* Downers Grove, Ill.: InterVarsity Press, 1997.

Morris, Leon. Revelation. *Tyndale New Testament Commentaries.* Grand Rapids: Eerdmans, 1987.

Mounce, Robert H. *The Book of Revelation.* The New International Commentary on the New Testament. Grand Rapids: Eerdmans, 1977.

Walvoord, John F., and Roby B. Zuck. *Bible Knowledge Commentary: New Testament Edition.* Wheaton, Ill.: Victor, 1983

INDEX